The Scent of The Roses

Long, Long be my heart with such memories filled
As the vase in which roses have once been distilled
You may break you may shatter the vase if you will
But the *Scent of the Roses* will hang round it still.

Thomas Moore

The Scent of
The Roses

Mary O'Hara

Michael Joseph : London

First published in Great Britain by Michael Joseph Limited
44 Bedford Square, London WC1
1980

© by Mary O'Hara 1980

ISBN 0 7181 1733 6

Photoset, printed and bound in Great Britain by
Redwood Burn Ltd, Trowbridge and Esher

Contents

ACKNOWLEDGEMENTS

The Publishers would like to express their thanks to the following for permission to reproduce various photographs used in this book:

Allegro Photographic Studios (no. 20), The BBC (no. 19), Fergus Bourke (no. 28), Charles Collins Photo Agency (no. 31), Paul Chave (no. 37), Paul Cox (no. 36), Brodrick Haldane (no. 22), Ross Halfin (no. 33), Sarah Hook (no. 35), Doug McKenzie (no. 30), Tony O'Malley (no. 26), Steve Oroz Associates (no. 21), John Sarsfield (no. 12), and Peter Stuart (no. 34).

Prologue

Mid-morning, Easter Thursday. In the sunlit Methodist Hall the tension was almost tangible. A singing competition of the Sligo Feis Ceóil, the annual Festival of Music and Drama which attracted competitors from all over Ireland was drawing to its close. Anxious mothers sat beside their small fidgety bairns who had been thoroughly scoured and relentlessly groomed down to the last white sock (and gone through their songs until they could sing them in their sleep). Some pestered their parents with whispered questions such as "Mummy who do you think will get First?" But the fond mamas had their eyes and attention riveted on the god-like adjudicator, an august musical pundit down from Dublin, seated in potent isolation in the centre of the Hall, scribbling (endlessly it seemed to the watchers) page after page of criticism. The most miserable person in Ireland at that moment was competitor number twenty-eight; a slender, pale and freckle-faced little girl of eight, with a huge bow on the side of her straight light-brown hair sitting near the back of the hall. Heavens above, she was thinking, she hadn't wanted to enter the wretched competition at all, but realising that to have said so would have made no difference, she'd gone ahead with it. Even at that tender age she'd sensed it was good for her character to do things, innocuous in themselves, but which she personally disliked doing. Oh but the terrible shame of it: she hadn't even been *recalled*. Out of those dozens of competitors only about ten had had their numbers called out which meant that the adjudicator, dismissing the remainder as not being good enough, would listen to their performances once again and then decide who would get First, Second and Third Prizes and 'Highly Recommended'.

The little girl number twenty-eight wished the ground would open and swallow her up. Floors had never obliged before so why should they be expected to do so now? If only she could slip away unnoticed, run home and play tennis by herself against the side of the house and forget the whole affair. But

7

since her mother was sitting beside her, escape was ruled out. She'd just have to sit through the rest of the humiliating business of hearing the adjudicator call out the names of the prize winners and analyse their performances.

The hush of expectancy now deepened as the adjudicator finally made his way to the platform with a bundle of papers in his hand. He paused for a moment, glancing abstractedly over the top of his spectacles, at the sea of ultra-attentive faces before him and then he spoke. "I've recalled twelve competitors to decide which of them should receive second, third and fourth prizes. I didn't recall competitor number twenty-eight because after she'd sung there was no doubt whatsoever in my mind that she would be the first prize winner. I've given her ninety-eight marks out of 100" I was number twenty-eight.

1 Easter Child

In early sunlight, small voices in the rain . . .

(from 'Return' by Richard Selig)

I was born in County Sligo in the west of Ireland. Soldiers figure along the line, including my great grand-uncle who fought as a cavalry officer in the Union Army in 1863 in the American Civil War; and during World War II my father served in the Royal Engineers in the British Army.

A small town on the west coast, Sligo had once been a busy port before World War II, with an extensive trade in timber from the Baltic, weekly services to Liverpool and Glasgow, trade in grain from South America and Australia and various goods from Europe.

Our branch of the family is descended from Oliver O'Hara, who took part in the Irish rebellion of 1641. Later, when Cromwell gave all Irish Catholics the ultimatum of going to hell or to Connaught, the O'Haras were not immediately affected as they were already in the province of Connaught, but Oliver O'Hara's family did forfeit their lands for participating in the rebellion. A section of the family conformed to the new religion and so retained their property.

I was born during Easter, the youngest in a family of four children. A fifth child had been born prematurely and died. When I was finally told about this when I was about eight, my reaction was "Thank God it didn't live". The unhappiness in our family was sufficiently palpable for me to have felt sad at the thought of another, younger child, having to live through it, too. But although the background of my childhood was unhappy, to a great extent I successfully abstracted myself from that ambience and was not an unhappy child.

By all accounts my parents' marriage was not the happiest of alliances. It is still very difficult to understand why my parents married each other. My father is a mild-mannered man, my mother was forceful with a tyrannical streak. I often think that

9

if my father had married somebody who was more of a home-maker it would have provided him with the foundation he needed to make him truly happy. And if perhaps Mother had shared her life with someone more firm, she too might have thrived: she needed to be controlled. Although there were admirable qualities on both sides, they tended to negate each other. A significant fact came to light some years ago when my father told me that at one time they had both considered doing medicine. But as far as I can judge neither would have been the right type. Their temperaments were unsuitable. The medicine dream was an aspect of their partial inability to come to terms with everyday life.

Father had always wanted to travel. At the age of sixteen, and still at Summerhill College, the boys' secondary school in Sligo, he left and went to Cahirciveen in County Kerry to qualify as a wireless operator. The course usually took a year, but he applied himself diligently and qualified in three months. The college principals were impressed enough to ask him to stay on as an instructor; as his only reason for having taken the course was to get away to sea, he declined the offer, and travelled the world instead. Three years later, enriched by his experience of globe-sailing, he decided he would like to continue his studies. He matriculated and entered University College, Galway, where he met my mother.

Father was reading for degrees in civil engineering and geology and Mother was doing commerce, so this meant she knew more about money matters than he – or thought she did. Later on, during their marriage, money became an endless source of dissension, Mother always the aggressor and Father never asserting himself – hoping for a quiet life.

When they first met, as undergraduates, Mai Kirwan is reputed to have been very attractive and vivacious. I've heard her referred to as a college beauty and as being very charming. Educated and consequently in one sense a liberated woman in her day, she was at the same time not *really* liberated, being somewhat enslaved by her undisciplined ways and capricious moods.

After he qualified, Father had planned to become a professional soldier in the British Army and go to India, but he changed his mind and was appointed to the British Colonial

Service and posted to Nigeria instead. In the meantime, my mother had a teaching job in the provinces. After two years my father returned to Ireland, married my mother and together they returned to West Africa. He was twenty-seven and she was twenty-nine. Mother was beginning even then to show signs of neurotic behaviour.

They were on board the West African Mail steamer which had just started to sail down the Mersey with the pilot on board. Mother decided she'd investigate the as yet unseen cabin. Seeing the low bulkhead, she turned on father and snapped: "The ceiling is too low; get me off this ship at once." He replied, "If you really mean it, then you'd better hurry up so that you can leave with the pilot and get down by the Jacob's ladder." Mother stayed.

This irrational strain in her character lingered on. Years later when we were living in Sligo, close to the harbour, and when for some reason or other Mother was in bed, during the day, the heavy dray horses pulling their noisy carts over the cobbled stones alongside the house got on my mother's nerves. She would order Father to go to the Town Hall and get the traffic stopped. He never did go.

It always seemed an extraordinary partnership. I do think that Father really loved Mother, in his own way. All his life he was very loyal and faithful to her, and he never mentioned to anyone outside the family their constant friction and quarrelling.

Because Mother died when I was seventeen, I was too young to have had a chance to try to understand her. Now I will never know what lay behind my parents' enigmatic relationship, but the memories are fairly vivid. After the war, I started to be used, perhaps unintentionally, as the go-between. I was known to be very fond of Father but I was also genuinely fond of Mother – and they both knew it. The fact that we grew up in an atmosphere of bickering and sometimes vituperative language in no way inured us to the distress it engendered. Nevertheless I developed ways of disengaging my inner self from the misery, as a means of survival. I think I was affected but not damaged by it all. And there was a very positive side to it. From an unusually early age I could see something was radically wrong, and I learned a lot about what a marriage should be from observing one that was, as far as I could make out, a fiasco.

Mother's relationships were nothing if not striking. Once, my parents were queueing to see a very popular film. The line was long and slow and they were nearing the top. Someone crashed the queue and Mother simply walked up to him, bashed him over the head with her handbag, gave him a piece of her mind and told him to get to the end of the line where he belonged. She was also a great one for smashing crockery. The lifespan of every dish and glass that entered the house was destined to be very brief. I doubt if any family had as many oddments as we did. We as a family had no difficulty in believing in flying saucers – invariably aimed at Father.

Mother had an eccentric streak in her. She brought back a monkey from Africa. He was called Yonk and eventually became as neurotic as his mistress. She liked to go out walking with Yonk perched on her shoulder, all dolled up in the woollen outfits that she specially knitted for him. One day my parents arrived home to find Yonk keeping the housekeeper at bay by throwing every moveable object he could lay his paws on in her direction, having, no doubt, taken a leaf from Mother's book. In Sligo he entertained the boys at Summerhill College with his capers on the school wall, and was the bane of the local housewives. He had a habit of sneaking in through kitchen windows and purloining potatoes from their pots. Eventually Yonk's anti-social behaviour landed him in a cage in the Dublin zoo, where the family regularly visited him. Things had come to a head when baby Joan was born and the monkey showed signs of jealousy. Then he took a swipe at the cat and knocked its eye out.

I have a theory that Mother wanted only one child. This child was my elder sister, Joan. Thinking about it years later as an adult, it seemed to me that Mother saw Joan as an extension of herself. There was a companionship between them that was not shared by the rest of us. Joan had the dubious privilege of having her cot in mother's bedroom. Later on, when my brother and I came along and we used to be taken out for walks by the maid, Mother would say, "Now the babies are all out we can shout and dance together," and she and Joan would dance around the room.

One year after Joan was born, my sister Angela arrived. Mother decided she simply could not cope with another small baby, so Father entrusted her to his parents, by whom she was subsequently reared. As there was antipathy between my grandmother and mother we were rarely allowed to visit. Sometime during the war years, Angela came to live with the rest of us for a short while, but soon she was away again. (She was destined to have more than her share of misfortune and unhappiness throughout her life.) So, from the start and until her death in 1972, Angela was to me for most of the time a remote figure, and I never had the opportunity to really get to know and understand her. Dermot appeared on the scene two years later. Mother spoiled him in a different way from Joan – I think she felt sentimental towards him because he was the only boy. I was one year and twelve days younger than he, (though for many years I was telling people there were just twelve days between us), and we were very close up to the time we went to boarding school.

I think I must have sensed straight away that I would have to stand on my own two feet and fend for myself. Which is precisely what I proceeded to do at the age of seven months. My first steps were not only taken alone but were running ones. It was a mild December day and the family had driven out to Strandhill a seaside resort five miles outside Sligo. Leaving me lying safely on a rug on the strand, the grown-ups started to take a walk along the edge of the sea. Suddenly, there was a noise and turning round they saw me running towards them. To this day I love speed.

Very early on I also learned to pull myself up in my pram and would sit there unusually straight-backed, grinning at the world. Mother thought I must have something wrong with my back and took me to the doctor, but all was well. Later, I cultivated an upright stance and my boarding school reports, which got progessively worse, had one redeeming gleam of light. Beside the word deportment, "excellent" invariably appeared.

I do think that children ought to be told not only that they are loved but also that they are attractive or at least made to feel they are. I grew up assuming that I was physically inferior to everyone else: the Plain Jane of the family. Some of this was due to the

13

fact that Joan was blessed with an abundance of self-confidence about her appearance which was freequently endorsed by Mother's compliments; and now and then I'd heard her quoting admiring remarks made by others about my sister's looks. Matters were not improved by my mother's tendency to dress me in Joan's cast-off clothes, which, since her colouring is completely different from mine (Joan was dressed and looked marvellous in browns and dark colours) only emphasized my paleness. When I was older Mother once told me that when, as a small child, I fell and hurt myself I would run straight to Joan. I am delighted to know this now but when I was first told about it, it seemed very strange indeed because I recall finding Joan a cold and distant person who rarely smiled – almost a stranger. It wasn't until I entered my teens that I became aware of jealous feelings towards Joan. I suppose Mother's preference for her partly accounts for these childish pangs. Once or twice I discovered some new dresses of Joan's in Mother's wardrobe and I felt very hurt and envious.

Mother was conventional and curls were the 'in' thing in those days. My hair was very fine and straight and would probably have looked well with a proper cut, but curls were a must. She went to town where bows were concerned. Very large multi-coloured objects became permanently attached to the side of my head. I didn't object to these, perhaps because I couldn't see them. Then one day when I was about eight, mother decided I must have a perm. This was an awesome business, and secretly I felt I was getting preferential treatment. Stoically I endured the hot irons clamped tightly to my head and after several hours I emerged from my first visit to the hairdresser with a halo of fuzz. Everyone was delighted. In fact in the long term it did my hair good; and from then on bit by bit it became naturally wavy, and today there are times when it is decidedly curly, especially in damp weather.

Another time when I was very small, Mother suddenly got the whim to cut my hair very short and put me into a pair of shorts. I suffered the agony in silence, but after the job was completed I disappeared. Eventually, I was found hiding behind the pantry door, crying quietly. My explanation was, I'm told, "You're trying to make a 'shame-boy' out of me."

My unhealthy preoccupation with not feeling pretty was

partly due to the fact that Mother unwisely told me that as I was a thin baby she felt ashamed of me and kept me deeply hidden in my pram. This is again curious, for in any of the rare snaps I have seen of myself I am in fact a decidedly chubby, dimpled and blissfully beaming child.

Later, when I was out of the pram and the family was being snapped, Mother would repair to the kitchen with me in tow and endeavour to coax some curl into my hair with the curling tongs. By the time the operation was through the roll of film had been used up.

Although there were no really halcyon days, nevertheless Dermot and I shared many happy childhood times. Father was a great pal to us, and we played a lot together. Dermot and I used to tumble about on Father's bed, and he would be unendingly patient with us. We were extremely lively, but he never once admonished us for all the shouting and squealing and pulling at him that we delighted in. If he failed to wake up when we yelled into his ears, we would pull up his eye-lids and shout into his eyes!

Dermot and I frequently got into trouble; like the time, when we were three or four, our next-door neighbour found us lying on our backs systematically eating her carefully grown peas, row after cherished row, which ran alongside our fence. She chased us away into a field of shin-deep nettles, and when we came home in tears smarting from the stings we rightly got little sympathy, so we comforted each other over our bowls of soup.

People sometimes ask me if I ever smoked. My answer is that I gave up cigarettes when I was three years old: Dermot and I used to puff away *under the bedclothes*. My parents, who were both heavy smokers, noticed that their supply in the spare bedroom was dwindling. They suspected the maid until one day the little clandestine mound of cigarette butts, secreted in some private corner by my brother, was found. He got punished, I didn't.

Joan would come home from school full of her new learning and eager to impart it to the two little receptive ignoramuses. She would make us sit before a blackboard where she would chalk up her day's knowledge and, reversing her role of a short while before, she would make us be the pupils. She tells me that

15

she had a little cane and would whack the hell out of us if we gave the wrong answers!

Later on when we were a bit older, she started writing plays which we would all perform for the family. The one I best remember had a farmer in it, played by the maid who was swathed in a curtain, and shod in mother's white leather mosquito boots. I was a rather superior fairy and, adopting a dramatic stance, was carefully coached by Joan to stare at a certain Victorian print on the wall and proclaim with raised magic wand, "I am the fairy Zakufranzpenromanisk." Dermot stole that show, dressed up as an exceedingly pretty fairy in a confection of yellow tulle, wearing bright red lipstick, and halfway through his bit he got an uncontrollable fit of the giggles and the "curtain" had to be drawn.

Like all small children, we had our share of the giggles. Sometimes the attack would descend during tea and the said beverage would cascade through our noses. That, of course, led to instant bed.

I was four years old when I started going to school. Dermot started at the same time. I remember it vividly. Father drove us there and having said good-bye left us at the little gate which was too small for a car to drive through. It was the national school, St Vincent's, run by the Ursuline convent and staffed by some members of the community, but mostly by lay women. We must have arrived late for there was no one to be seen anywhere. For some reason I was carrying Dermot's coat over my arm. We knocked on the door of the Low Babies' section of the building. (The next year would find us in the High Babies class.) At the sound of Father's car starting, Dermot let out a wail and, dashing into the yard, belted towards the gate crying his heart out, leaving me alone with the coat to face the music. My new teacher, conducting me inside, put me at a desk near the front. Smiling to hide my painful shyness I produced a hankie and held it pressed to my face. The teacher, gentleness itself, finally managed to get the hankie away but I spent the rest of the morning with my face buried in my hands, my head down on the desk, too bashful to face all these new children.

I was full of admiration for these self-confident ones. Even Dermot, when he was finally lured back, settled down with no apparent self-consciousness and with his customary charm. I can see him now, walking into the Low Babies' classroom, having attended to the necessities of nature, his trousers still undone, and in an enviable matter-of-fact way heading straight to the teacher's desk saying, "Please, Miss Ruhane, will you do me braces?"

I think it was before I started school that I had the experience of my first unwelcome suitor. He lived in our neighbourhood, was my own age, had flaming red hair and could not pronounce the letter "r". Every Saturday morning he would make his pilgrimage to my back door and present me with his milk bottle tops, devotedly collected, and which he called "money cows for Maly".

It was about this time that we moved to Harbour House, formerly the Harbour Master's house. It was a large, 18th-century stone building, supposedly haunted by a sea captain. Areas of the house inside were in permanent twilight and there was a particular passage between the breakfast room and the kitchen which was decidedly stygian and figured in my nightmares. I could not go down this passage at night without a tightening of the abdominal muscles and *very* loud singing, moving at top speed. When at night, I was sent upstairs to fetch something, I would sing with such volume and intensity that I'd forget what it was I'd been told to bring down and would have to call out "What did you send me up for?" Joan told me that she was so scared in Harbour House after dark that if she happened to find herself alone in it, nothing – not even inclement weather – could persuade her to stay inside. She would simply wait outside, swinging on the railings, or sauntering up and down, till someone arrived home. Father says he believed the house was haunted: for instance, doors would close unaccountably. The four large attics were so spooky that I couldn't so much as look at the winding stairs leading up to them once darkness had fallen. In the morning we would ask Father, "Did you see any ghosts last night?" and he would reply something like, "No, but I saw some pixies." (These were the Little People or fairies which we used to read about in our story books.)

"What did you say to them?"

"Well, they asked me if I would like to be a pixie too, but I said no thanks because I think Mary and Joan have enough pixies already."

He was referring to our little woollen pointed hoods which were also called pixies. This would have us laughing delightedly and our fear of the dark night and the ghosts would be temporarily allayed.

Most children are afraid of the dark but my fear persisted into my late teens. It was only later when my faith became active and the omnipresence of God a conscious reality in my life that it left me. In fact, the tension of opposites, the concept of light and darkness, sorrow and joy has exercised my mind considerably since I grew into adulthood. In one of my songs "Prayer of the Badger" the badger sings:

> Lord I do love the darkness
> The hours folk call the night
> Where others see but blackness
> I know a lordly light . . .

Not only am I no longer afraid of the darkness or of being alone, but I relish the opportunity for quietness that darkness affords. Like badger, I too have come to sense the light behind every darkness.

The Sligo National Primary School was just down the road from Harbour House, and from our windows you could see and hear the children playing at recreation time. You might even hear the pupils in First Class, the part of the building nearest our house, chanting their lessons. It was a lovely surprise recently during an Irish tour when Imelda Farry presented herself backstage after one of my Dublin concerts in the Gaiety Theatre. This charming lady had taught me in First Class when I was six. I'd forgotten how handsome and gracious she was. Looking back, the schooling system seems a curious set up. There was St Vincent's, the national school, where the teaching was excellent, and it was free and attended by a mixture of pupils from both professional-class and working-class backgrounds. Not far away, separated only by a camogie pitch, was a small private fee-paying primary school, and then there was the big secondary school which catered for day-students and boarders. Each member of our family started off at St Vincent's, until he or she was ready for the secondary school.

But I only stayed there until I was eight. One day during recreation I was accidentally charged and broke my collarbone. Mother decided the school was "too rough for Mary", and I was sent instead to St Anne's, the private school further down in the grounds, where I spent the next two years before graduating to the secondary school and joining my two older sisters.

At the start of World War II Father joined the British Army as a commissioned officer and for some time was stationed in Northern Ireland. We used to drive up and spend long weekends with him in Ballycastle, County Antrim, while he was there. I recall loaves of white bread being smuggled into the Free State in the boot of the car. There are other memories too. There was 'Snowball', a charming woman who stayed in our hotel. She had prematurely white hair and the luxury of two swimsuits – a pale pink one for swimming in and a pale blue one for sunbathing. Years later we heard that she had been a spy for the Germans. *442,095/920/O'HAR*

After County Antrim, Father went to India. From there, he wrote to each one of us. I looked forward to his letters (which towards the end I could read for myself), which were chatty and affectionate and always ended up with "take care of Mumsy" or "do what Mumsy tells you". Throughout the most appalling rows at home he would never countenance our speaking against her. He would say, "She is your mother and you must not talk about her like that!" For grumble away we did at times, we would get so fed up with the whole blessed thing. He was very loyal to her.

The day father came home from India I was given the day off from school. There was great excitement. He had trunks full of exotic presents for us: silks, rings, silver-ware, swords, sandals, to name just a few. And there was all the news to tell him.

Meanwhile the rows and endless bickering continued. Even as a very small child I used to pray that my parents would separate. I knew if they did that I would stay with Father – everyone knew I sided with him in the interminable conflict. Joan, I assumed, would stay with Mother. Both parents by now were drinking a lot more than was good for them. I took to playing tennis 'out the back' on my owney-o, bashing the tennis ball against the side of the house. I used to be as happy as Larry there

19

all by myself, absorbed, and away from the tensions inside the house. It was my big release. By the standard of the times we were well off, but my parents were unwise with their money. There were many times when Father would have preferred to go abroad again and sometimes they reached a stage where a house would have been purchased, whether it was Sheffield or Malta or wherever and at the eleventh hour mother would have a 'health crisis' and say she was not going and would "take to the bed". She thwarted many of his best plans. He was, and still remains, a very gifted man – if only Mother could have been flexible and met him half-way. Of course, there must have been failings on Father's side too but I can only write as I recall. Mother's failings were more glaring in my youthful, inexperienced eyes. Perhaps she tried harder than any of us ever knew.

Even though a slender, pale child, I was stronger than I looked. Going off to school in the morning someone might comment, "Mary looks pale". ("Dawney" was a favourite word of Mother's.) Small wonder since I didn't get enough sleep. During the nocturnal frays I tended to get shifted from bed to bed. Tonsillitis dogged me for years, and mother was very careful about keeping me in bed when I had an attack, even though the inflammation and swelling were never serious enough to warrant the removal of the tonsils. So, Mother did care about me in her own peculiar fashion, but I think that she became absorbed in and preoccupied with her own unhappiness and was incapable of pausing and objectively working out what was the best for her children. I question whether she had any deep maternal feelings.

Father's sense of humour was his safety valve. At times when the situation was becoming unbearable he would crack a joke, and even if it was in the middle of a monumental row Mother would laugh – in spite of herself.

Years later, when I was in the monastery, I started having a recurring dream. In it mother had become a totally reformed character: an attentive caring wife and mother. She never spoke a harsh word and was frequently engaged in gardening, something I don't ever remember her doing. Perhaps this was a sign that she had attained complete happiness at last. This dream had an unfailingly soothing effect on me too.

Mother was forever threatening to leave. One day Dermot and I were collected from school by father who said, "Mother has gone. I've left her at the station." Dermot and I burst into tears. Father drove us to the home of a good friend of theirs in Sligo, where his wife gave us soup. Dermot and I cried all the way home, only to find Mother was back in the house again. She was always doing this to us.

But there are happy memories too. She played the piano well and liked to sing to me. She taught me my first song, "Little Sir Echo", when I was about two or three; we would do it together and I'd be the echo. Mother would make me miserable by getting me to sing it for her friends, and although because of my shyness I hated doing it, I would never say I did not want to in case I got a clip in the ear, something which was liberally and gratuitously dispensed without too much warning.

Then there was what I called "the bouncy thing", which I adored. On the way into town to do the shopping she would hold out her arms and stiffen them and, holding on to her hands, I would leap into the air. I loved that bit of the trip. There was always a break in the shopping for a delicious sit-down ice-cream. She'd bring bars of chocolate and cakes back to all of us, for although this was wartime there was minimal rationing in Sligo. And Tuesday was a big day because that was comic day. Who would read the *Dandy* and the *Beano* first! Dermot usually won.

I was not a great reader (Joan was a voracious one), but there was one particular book that I read over and over again. It was called *Long, Long Ago* and was the Greek and Roman myths retold for children. I'd probably be very disappointed in the illustrations now, but to me, then, they were exquisite. It takes no effort to conjure them up over thirty years later: "While Proserpine danced the great king watched her", and poor old Pluto looking so innocent and well-intentioned. "Prometheus chained to a rock" with that vulture at his liver. "Europa and the bull" – all those daisy chains; yet another chain: the one binding the diaphanously clad blonde-haired maiden to the sea cliff where she waited for the unseen monster to come and gobble her up. But of course, Perseus always got there first.

Every Easter week found Sligo in the febrile grip of the annual

21

Feis. Feis is the gaelic word for festival. There were two organisations: the Feis Ceóil and the Feis Sligigh. Both involved competitions for singing, reciting, the playing of musical instruments and dancing. There were solo, duet and ensemble contests. The Sligo Feis Ceóil was the older institution and the standard was reputedly as high as, if not higher than, that of the Dublin Feis Ceóil. There was a preponderance of competitions in the Gaelic language in the Feis Sligigh.

As a child I dreaded Easter because the very word evoked thoughts of a week of unmitigated discomfort, occasioned by my having to perform at innumerable competitions. Competitiveness is alien to my nature, so I would never have voluntarily entered the Feis arena. It was my school teachers who did me the bad/good turn. I considered it a penance: all that relentless assault on the nervous system. But it was also a blessing in disguise, for it trained me successfully to cope with and effectively to control that agony of nervousness which is the common lot of most performers and artists, whose ranks I was destined to join nearly ten years later. The exhilaration of winning was tempered by the knowledge that one would be "sent in" again the following year. How incredible to have thought then that a time would arrive over twenty years later when Easter would become of paramount importance to me. That at the mention of this feast of the Resurrection "blood and bone would thrill", and that dwelling on the mystery, joy would invade the nooks and crannies of one's being.

Preparations for the *Feis* started months ahead: some parents I suspect may even have built their year around it, becoming obsessed with the performances of their offspring. With single-minded dedication they would have their child licked into shape well in advance of the Big Event. Then, at the appointed hour, they would lead them forth to the venue, thoroughly scrubbed and dolled up in their best outfits. While their children went through their paces, some parents could be observed in the audience following every syllable and mouthing it with them. (The rivalry could be quite acute. At least one year I know that there was a dark rumour afloat that certain parents had invited the adjudicator to tea. Rank bribery was intimated!) The high point of each event was reached after that awesome interval when the competitors had retired and the adjudicator scribbled at his desk before mounting the platform. At this stage breathing was more or less suspended. Then the winner would be announced, the charged atmosphere clear, the audience discuss and compare notes among themselves and slowly the hall would empty and wait patiently for the following competition.

The ability to bi-locate would have been invaluable for those of us who found we had been entered for two or more competitions at more or less the same time on the same day. Believe me, it did happen.

I've already described how I won a singing competition at the Sligo Feis Ceóil at the age of eight. In the same year I had been entered for a Feis Sligigh competition with equal reluctance and trepidation. The venue was the Town Hall. No memory of sunlight then but a sense of dust and dryness everywhere. My first song was "An Caitin Bán", a lament for a little white kitten. The other was about a little girl called Mary, "*a bhíos i gcómhnaí' gáire*", or, who was always smiling. That adjudicator had also caused me unnecessary agony, this time by reading out the prize-winners in reverse order. I wasn't even among those highly recommended. Nor third or second prizewinner. To my amazement, I heard my name and number being read out as First prize-winner. To compound my painful confusion at this unexpected turn of events, shot through with pleasure of course, I heard him say, "Would this competitor please come up on stage so that I may congratulate her". Veiling the acute shyness with my customary giant-sized smile, with thumping heart I gracefully climbed on to the stage. So far, so good. But my exit was less graceful. I slipped on the wooden steps, bumped my head and landed on my back completely winded at the foot of the stage. I was carried out by the adjudicator, with Mother close at his heels and very worried indeed. A concerned crowd gathered. As I regained my breath the adjudicator gently remarked, "You have a lovely voice and I hope you'll never get a swelled head." I almost did.

"Out the back" was our favourite place for sulking, being alone or nursing a hurt. During the war Mother tried to economize on children's new clothing. She gave one of her suits to a

tailor to have it reduced and made into a "new" suit for
Dermot. Now reduced is the operative word for the man did
more or less just that with the jacket. He turned up the hem
leaving the pockets where they originally were and, worse still
also left the waist as it was. The first day Dermot was put into
the outrageous garment he vanished almost immediately – and
was missing all morning. He was finally located "out the back"
in tears. When he was asked what the broken heart was all about
he said: "It's this suit. I wish that a lion would come and eat me
up – me and this awful suit." He'd been listening to those verses
about the little boy who let go his nurse's hand and got eaten by
the lion at the zoo. Thereafter it was referred to by all and
sundry as "the lion suit".

It's probably true of many mothers that they don't realize
how sensitive little children are about the clothes they are made
to wear, and how hurt they can be. My Confirmation Day was
a mortifying experience. Mother had decided that, for the ceremony, I should be clad in Joan's once-best dress. It was an expensive dress, but salmon pink – beautiful on Joan but a disaster
on me with my different colouring and skin tone. It was also
short. I loathed the garment but knew better than to argue and
provoke a scene. Being wartime, ever since the supply of petrol
for civilians had ceased, the car had been laid up on blocks in the
coach house. There was only one man in the town who ran a
taxi service, and he had been booked to bring my brother and
myself to the cathedral. For some reason the taxi failed to turn
up. It was getting perilously close to the hour of the service so
Mother decided to get out her bicycle and ferry us on the carrier
through the rain, one at a time. The church was a good ten
minutes' cycle away. By the time we were both deposited
inside the door of the cathedral, Dermot was lachrymose. The
ceremony had begun. The boys in an assortment of garments
were seated on one side of the church. On the opposite side sat
the girls in serried ranks, all vested – to my utter consternation –
in *long white* dresses, complete with white *shoes* and socks.
Dressed glaringly in my short salmon pink dress, white socks
and *brown* sandals, feeling like a cross between a fish out of
water and a Christian martyr, I had to march up the aisle in full
view of everyone to join this radiantly white troop of potential
soldiers of Christ. I deserved an award for bravery.

Out for a walk one day and skipping ahead of my mother and a friend of hers, I overheard the latter remark: "Mary's got dancers legs." Since compliments (I took it to be one!) were thin on the ground where I was concerned, I was thrilled; but too diffident to enquire what was meant. Mother then decided I should learn ballet. The prospect of learning to dance gave me unspeakable pleasure. There was one woman in Sligo who taught ballet, and though I was never taken to meet her, Mother made all the arrangements for me to start having lessons. Then unexpectedly my would-be teacher left town. That was that. I took it all philosophically. I would have loved to have tried dancing. It seems to me to be the most satisfying form of self-expression, engaging as it does the entire body from head to pointed toe; also the silence of the art appeals to me. It wasn't until I was nineteen and living in Dublin that the opportunity of having lessons presented itself again. I attended ballet classes there and enjoyed every second of them, but by then my singing career had begun to get underway and occupied most of my time. Besides, I'd always been told that dancers must start as young children and as I am five feet seven and a quarter inches in my stockinged feet, my height was against me too. I think perhaps one reason why I enjoy tennis so enormously is because of the grace of the game. Some movements on court approximate to the dance.

I've always had a natural aptitude for sports. When I moved on into the senior secondary school in Sligo, I started to play camogie, which is hurley as played by women: a ball and stick game. The only time I took part in the Annual School Sports, I won the running competition. I loved movement, and when I was chosen to act as goal-keeper in my first and second year at day school I was too inhibited and diffident to say I hated the in-activity and could I please be allowed to play out in the field. So for two whole years I endured the restrictions, until I was sent elsewhere to boarding school.

As we grew older I played less and less with Dermot, for now he was at the Christian Brothers' school on the far side of town (while I was at St Anne's) and immersed in a world of gangs to which, of course, little girls were never admitted. Dermot had an endearing habit of getting some words slightly wrong. He announced one evening that he was "clergic" to eggs. And my favourite one is this: he was trying to do his homework and the rest of us were being noisy when he flung down his pen and cried, "Can't you have a bit of *constipation* for someone who is trying to study?" He was a very affectionate little boy and very protective of me. When I broke my collarbone and he heard the news from a school companion who said, "I hear Mary was taken home in a coffin", he was so frightened and angry that he fought the other boy. And later, when I had to have my appendix out, he burst into tears, ran upstairs, locked himself in the lavatory and cried for hours.

On the two occasions that I spent in hospital, Mother would not visit me there. For some reason she could not face it, but I was prepared for this, remembering her reaction to my first accident. I'd been wheeling a dolls' pram and a very plump girl I was playing with, sat on the pram causing the whole thing to tip over. My hand caught in the handle and, unable to free it, I was dragged down the slope of the concrete road for several yards. Spurting blood, I dashed into the house and Mother was so upset that she promptly disappeared, leaving Father to deal with me. He held my finger under the running cold water tap. The finger was broken and the chemist fixed it up. Mother didn't come in with us, and I fully understand now that she just did not feel able to cope. She knew I was fond of her, but I took it for granted that she would stay away from the hospital and that Father would take over as usual. She was inordinately fearful of illness. She suffered from bronchitis, but would never have her chest examined in case she had tuberculosis. She grew up at a time when the disease was rampant in Ireland and entire families died of it. I do think that she could have benefited from psychiatric help, but in those days and in that part of the world, ailments of that nature were synonymous with mental sickness and treatment was not available as far as I know. She was subject to black depressions. Her physical violence, betrayed an imbalance, and as time went on she became dependant on barbiturates and alcohol which led to her death at the age of fifty-two. A week before she died she was admitted to hospital and operated on for internal cancer. It was so far advanced there was nothing the surgeon could do for her.

I had a reputation at school for being gentle and biddable, but I must often have been very difficult and fractious at home; for I remember Mother once turning on me saying, "You're a street angel and a house devil." Boarding school was soon to put an end to that – the street angel bit.

Father wanted to send Dermot to Stonyhurst, the Jesuit School in England. There was a family hitch at the last moment and Dermot was rushed, into Blackrock College, County Dublin. The following year when I was thirteen it was decided that I should go to Sion Hill, run by the Dominican Sisters which was right next door to Dermot's school. That was handy for everyone, especially for my parents when it came to visiting us. As things turned out, with Joan now at the Abbey School of Acting in Dublin and two of us at school there, my parents sold the house in Sligo and moved to Dublin. Going to boarding school was something I'd never dreamt of. Joan told me that she used to which she'd been sent to one, so in a way I felt privileged.

I was intrigued by the Cash's name tapes, the long list of required clothing and excited by the shopping it entailed. I was put on a train and met by friends of the family who drove me to Sion Hill. I was clad in one of Joan's coats. Originally brown, Mother had had it dyed navy blue, the prescribed school colour. It was noticeably shorter than my very long new gym-frock and I tried hard not to feel self-conscious. A couple of years later, Mother bought me a very beautiful new princess line navy blue coat which was so admired by some of my more glamorous school friends that they used to borrow it for special occasions. It was well worth waiting for. And, instead of the dull mass-produced long white dresses which came from a leading Dublin store to be worn on prize giving days, Mother had a very pretty one made specially for me by a private dress-maker.

Everyone was kind, welcoming and pleasant and in no time I settled in. Going to secondary school was a turning point in my life. It may be an exaggeration to say that there I kicked over the traces, but something akin to that did happen. I sprouted wings.

I had always done very well at school in Sligo. Academically, the standard there was very high. Sion Hill was not in the same league. After the first few days of classes I could see that in

Third Year in my new school they were covering the same ground I'd already successfully traversed in Second Year in Sligo. So I simply sat back and lazed. My days of being a diligent student were over. At the end of that year I sailed through the school examinations without doing any work for them. The following year I got honours in the National Intermediate Examination Certificate. By then the rot had set in and thereafter it became increasingly difficult to apply myself to my studies.

As a small child, my parents used to quarrel in my presense so often that I got used to switching off as best I could. I tried not to listen, though I couldn't prevent myself from hearing. Maybe this was partly why, during boarding school, I became unable to take in very much in class.

If my brain was not being exercised enough, my body certainly was. Father had brought back some fine hockey sticks from India, but the game was not played in the Sligo school and the sticks had lain there unused. One of them arrived with my luggage at Sion Hill. The first day on the field I discovered that, although I am not left-handed, I have more power and control on my left side and since hockey is right-hand swing I decided the game was not for me. I swapped my hockey stick for a camogie stick (a lovely springy one which lasted me all those four game-packed years), and a new world opened up for me. I found that I simply adored the game. I was nimble-footed and revelled in the swiftness and speed of the game, and from then on played either centre field, or much more often, left wing. Camogie was more in tune with my temperament than hockey. Like the latter, it too has it's discipline, yet it is less restricting. For instance, unlike hockey, the player may swing her stick as high as she likes on either side; the ball may be bounced on the stick whether standing or running. In my opinion camogie is the more spirited game; rather like having wings instead of being on wheels. It certainly had a liberating effect on me. Later, the summer term brought tennis and an attendant new dimension of pleasure. A lot has been written about the virtue of games for growing children; I can vouch for their salutary effect on me. Out on the camogie pitch and tennis court I became unshackled, and knew a glorious sense of freedom. I loved games for their own sake, which is also the way I feel about singing. Two things mar that pleasure. Competition and organization. For example, I would prefer to rally for a couple of hours rather than play sets of tennis. And organization: it was an honour to have been voted Games Captain by my school fellows during my last year at Sion Hill but it most certainly took a lot of the zest out of playing. I am not an organizer and I disliked that particular kind of responsibility "being in charge" entailed. But, nevertheless, I spent any free time I had out on the playing fields. It was fortunate for me that games in Sion Hill were so encouraged. During my years there, our First Eleven camogie team was never beaten by any other Dublin school.

Not long after I arrived at Sion Hill it was discovered that I could sing, so I continued to be put through the Feis mill; this time the Dublin Feis Ceóil. My teacher was a very amiable, gentle person called Sister Angela Walsh. She continued to teach until she was almost ninety. I count her amongst my most cherished friends.

An annual pageant was performed by the school girls and students of the Domestic Science Training College attached to Sion Hill. The scripts were written by a member of the community. Each year I secretly hoped there would be a part in it for me. One year I played St Francis, a very small rôle with some lovely lines I had to speak about love and Brother Sun. During my last year at school the new pageant was about the life of Thomas Moore, the Anglo-Irish poet (a great friend of Robert Emmett, the patriot) who was the darling of the London drawing rooms in his heyday at the beginning of the nineteenth century. His verses are full of references to the harp as a symbol of Ireland. It was decided to bring in Máirín Ní Shéa to teach the harp for the occasion. Since I was known to have a good voice and had also been learning the piano for eight years I was one of the three chosen to take lessons on the small knee harp. The other two were Déirdre Flynn (later Kelleher) and Kathleen Watkins. We were not particularly pally at that time, but finding ourselves frequently thrown together during the ensuing couple of years, friendships were formed and to this day we have kept in touch with each other. After some years Déirdre got married and gave up singing and playing the harp altogether. Kathleen still performs on occasions and is married to another friend of mine, Gay Byrne, the Irish television personality.

Our new teacher worked hard with us and taught us enough so that we could accompany ourselves during the pageant. As things turned out she stayed on and we continued with lessons. Being our last year at school (I was sixteen), I decided that I'd better give up the piano. Just as with all my other subjects I did the minimal amount of work yet always managed to emerge with first-class honours for my piano examinations. In the late spring of that year Máirín arranged for each of the three of us to broadcast live from Radio Eireann, two songs apiece, on a programme called 'Children at the Mike'. Both my songs were in Gaelic, despite the title of the first one: 'Habit Shirt'. The other was 'Ard Tighe Cuain' – a beautiful exile's song from County Antrim. After I left school my sister Joan translated it freely for me into English and called it 'The Quiet Land of Érin'. As time went by I became identified with this song and later used it as the opening and closing theme melody for my BBC Television series in 1956 – and indeed for innumerable subsequent radio and television programmes.

By the time I'd reached my penultimate year in school my studies, or rather my capacity for study, was in a lamentable state. Work I did not and indeed could not do. When I sat down before my history examination paper and read the questions I decided I could not answer a single one. So, while everybody else scribbled industriously, I produced my needles and wool and proceeded to knit my white tennis socks. When the papers were collected up, mine was in its pristine state of blankness. The supervisor, with a glare of disapproval, took the tennis sock from me and pinned it to the examination paper. In due course I was admitted to the unamused presence of the Mistress of Studies, who promptly despatched me to the now deserted examination room to re-do the examination. To my astonishment, I passed.

Bit by bit in my final year, I began to drop subjects. I had already, foolishly, temporarily jettisoned music after my intermediate year (even though I'd got honours and the highest marks) partly because of disharmony between me and the teacher. Perhaps she saw I wasn't working. I'd have dropped every subject if I could have got away with it. Most people do

30

the leaving certificate examination with seven subjects, but I opted for the minimum number of five. Although I got honours in Irish and French, my marks for the other subjects were nothing to boast about.

I could never be classified as wild: I never went out of my way to infringe rules and regulations. It just happened. From the time of my arrival I became more and more irrepressible. My transgressions were largely of the schoolgirl giddiness variety: talking in class, in rank, in the dormitory after lights out (I had only one midnight feast and found it utterly boring), reading comics under the desk lid while class was in progress (I always made sure of a seat at the back so as to engage undisturbed in such undercover pursuits); running when I was supposed to be walking and so on.

Then there was the baffling episode of the pony tail. Without the slightest intention of setting a trend, one afternoon I innocently gathered my hair into an elastic band at the crown of my head and presented myself at my desk in the study hall. Its effect on the presiding Sister was startling. It was, I suppose, a hitherto unknown hairstyle. Anyway, I was called up to the Sister's desk and roundly reprimanded. During a recent visit to my old school I was told that the said sister had had difficulty keeping a straight face while the ponytail bobbed up and down as I argued earnestly with her over the offending coiffure. The next day the school was peppered with juniors sporting pony-tails. . . . The damage, whatever it was, had been done.

Another time, I slipped into town with two companions to meet some schoolboys. We'd met at a school function and went to the cinema with them. As they were saying their innocent good-byes to us at the gate the lights of an oncoming car revealed the delinquents, and of course the authorities heard about it at once. Next day my companions and I were dramatically called forth from the study hall and each one seen separately by the Prioress. She was such a remote figure that this was the only occasion I can recall having dealings with her – which indicated the enormity of the misdemeanour. My parents were sent for and told about the incident.

I had a hefty appetite (though you would never have thought it to look at me) and was the best eater at my table in any given

year. Everything I ate was quickly burnt up – games and
nervous energy I suppose. When autumn came we threw our
camogie sticks up at the walnut trees and the fruit tumbled
down. We used our desk lids to crack the shells. There was a
well-stocked apple orchard which also suffered from our
periodic raids. Being one of the more gracile ones, my job was
to slither through a gap in the hedge and collect the windfalls.
Having stuffed the tops of our gym-slips to capacity, the other
method of transport for the plundered fruit from orchard to
school dormitory was the capacious elastic-ended legs of our
uniform school knickers. If any of the Sisters noticed my
curious and uncharacteristically slow gait on an autumnal afternoon around 4.15 p.m. (the apple-gathering hour) they made
no comment.

A few months before I was due to finish school, soon after the
incident with the schoolboys, I was talking away in the rank
when leaving the refectory after breakfast. Suddenly, Sister
Petra, the Mistress of Studies, made a noise like a clap of
thunder with her wooden clappers. We all stood rooted to the
spot. "Mary O'Hara," she said, "the community has decided
that if you continue to break as much as one more minor rule we
cannot shoulder the responsibility of you any longer." That
shut me up for a bit, but not for long.

In our school, once a girl was in Sixth Years she almost auto-
matically became a Child of Mary. This was a religious sodality
dedicated to the Blessed Virgin, Mother of God. It carried
certain connotations of "goodness". When in the Fifth Year,
each girl received a blue ribbon and medal to pin on her uniform
to signify that she was a candidate for this coveted honour. I
didn't even get as far as the blue ribbon – something unheard of
in our school. I was unruffled about being passed over, for I felt
that I was Mary's child anyway.

Despite my almost incessant contravention of the school
rules and the annoyance it must have caused them, I know that
the Sion Hill community nevertheless loved me – and none
perhaps more than Sister Angela. After my husband's death I
was showered with letters from them, and one wrote "Nuns
seldom cry, but you would have been touched by the number
of people here who wept when your telegram reached Sister
Angela." They had never even seen Richard. I was deeply

1

Mary's mother Graduation
Day. University College,
Galway.

Mary's father, Major J.C.
O'Hara of the Royal
Engineers.

2

Mother – with Dermot, Joan, and Mary (*far right*) just before Mary's second birthday.

Mary, aged about three, and her two left legs.

(Front row, second from left) the shyest member of the First Communion group.

Mary, aged about eight 'out the back' playing tennis and getting used to the perm. The dress is her very own and not one of Joan's cast-offs.

7

8

Opposite page: Joan, Mother, Mary and Angela, in the days when bananas were a luxury.

Camogie group, Sion Hill. Mary encircled, wearing her Games Captain badge. (*Centre, front row*) Kathleen Watkins, now married to Gay Byrne.

Above: Jill Fisher's School of Beauty, Dublin. Mary aged seventeen. (*Left to right*) Rita Rooney, Mary, Berta Purner, Margaret O'Shea.

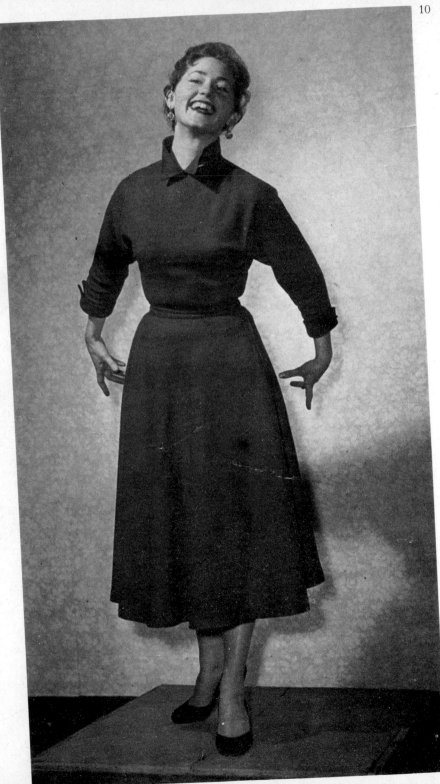

Opposite page: A modelling publicity photo of Mary, aged eighteen.

Above: Mary's sister Joan, an actress

12

13

Above: Mary, aged nineteen.

Mary on the Gold Coast
(Ghana) at nineteen.

moved. The connection between myself and Sion Hill from the time I left school until my marriage – and Richard's death – had been a very tenuous one, through my sporadic singing lessons and a letter about once a year to Sister Angela. But after Richard's death I visited them and started to keep in closer contact. Over the intervening years I have been the recipient of considerable love and friendship from several people there – and I know that my life has been the richer and warmer for it. I never think of myself as a past pupil but as a friend.

2   Growing Up

One day I sat down on the grass by the pond because I was tired of stand-
  ing.
"You are an idle creature," said Swan.
"What would you have me do?" I asked her.
"Count the stars!"
"But, Swan, it is daylight, I can't even see the stars."
"You are an idle creature," repeated Swan.
"Please, Swan, be reasonable. How can I count the stars if I can't see
  them?"
"If you counted the stars only when you could see them you'd never
  finish," Swan scolded.

(from 'My Friends: *A Fable*' by Richard Selig)

When I left school Joan was established at the Abbey Theatre as
a promising young actress. She'd known since she was five
years old that she wanted to be one. My lack of direction
bothered Joan and she suggested I do a course in beauty culture.
So that winter I attended classes and got my diploma at the end
of the course but neither collected nor used it. But it proved to
be a very useful thing to have done, helping later on where stage
make-up was concerned.

Then Joan got enthusiastic about my doing art. My talents
there were slender and undeveloped. I'd always thought it a
shame that in the senior school at Sion Hill the choice lay
between music and art. Naturally, I'd chosen music but I
regretted having had to forego art classes which I'd enjoyed as a
junior. So off I trotted to be enrolled in the College of Art in
Dublin. I did precious little work, but I had a very enjoyable
time. After about six months of relative loafing, the director
(rightly) sent for me and very simply said, "Miss O'Hara,
would you mind telling me what exactly are you doing here?" I
replied, "Oh, don't worry, sir, I'm leaving next month
because I'm planning to go to Africa," which I was.

While all this was going on I was singing; getting sporadic

engagements on radio and in variety concerts in the provinces. At the end of the summer after I'd left school, encouraged by Sister Angela, I decided to continue with my singing lessons and although at first I didn't intend to carry on with the harp, my mother persuaded me to do so. Joan too was anxious and willing to do whatever she could to get me interested in a career of one kind or another, to instil some of her own ambition and enthusiasm for work into me. While acting at the Abbey Theatre she also did occasional radio work on commercial programmes (there was no television in Ireland until 1962). One day she mentioned to the radio producer that her youngest sister sang and played the harp. He expressed interest, and it was arranged that Joan should bring me along for an audition. I sang my entire repertoire: a handful of songs which included Joan's 'The Quiet Land of Érin'. The producer said he'd use them on his programme and gave me £2.00 for each song, a princely sum of money in those days. I was very pleased. I was invited back and started seriously to build up my repertoire, and every few weeks I had a recording session. Quite unexpectedly I was earning my own money.

During the following twelve months, Máirín Ní Shéa took Déirdre, Kathleen and me along with her to various concerts and entertainments in England organized by Irish Societies, especially around the month of March and St Patrick's Day, where we would sing and play together. Máirín's sister, Roisin, sometimes joined us too. We wore long green woollen Irish costumes, hired from Ging's theatrical outfitters in Dublin, which we irreverently referred to as "our flowing togas". Déirdre and I were never really comfortable in them.

It was round that time that I was introduced to Seán Óg O'Tuama, who was to become a key figure in my musical career. He was related by marriage to Máirín Ní Shéa through whom I first met him. We became and remained, to the time of his death in April 1980, very good friends. Séan was a gifted and generous hearted man. Science was his profession, music of all kinds his passionate interest. In my opinion few people in the mid-twentieth century in Ireland can have done as much as he, indeed, none more than he, to foster a knowledge and love of traditional Irish song among two if not three generations.

For years he held a class on Saturday afternoons in the Royal

Irish Academy of Music in Dublin. Anyone who wished to could attend. They were free. And they were great. Seán Óg stood before us and taught us songs by singing a phrase at a time, which we would repeat after him.

His fund of songs seemed endless. I think that Máirín brought the three of us to one of his sessions at the academy while we were still schoolgirls. During the following few years, needing to build up my repertoire because of the increase in my radio broadcasting programmes, I attended the clascea-dal, as it was called, as often as I could. Out of those who regularly came to the RIAM, Seán assembled a small group which broadcasted regularly from Radio Eireann.

Sometimes I sang with them; and Róisín Ní Shéa accompanied us skilfully on the harp with her own imaginative arrangements. To my way of thinking learning a traditional song from someone as informed and as steeped in Irish culture as Seán Óg, is incomparably better than learning from the printed page. Besides, scores of these songs had never been written down. The delicate subtleties of many of the classic Gaelic songs defy entrapment between bar lines. In a very real sense Seán Óg and exponents like him, by transmitting them the way they did have kept these songs alive.

His singing voice may have left much to be desired, but behind the voice was a mind and heart charged with an intense love of his country and her music, so that he was more than a mere teacher of notes. All the Gaelic "big songs", which I find elicit strong praise from music critics all over the world when I sing them in my concerts, I learnt from Seán Óg Ó'Tuama.

I felt I needed further instruction on the harp so I started taking lessons on the concert harp from Mercedes Bolger, who had just returned from a season with the Hallé Orchestra and was now playing with the Radio Eireann Light Orchestra. A shy and amiable person, Mercedes and I became good friends. I continued with lessons from her until frequent absences from Dublin, and eventually my engagement, took me away from Ireland altogether.

A big event during that winter was when Máirín, Déirdre, Kathleen and I were flown to London to take part in the entertainment side of the publicity for the first "An Tóstal", a project launched by the Irish Tourist Board to boost the tourist industry (*tóstal* means welcome). It included tea at the Irish Embassy and an appearance on a TV programme called 'In Town Tonight'. It was then that I first met Richard Afton who was to play an important rôle in my career some time later. He brought me over from Dublin to make my first solo appearance on British television in his programme 'More Contrary', which led to my own series. On that first occasion he took us all to lunch at the Café Royal and saw to it that we were comfortably set up at the Piccadilly Hotel. There we tasted the sensuous delight of our first heated bathroom. Déirdre and I, who shared a room together, cavorted ecstatically about the suite, scantily clad, delighting in the warmth of the rooms – for central heating in those days was virtually unheard of in Ireland and it was warm only near a fire, beyond the radius of which chill and draught prevailed.

It was during that first year after I'd left school that the producer of Radio Éireann's 'Children at the Mike' approached me and asked if I would do a fifteen-minute programme of Irish songs (in Irish) on my own. They were satisfied enough with the result to continue to ask me, and from then on a blue contract form would arrive in the post at regular intervals. I also sang as soloist with the Radio Éireann Light Orchestra every couple of months or so 'Take the Floor' was a light variety programme in which I took part many times. It included, besides myself on the harp, a storyteller, dancers (believe it or not on radio), another singer, and a compère and comedian. 'Gael Linn' was another sponsored programme for which I recorded individual items from time to time. As I did not have an agent, amateur concert organizers around the country contacted me through Radio Éireann. Without having to seek it, a fairly steady flow of work was coming in.

A strange thing happened to me during one of those 'Take the Floor' live programmes. Shortly after Mother's death the surgeon who had operated on her had a look at an unusually large and curious mole between my breasts. It was dark brown, almond-shaped, three-dimensional and for some years had been deteriorating, so the doctor decided it had better be removed. Given the choice, I opted for a local rather than a general anaesthetic. Memories of the effects of a general administered to me when I had had my appendix out were uncomfortable enough to warrant my wishing to avoid it if possible. Stoically I lay down on the operating table and allowed myself to be carved. I felt no pain but I was aware of most of what was going on. I heard the measured tones of the surgeon, sensed the tension and the serious atmosphere and experienced the trickling of blood down my sides. The deed done, I was stitched up and bandaged. Two lengths of plaster, about two inches wide, were criss-crossed over my shoulders from the front to the back of my waist to hold the dressing over the wound securely in place. One of the nurses told me that word had got around the nursing home that I was a remarkably brave young girl; how I'd chosen to have a local anaesthetic and appeared not to bat an eyelid before, during, or after the operation. I was discharged from hospital a day or two later in time for a 'Take the Floor' broadcast. I wore a very loose, black sweater to hide the shape of the bandages. In the middle of my song, to my horror, I felt blood trickling down my side, exactly as it had done during the operation. Hiding my consternation by smiling even more broadly than ever at the live studio audience, and convinced I was bleeding to death – the trickling had become a veritable rivulet by then, I finished my song and made a dash for the ladies' dressing room. Steeling myself for the bloody sight I was expecting, I removed the sweater and doubled up with relief and laughter when I saw that the 'stream' was one of perspiration due to nervousness. There was no clothing to absorb the sweat so it had begun to run down my body. A few weeks later I went to have the stitches removed. In the deserted waiting room the surgeon asked me to remove my sweater and turn my back to him. Suddenly, I felt a sharp stab of pain at my waist and irrationally thought I had been knifed. There and then I vomited on the floor with fright. The surgeon was only removing the plaster bandages. He had to give me a glass of brandy to settle my stomach. So much for my bravery.

Mother died in February 1953. She never recovered from the operation she'd had for cancer. During that period in the nursing home, Father, Joan and I used to spend a lot of time with Mother – Dermot came occasionally. She died very peacefully; it was the first death I was ever present at. Father was distraught and early in 1954, as soon as he could after straightening out his affairs, he returned to the west coast of Africa in the employment of the Colonial Service once again. This time it was the Gold Coast which has since become Ghana. Dermot and I shared the house in Dublin. Sadly, we had grown apart and were most of the time at loggerheads with each other.

In April 1954 Joan married Frank Barry, the Dublin architect. Her years of sharing a bedroom with me were at an end. No more for her the discomfort of having to put up with the foibles of a younger sister. One particular incident I shall never forget. I'd read in some woman's magazine that buttermilk left on one's face overnight takes away freckles. Arriving home tired from the theatre late one summer's night, the stink of buttermilk assailed Joan as she opened the bedroom door. She made me get up and wash my face, so I'll never know whether it works or not. I still have freckles in the summer. We had only one set of curlers and they belonged to me. Joan wanted to borrow them the night before her wedding but I was too mean to lend them! I put them in my own hair. But I did lend her my special green sweater for her honeymoon. Since her falling in love with Frank, Joan had blossomed and the relationship between her and me improved immeasurably. It was as if I was getting to know her for the first time in my life. The cold, distant eldest sister of my childhood had become warm and responsive. We became great friends, and there were few things I enjoyed as much as visiting Joan and Frank in their flat in St Stephen's Green and going places together with them.

During the summer holidays of my last couple of years at school I was a member of the local tennis club. The standard cannot have been all that high for I once arrived home with three cups (and a hairbrush!). Most Saturday nights after I had left school I attended a dance either at a tennis club or at the College of Art. Occasionally I went out with boys but I was easily turned off. The type of shoes they wore or the colour of their shirts, a mismatched tie or other such trivia would invariably put me off. Obviously the right person hadn't yet come along. I knew I would recognise him when he did.

I went to Africa on June 1 1954. It was just over a year after Mother's death. My father had invited me out for the summer and I was jubilant at the prospect. Some of my friends were apprehensive about the venture and issued warnings about the risks involved. When I communicated these fears to my father he brushed them aside and assured me that in that day and age those hazards no longer existed.

Frank and David, a painter friend, saw me off at Dublin Airport. David had proposed to me a few days earlier. That was an embarrassing experience in that I had no previous inkling that he was serious about me, and I was joking insensitively about 'popping the question' just as he was bracing himself to ask me to marry him. He had a gentle, delicate mind. A gifted painter, I still have the very fine woodcut print he made and gave me for my birthday (Christ walking on the water). He was also a talented musician who opened up to me the treasure-house of Elizabethan song, and who sometimes accompanied me on his lute. Father met me at Accra Airport, where we stayed a few days at the home of an RAF friend. Then we set out for Secondi about 200 miles away where Father had a house.

On the way I had my first introduction to the colourful mammy wagons. These are open-sided lorries which transport humans, domestic animals and general merchandise, in one happy pot-pourri. Along the sides of the wagons an endless variety of imaginative slogans are written: "Jesus saves us"; "Freedom forever"; "Caution Best"; "Kwame Nkrumah the Saviour"; "Sweet pas Takoradi Harbour"; "Love thy neighbour"; "Sea never dry" and so on. Years before, my parents had brought back a drum from Africa. It looked forlorn and out of context in a west of Ireland home. Now, I was to see and hear them in their proper setting. "In the beginning," says African folk-lore "the creator created the drummer, the hunter and the smith." Drums do indeed talk; they warn of danger, call the people to council, bring news from afar, provide rhythm for the tribal dances and give prestige to all kinds of ceremonial gatherings. They are made from hollowed logs with animal skin or an elephant's ear stretched across the top and held taut by pegs. There is a legend in some parts of West Africa that the man-in-the-moon is a drummer.

When we finally reached Secondi, Kofi the cook greeted me with a shy smile and a splendid meal. My favourite dish to this day is West African curry, and Kofi was a past master at producing it. The basis of this dish is chicken, guinea fowl, native goat, lobster or rabbit. The meat is stewed in palm oil which is derived from crushed palm kernels, and is a heavy deep reddish brown coloured liquid. Madras curry powder is mixed into this and swimming around in it all are whole, hard-boiled eggs. An accompanying mountain of fluffy rice is borne in a separate dish. But it is the variety of side dishes which is the crowning gastronomical glory. Fruit of every available description – mangoes, avocado pears, paw-paw, oranges, limes, grapefruit, bananas, pineapples; and vegetables: tomatoes, garden eggs, okras and ground nuts. For those for whom the dish is still not fiery enough, little dishes of red peppers are on the table. This meal is ambrosial.

I was there in the rainy season, and when it rained it did so in style – the tropical, torrential rain that one sees in films. But the days of glorious sunshine far outnumbered the wet ones, and I took advantage of all the swimming, sunbathing and exercise in the fresh air. I had never been in better health. My catarrh vanished, the attendant swellings under my eyes, which are, I believe, connected with sinus trouble, completely disappeared. I slept well, ate supremely well and came back to Europe after those three months with a smashing tan, fortified against the awful colds and chest coughs that I was victim to, winter after winter.

I made many new friends in Africa, one of whom was a young Greek called George. He was a quiet, courteous, thoughtful person. The fact that I neither smoked nor drank intrigued him so much that he made a wager. He wrote me a cheque for £100 which, in 1954, was not exactly buttons, and post-dated it 1964. If, he said, I was still a non-smoker and didn't drink by then I could cash it. Highly amused, I pocketed the cheque and promptly forgot about it. A few days later, Father got a 'phone call from his bank manager: did he have a relative called Mary and, if so, could she come and see him. An African had picked up the cheque in the street and, signing it Mary O'Hara, had attempted to cash it. I tore it up. Poor George, who had also presented me with a gold watch, kept wanting to take me out; but I wasn't at all keen on him (in that way), so I said I'd go to the pictures with him provided Father came too! Not that I wasn't able to look after myself, but I didn't want him to get any wrong ideas and risk hurting him.

At a luncheon party aboard a visiting Portuguese naval ship

one day, I met an older man of great charm; I suppose he would have been in his late twenties then. He was an officer in a Highland regiment. On the strength of that meeting and a couple of brief encounters in the open-air swimming pool, and possibly at the officers' mess of the Gold Coast Regiment – of which Father was an honorary member – Dougal got romantic ideas about me and wrote declaring his feelings after I returned to Europe. He actually asked my *father* if I would marry him! But confidently I declined. I waited. . . .

Arrangements were made for me to give a recital at the British Consulate. I visited a Danish lady, who was a very good musician, and practised at her home in preparation for the event. She accompanied me expertly on the piano. My programme included traditional Irish and Scottish songs; a Mozart, some Elizabethan songs, a Max Reger lullaby in German, and others. It seemed to go down well. A black member of the audience wrote me an enthusiastic letter afterwards and said, "Your voice is beautiful and you sing like a devil." Could he have meant angel? Later I broadcasted some songs over the Gold Coast radio. The studio was a non-airconditioned room, with a piano that had suffered long from the humidity of the rainy seasons. The broadcaster preceeding me gave a learned dissertation on tropical fish.

Despite the warnings of my Celtic friends back in Dublin, I never met the black mamba, said to be a killer, who craftily managed to deceive the human (or any) enemy by looking convincingly like a discarded car tyre by the road side. Mosquitoes inevitably made a meal of me, but my daily intake of mepacrin obviated my demise by way of malaria.

Father moved to a new bungalow in Takoradi while I was staying with him and life there was much more pleasant. From there I made my first abortive attempt at learning to drive. Father gave me lessons on Takoradi air strip, but the lessons ended abruptly when I almost overturned the car. However, I was leaving West Africa the next day anyway and I didn't sit in a driver's seat again until I'd resumed my singing career after I emerged from the monastery, twenty years later. Driving is now one of my great delights.

Back in Dublin I took up singing again and was kept comfortably busy through that winter and spring of 1955. I broadcasted on radio, as soloist with the Radio Éireann Light Orchestra, doing sporadic fifteen-minute radio programmes and also appeared, again as a soloist, with the Radio Éireann Singers. I don't envy people who have to accompany others. The first and last time that I got involved in that sort of team work I made a right hash of it.

Sometime in 1955 John Reidy (Seán O' Riada) asked me if I would accompany the Radio Éireann Singers who were singing a piece of his on a programme in which I was also singing a solo. In John's contemporary composition I was required to count seventeen and a half bars of silence before coming in with a vigorous discord. Then another dozen and three quarter bars of silence followed by a dissonant twang from me. After that some more silence before my next caco-phonic contribution. The strain of counting those bars of silence was severe. During rehearsals I managed to come in at the right time, but when the live performance was in progress I slipped up somewhere in my figures and from that first inaccu-rate entry to the bitter end I didn't know whether I was coming or going. Exacerbation and resignation vied for supremacy on John's poor distraught face as he conducted his esoteric work to the end. In my philistine way I wondered if my mistakes sounded that much different from what the composer orig-inally intended. . . .

It was during this period that I took ballet lessons; and it was about this time, too, that I got interested in modelling. The latter was probably more of a curiosity than an interest. I still did not know what I wanted to do, so I was willing to try several things for a while. Jill Fisher, who ran the School of Beauty Culture which I'd been through, had suggested that I have a go at modelling. I was accepted for the course at one of the top agencies. At the time I was self-conscious about my bottom, for I felt it stuck out slightly when I was in a straight skirt; but I remedied this by placing a small, flat woollen cap inside my skirt at the back. I got away with it for about a week, until one day in class the instructor detected it, and, to the great amusement of the others, she extracted the woollen cap. After the course, I got bookings and did three fashion shows – quite successfully, as far as I could judge. My fourth appointment clashed with something far more significant: I chose instead to be with Richard Selig whom I was eventually to marry. That was the end of my brief modelling career, and I never went back.

3 Dublin

When, at such hour that we meet to change our myth . . .
(from 'Horoscope' by Richard Selig)

I used to get some work through Ciarán Mac Mathúna, the
Radio Éireann producer, who from time to time included
songs in English and Scots Gaelic in his programmes. In the
spring of 1955 he used me on a programme singing a Hebridean
song, "The Uist Cattle Croon". He told me that Calum
Maclean, a good friend of his, was in Dublin just then, doing
some work at the Irish Folklore Commission; this is the Irish
counterpart of the School of Scottish Studies in Edinburgh
where his friend worked. He was a Hebridean Islander, a
renowned folklorist and a native Gaelic speaker.

Ciarán suggested that I see Calum Maclean and have him
coach me in the correct pronunciation of the "Uist Cattle
Croon". Irish Gaelic is very close to Scottish Gaelic – Irish
being the mother language – but the pronunciation differs. I
agreed, and Ciarán made an appointment for me. It was a gloriously fresh spring morning as I crossed St Stephen's Green,
making for one of the Georgian houses where the Folklore
Commission has its headquarters. When I entered the room, a
small, slightly built man, with large brown eyes and a long pale
Highland face, was seated at a desk with his back to the
window. On either side of the desk stood two men. As soon as I
appeared all three exchanged knowing glances.

Later Calum told me that he'd also been expecting an eccentric American that morning, who wanted to buy one of the
Hebridean islands and that's who they thought I was.

I sat beside Calum and proceeded to go painstakingly
through the song, syllable by syllable. After the programme
went out over the air I had an enthusiastic letter from Calum
saying how pleased he was and would I consider going to the
Hebrides to learn more of their songs. He wrote that his brother
was the local doctor on South Uist and would see to it that I

would be put up in one of the crofts. Calum didn't even wait for an answer, and another letter from him followed saying that his brother Alistair would be delighted if I would stay with him and his family. I accepted the invitation and I was expected in South Uist towards the end of July.

I planned to stay one week, as I had a broadcast coming up and wanted to be back in Dublin in time. I flew to Glasgow and spent the night with a Scottish journalist friend Ian Coulter and his wife, Angela. From there I took a train to Oban in time to get the boat to Raasey where I broke the journey to pick up Alistair's eight year old son Cormac. The Macleans are natives of this small inner island and Calum's brother Sorley, the Gaelic poet, and his family were there that weekend.

Like many of the islands Raasey is Calvinistic (South Uist is a Catholic island). Calvin and his followers have a kill-joy attitude to life which includes not allowing such things as singing and playing on Sundays. So when I took Cormac along with me to go swimming that Sunday morning, I felt I was doing so with their tacit disapproval. Later on in the evening we called on one of the uncles, a farmer who lived further up the hill. While the preacher's voice could be heard resounding through the valley, Uncle Hector, who was milking a cow at the time, carefully closed the cowshed door and asked me to sing. Which I did. Next day Cormac and I continued the boat journey to South Uist.

It was a good week. The Maclean children and I went swimming whenever it was warm enough. There is nothing to compare with the miles of deserted silver strands that one finds in the Outer Hebrides.

As it turned out I didn't have to go far to collect songs. Alistair's wife, Rena, a native of Skye, taught me several lovely songs at her kitchen table. In fact things were going so nicely that I decided to accept the invitation of my host and hostess to stay longer. To do this I was prepared to cancel my radio broadcast. Then an odd thing happened. Never before had I had two live broadcasts on the same evening, nor indeed ever again. But towards the end of that week I received a contract for a second broadcast for the same date as the other one. I discussed it with the Macleans and we decided it would be best for me to return to Dublin for the two broadcasts, after which I'd go back to

South Uist for another week or two.

I flew from Benbecula and was met at Dublin airport by my brother-in-law, Frank. He had been approached by some undergraduates he knew at Trinity College, Dublin. Amateur actors, they would be performing three of Yeats' one-act plays as a fringe production at the Edinburgh International Festival of the Arts. They asked if I would come and perform between the plays. They would pay expenses but could not afford a fee.

I was decidedly insulted by the "offer", for I could see it only as a stop-gap: to keep the audience entertained while the students shifted scenery, and I summarily said no. But Frank wisely pointed out that, as there would be two performances, one at 5pm and another at 11pm, I would have the splendid opportunity of being free every evening to go and see performances by internationally top-ranking actors and musicians if I so wished. It was an inviting prospect, so I told him I would think it over. As it happened my decision was to have significant repercussions in my singing career and personal life. A couple of nights later I fulfilled my two broadcasting engagements.

The summer of 1955 was an incredibly hot and sunny one by Irish standards. The farmers groaned but the rest of the population rejoiced, and often we would go swimming at midnight. To this day I meet people who can remember the "great summer of 1955". But I was to remember it for another more personal reason, which was to determine the course of the rest of my life.

The morning after the two radio broadcasts, I was strolling along by The Green enjoying the radiant morning and mulling over the Edinburgh Festival proposition. If I accepted, then of course I'd forfeit the rest of that holiday on South Uist. Should I, should I not. A voice broke in on my thoughts: "Hello, Mel, I'm glad I met you because I've been trying to contact you." It was Tom Kinsella, the poet. He wasted no time: "There's a young American Rhodes scholar called Richard Selig, a minor poet at Oxford, who wants to meet you!" Now, at that time the idea of having to meet another American was anything but welcome. Only a couple of weeks before I'd managed to fob off an American, and oddly enough he too was called Richard. He had been one of a group of international students attending a

47

summer school at University College Dublin. I had taken part in a one-act play 'An Imaginery Conversation' put on during that week. I was the only non-undergraduate in it, and consequently had met this man along with many others at a reception in Newman House. He'd kept asking me out and finally I'd agreed to go to the cinema. I thought *Bad Day at Black Rock* would never end... After the pictures we'd repaired to a trendy coffee shop and while I was sitting there trying not to look too bored, a friend from Oxford passed our table, and said hello. As he went to pay his bill at the cash desk the young man with him turned and gave me a long, penetrating, singularly un-selfconscious look. Although I couldn't have known it then, this was Richard Selig.

"Tom," I said, "I'm not interested in meeting your American. I've just got rid of one!"

Undaunted Tom pressed on: "Mel he's *very* good-looking and has a jaw like Rock Hudson".

"Well," said I, "I happen not to like Rock Hudson, neither his looks nor his jaw."

Tom went on to explain that Giovanni Costigan, an American professor from Seattle who had taught Richard Selig at one time, was giving a party in his flat in Fitzwilliam Square. The party was so that Richard and I could meet.

Tom and I went our respective ways and I'd still not committed myself to the arrangement. When I got home there was a message that some stranger had phoned. Next morning as I was coming downstairs the phone rang. When I picked it up a voice said: "This is Richard Selig."

Oh God, I thought, it's that American! His accent was very, very slight. I think his years in England, combined with repeated listening to Yeats reading his own poetry on records, had resulted in a neutral sort of accent entirely his own, and very pleasing to the ear.

Richard went on. "There's a party tonight at Tom Kinsella's. (So they'd changed their plans.) Would you have dinner with me at the Bailey beforehand?" Richard always came to the point.

Now, I did *not* want to go but I couldn't see how I could gracefully get out of it. I envisaged another weary evening similar to the previous "American" one. Moreover, this wouldn't end with dinner but would drag on into a party. And I didn't enjoy parties anyway. Oh Lord, I thought, what am I going to do? I was stuck. Warily, I agreed to meet him.

How would we recognize each other, was the next question down the phone. Aha, I thought, this'll fix him! Then, out loud, "You'll have no trouble identifying me. I am disfigured with freckles and I am inclined to drool."

He laughed, "I too have freckles and I'll be wearing a pea-soup green suit."

What I didn't know then was that he had not only seen me (at that café) but had also heard me sing. He was renting a room in Waterloo Road, and from this Dublin base, Richard had travelled to the west of Ireland, hired a bicycle in Sligo and headed for Drumcliffe Churchyard to visit the grave of W.B. Yeats, whose poetry he'd admired for years. He'd also visited Galway and Connemara. Back in Dublin, he circulated amongst the Dublin intelligentsia, the poets and artists of that colourful city. As it happened, a thin wall of Richard's room separated him and John Reidy, a composer and mutual acquaintance, who later adopted the Gaelic version of his name, Séan O'Rīada, and was to do much for Irish/Gaelic music before his death. One evening, Richard had been chatting with some friends in the flat below, with the wireless on in the background, when my voice came across the air. Silencing the others, he listened. He didn't know whose voice it was until, at the end, the announcer read out the names of those participating in the programme. It was the earlier of the two live broadcasts that previous Monday evening – the ones I'd come back from the Hebrides to do. So, he'd heard my name mentioned on and off by mutual friends, then seen and later heard me; and had decided now that he wanted to meet me.

Richard was very direct. After we'd got to know each other I once asked him why he'd stopped in his tracks to listen to my singing. "Because," he said, "I had to listen. There was a sadness in your voice." The song was a Gaelic lament "Caoine Cill Cais".

Our date was for eight o'clock. Typically, I arrived late. I was wearing a sleeveless cotton dress. My hair was long and flying all over the place because I'd just washed it. Since those three months under the African sun people had often remarked on how much more golden red it had become. The thin red "Alice band" I wore on it was for decorative rather than functional purposes. As usual I was without stockings and minimally shod in very open, flat sandals.

Sensing that I'd be late, Richard did not meet me at the Bailey, but sat in Davy Burns, the fashionable pub across the road frequented by the Dublin literati, and watched my arrival. Much later he told me that I reminded him of nothing so much as a young wild pony.

I swept upstairs and went to the appointed room. There was no young man in a pea-soup green suit. I went off to the ladies to do a small repair job with the comb. When I came back to the room, minutes later, sitting at a table was a serious-faced young man, smoking a pipe and clearly waiting for me. I was very impressed by his unusual good looks, but all evening I was careful to conceal this. Had I not been told I would never have taken him for an American. On the contrary, he looked very "county" to me. Later, when I discovered how cosmopolitan he was, this made sense.

I don't remember what we said to each other, but I recall the meal. It was vast and excellent. The Bailey was at that time one of the two top restaurants in Dublin. But in spite of my customary shyness I felt a certain at-homeness in his company. My habit of sitting up very straight, caused Richard to ask at one stage "Do you by any chance have a poker down your back?" During coffee, Richard Murphy, the Irish poet, came in with his wife and joined us. He and Richard were both Magdalen men and shared the same tutor.

As we emerged from the restaurant, taking a deep breath, I made the both innocent and sincere remark: "Thank God for the fresh air". Richard told me afterwards that Mrs Murphy had taken him aside some time later and warned him against "these deceptively charming Irish girls". Her brother had been hooked by one and she'd turned out to be a bad lot. She'd misconstrued my remark about the fresh air and thought I was being affected.

It was time now to head up to the Green for Tom's party. "Aren't you going to bring the harp?" Richard asked. A rhetorical question as it turned out. Stifling annoyance, I said, "Do I have to?" I had to. The instrument was still in the studio where

it had lain since Monday night. Radio Éireann, above the GPO
in O'Connell Street, was a good ten minutes' walk away. We
collected the harp and made our way back through the city to
Tom's place. Every time we had to cross the road, Richard took
my hand. It was a friendly, matter-of-fact, protective gesture.

It was close to midnight and the party was in full swing.
Frank was sitting on the floor in one corner and I gravitated
towards him. Joan had had her second child Sebastian that very
week and was still in the nursing home. Both of them, my sister
especially, were forever plotting and hoping that I would
develop a sustained interest in someone worthwhile. So Frank
asked as usual, "Mel, is he an egg and rasher?" (Dublinese for
smasher.)

This time it was an unqualified Yes.

Richard had deposited himself in a far corner and was soon
surrounded by people. So far as I knew for the rest of the night I
might as well not have existed, but I didn't let it bother me too
much. That's it, I thought. And anyway, I was good at hiding
my feelings. Later in the evening individuals were called on to
sing. I sat on the edge of Tom's bed and sang. 'The Quiet Land
of Erin'. Richard obliged with two American folk songs I'd
never heard before, and which I thought were very lovely:
'Black is the Colour of My True Love's Hair' and 'The Riddle
Song'. He had a sort of Gene Kelly voice – a husky baritone. In
1976, when I gave a recital at the American Embassy in Dublin
and needed American songs, I remembered "The Riddle
Song", made an arrangement for the harp, sang it there and
have kept it in my repertoire ever since.

At about three in the morning people started drifting outside
for soup. As I came to the centre of the room I found Richard
was there too and in a rather cool voice he asked if I'd like some
soup. I said I would. Thinking we would be away for about
thirty minutes or less, I didn't even bother to bring my little
straw handbag. We wandered into the warm night. We
couldn't locate the others so we had soup on our own in a little
coffee shop on Stephen's Green at the top of Grafton Street.
When we'd finished, Richard suggested we go for a walk. We
headed down the now deserted Grafton Street and on through
the city till we reached the docks. We sat down on a bench and
talked a bit. We continued our stroll on into Sandymount and

beyond. With the dawn, we turned back and made for the city again where we breakfasted. My handbag was still in Tom's flat, so I had to go to where he worked to get the key. I decided not to keep the modelling interview that had been arranged for me that morning and we agreed to spend the rest of the day together.

Killiney is to my mind the finest beach outside Dublin and I decided we should go there. After lunch we borrowed swim-suits from a friend in the city and took off. Now I'm a bit bovine when it somes to a sense of direction. First I took some mis-guided short cuts by foot and then hopped on the bus, only to find ourselves unloaded at Bray, the other end of the spectrum from Killiney. All those pebbles and stones, ice-cream shops and crowds precluded the idyllic day I'd planned. With no beautiful stretch of sand and no people-free sea we didn't go swimming, we just talked. I had a date that night with two undergraudates from Trinity who were taking me to the theatre, and I had to go home, wash and change and come back into town again. So we stayed by the sea a few hours.

We talked about many things during those first twenty-four hours together. Later I came to realize that during that time he gratuitously told me facts about himself, and certain of his atti-tudes towards life in general which many of his close friends did not know. It was a measure of his intuitive trust in me, to have shared so much, so soon.

There has been a lot of codswallop written about how Richard and I fell passionately and madly in love at first sight. I personally don't believe in that burnt-out, unrealistic cliché, "love at first sight". But there is such a thing as instant physical or chemical attraction, and it can sometimes be the first step towards a relationship that can continue to grow into love for the remainder of one's life. This happened to us. I believe that love is something that both people must work at, and daily. We had to work at ours and like everybody else we had our highs and our lows.

Richard was planning to leave the following day for the Aran Islands in Galway Bay, in the west of Ireland and would later return to Dublin for only one night. If I hadn't had those two broadcasts to entice me back to Dublin I would never have met him – and I would not be writing this book. . . .

During our day together we already had discussed the pros and cons of the Edinburgh Festival and decided I should do it. As it turned out there were many unexpected benefits. Before we parted that evening we talked of my joining him in the west after the stint in Edinburgh.

The week at the Festival proved to be yet another memorable chapter in that fabulous summer of 1955. The performances were so well received that I was invited back the following year to be guest star in a production in the official Festival. Members of the audience didn't seem to notice the irregularity, at one point in my singing, when one night I got a belt in the back from some scenery being shifted behind the curtain.

While in Edinburgh I became very friendly with some of the undergraduates from Durham University, and with a few of the Oxford crowd whom I was to meet again the following winter in Oxford with Richard. There was a gay, festive atmosphere in the city with entertainment of a high calibre at the theatres, followed by innumerable parties, whether thrown by undergraduate amateur actors or the more sophisticated. Sir Compton Mackenzie was a prominent figure in the social life of the city, but never more so than during the annual Festival. His generosity was legendary. Every evening for those three weeks in August and September the famous and the obscure flowed in and out of his elegant house in Drummond Place. He and the charming Hebridean, Chrissie MacSween, whom he was later to marry after his wife's death, extended a warm Highland welcome to all who crossed the threshold. Most nights during that particular year Sir Compton was suffering from sciatica, and held court from his large four-poster bed, clad in bright orange pyjamas. Word of me and my work had got around and they invited me to one of their parties. Ulick O'Connor phoned me and offered to take me there. I told him I wasn't keen on going and that I'd already accepted an invitation from one of the Oxford undergraduates to accompany him to a Dieter Fischer-Diskau concert.

As it happened, I changed my plans and went to the party with George Scott-Moncrieff, the Scottish playwright, who was, among other things, the theatre critic of the *Glasgow Herald*. He had presented himself backstage one evening, and we had become friendly. After Richard's death he was to

53

become my closest friend.

I was asked to sing at the party. I did and everyone seemed very pleased. From that meeting on, Sir Compton interested himself in my career. It is well known how he recognized and fostered Father Sydney MacEwan, the tenor, and wrote about him to John McCormick, who launched him in the international field. I'd met this exceptionally fine Scottish singer about a year before when we shared the concert platform together in the north of Ireland, for a number of concerts.

There were others in the literary as well as the music world for whom this generous knight opened the vital door. Now in his customary altruistic way he set about doing the same thing for me. He invited me to be his house-guest for the remaining two weeks of the Festival. I explained that I had something to attend to in Ireland the following week. The something was someone: Richard. Sir Compton said that if I felt like it I could come back for the third and last week of the Festival. All I needed to do was send a telegram from Dublin.

I flew back that Sunday and spent a good deal of time on the journey home speculating about whether there would be the half-promised letter from Richard awaiting me or not. One minute I ardently hoped there would be a letter, the next I told myself I didn't care if there wasn't. On and on I vacillated until I reached the house, and there it was.

> 24th August 1955
> Inishere, Aran Islands,
> County Galway, Eire.

Dear Mary,

I am writing to you late at night by the light of a candle and an oil-lamp and intend to make this the longest letter I have ever written. Seán Coneely, the keeper of the pub, store, and guest house, a man nearly fifty, father of eleven, kindly and toothless, has just shown me home from an unexpected *ceilidh* during which other guests from Dublin and myself sang. Some of the children and Seán's splendid wife, Juda, sat about with long hands on faces that delightfully resembled one another. Most of the singing was done by a young Dubliner, Leo, aged 22, whom Mrs Holbrook, the old and witty American lady, referred to as "the boy scout", and by a small, ingenuous employee of Guinness who was accompanied by his wife whose large eyes, thinness and pallor bespeak some recent suffering. Most of the guests are leaving on tomorrow's boat. (A donkey has just brayed passionately into the night nearby and a dog answers now with a howling, and then another.) I walked to the lighthouse today with Ernie O'Malley, on the way exchanging the less personal of our views on life. A dour man from Cork City is one of the keepers and was kind enough to show me the workings of the light itself. It is over a hundred years old and still operates on the original equipment. The Atlantic was there with all its threats and glories, rolling intractably between birth and eternity on the small sphere which is our present domicile. I could not help thinking, as I often think, that the waves no matter how big are only bigger than men. On the way back we visited the burial ground in the middle of which is a half-buried chapel from the time when the holy men of Ireland held their "midden" in tough places, nourished on mist and shellfish. After tea I went out fishing, "Killing mackerel" as they call it, in one of the currachs with three men rowing and Ernie O'Malley's red-haired son, Cormac, in the bow.

I have an inveterate, though now a long-restrained, propensity for romance; and I hope you will not be embarrassed by the fact that after less than twenty-four hours' acquaintance with you I wish to confide the details of my travels thus far as an expression of the warm affection I already feel for you. It satisfies some strong demand of my nature to have some one person to communicate with. You are the most likely candidate I have had in a long time. Taciturnity grows on me in proportion to a lack of love. To conclude this paragraph and to get on with my story, suffice it to say that I enjoyed your company very much.

Good morning! It is the next day after breakfast. Leo and I took a chilly swim before eating so I am more awake than I usually am at this hour. The *Dun Aengus*, the steamer, is expected at about three in the afternoon. I'll spend the rest of the morning writing what has already happened rather than acquire some more adventures by wandering out under the day. Today is Wednesday and the next steamer comes on Saturday. To be sure you receive this on your return from Scotland, I'll post it today.

On Sunday at six in the evening at Kilronan, I began taking notes of my experiences on these islands. It is a long time since I have been able to keep such notes. Laziness and a lack of faith in the interest anything I might set down would have, and a contempt for words as poor vessels to hold the myriad coruscating qualities of the world, flashing, all too delicately, across my senses. I am encouraged by Synge's sensitive companionship and by the fact that the islands themselves are sizeable and simple enough to comprehend as a whole and to describe in full. One of my basic problems, and one which is traditional to Americans of my calling, is the vastness of our country and the amorphous complexity of our social life. One can monopolize some fragmentary corner – Faulkner succeeds best at this; one can sing of the Whole – Whitman, Hart Crane's Continent; one can revert to some kind of microcosm – Melville's ships, Hemingway's wars and fishing trips, Jack London's primitive Alaska; one can emigrate to a more stable and more comprehensible society as Henry James did etc. etc. In any case it is possible to understand the life of the islands, not that I have time to do so; but at least I can walk around the whole of our island, meet all the residents, and learn the methods by which they support their life here.

I remember one day in Dublin sitting on the steps outside 44 Waterloo Road announcing in a mood of arrogant discontent: "Dublin is a city where nothing happens except by accident, aberration or the machinations of the Devil. It is a place for respectable young ladies from the counties to earn money to send home to ther families." I also took note of a tendency to be morbid and superstitious. That gaiety is warlike and love is sad I also found. But the chimney pots of Dublin are comically elegant in their variety and elaborateness, the façades on the Liffey on a sunny afternoon have a special grandeur, the pillars of the Bank of Ireland end in the street. What else? What else is there to say to fix a city in words? A city to which I am and shall ever be a stranger despite all my words.

My chronicle begins at the dock at Kilronan. The sun is still quite high. If I look straight across the bay, at eye level, the sun is above my brows where the hairline is. It is very warm on the left side of my face and on the left hand which holds this book steady. The crossing from Galway began a little after noon under a layer of darkish clouds high up. The wind was from the east which is propitious in these parts. Coming down from lunch in the village an hour earlier there was something in the proportions of light and air, that tinge of desolation in the smell of the breeze, which reminded me of September days on Long Island years ago. Perhaps it is the proximity of the Atlantic on this and on the other side which makes this stony island and the neighbourhood of my childhood reminiscent of each other. The night in Galway was restful. That and the crossing to Kilronan have taken me nearly through Synge's book on the islands. I am waiting for a currach to take me either to Inishmaan or Inishere, preferably Inishere, being the more remote. The loneliness I experienced in Dublin was uneasy, but here I already feel at peace and being alone seems nothing but appropriate. I would dislike to meet many tourists. The island folk, the birds, the sea and the quiet will be enough for a while. I can hear myself thinking again and since my thoughts of recent months have been the product of painless, almost cheerful despair and negation, my self thinking is a very broken-voiced, prolix and fatigued affair and will take some coaxing to be restored to the abundance and optimism to which my nature has accustomed me.

I napped a little as the sun declined. A boy rode by on a bicycle, shouting something aloud which woke me. I went to the end of the dock and sat on top of a pile of boxes and ate a potato which I had stored in my pocket from lunch. Looking across the inlet I saw that two men were putting their currach into the water. It was about 7.15. I went quickly back to pick up my rucksack and yelled across to them to wait. In a few minutes I was there, asking if they would take me. We agreed on ten shillings. The man in the forward end of the currach was the elder, about forty-five, and was the one to whom I addressed myself. He asked me if I could row. I said yes and was quickly at the middle pair of oars and we were on our way. I had no trouble getting the knack of the oars, imitating the young man in front of me. Soon I was being complimented on my ability to pull. A young girl, perhaps fourteen or fifteen, sat in the stern with her feet folded under her. Her grey eyes and sternly handsome face presented me with a pleasant compendium of the sea, the receding island, setting sun, and the sky, to which she was the foreground.

They spoke an Irish softer than I had heard before. Occasionally the old man would interrogate me as to my nationality and my potential financial status. He seemed impressed with my rowing or at least he let on that he did in order to get me to row even harder. I did row hard and was quite pleased with myself and with the whole scene about me. The old man's often reiterated phrase of approbation was "good man, good man", to which my response was to increase the energy of my strokes. "Ah, man, dear, if I was a girl, I'd fall in love with you," he would say. "You're the nicest man I ever know." "Do you see that?" he asked. I turned as I leaned back on the oar and couldn't see what he meant. "No," I said. He spat into the water. I watched the spittle trail away. "The sea. And that to her," he said. There was no mood of propitiation in that man, I thought, the sea's his enemy.

The distance, they said, from Kilronan to Inishere is ten miles. It took us two hours to row it. Except for some slight blisters on my hands, I arrived none the worse for the effort. After pulling the currach up the beach with the help of a number of bystanders, my two companions and a third man who had joined us on the beach made straight for the pub. On the way I was asked whether I had brought any musical instrument with me. I was sorry I hadn't, I said. This was a disappointment. I and the older man had complained of a thirst most of the way over from Kilronan and by then the taste of my spittle was thick and salty. The pub was lit by a single kerosene lamp. It was expected that I buy the first round. After three pints of porter we strolled out under a clear night sky. I bedded down by a wall. The wind changed direction during the night and I slept badly, being cold. In the morning the older man brought me a huge mug of sweetened tea and some thick slices of heavy, yellowish buttered bread. This was very welcome to me; the combination of all that rowing and porter not being followed by food or good sleep, left me feeling slightly poisonous in the morning. The tea restored me completely and a chat with a fisherman revived my interests in things outside my still somewhat aching head. I returned to the place where the pub is which is also a guest house and arranged to have my meals there. I learned of a lake not far from here, sixteen acres of fresh water, beyond the school house and the graveyard to the east of here. I went over to see it this morning. The road passes to the left on the seaward side of the mound of sand the flat top of which is the burial ground itself. The sides of the mound are a torrent of sand and small sea shells. It seems as if most of the shells of the island were foregathered here.

I didn't learn about "middens" until later. On that part of the island each acre is delineated by the low puzzles of grey stone walls which are a characteristic of the island. In the winter making these walls is the islanders' chief occupation. I am told that they are paid by the government for every acre they make. The walls surround a plot of paltry green stubble. I stretched out on a dune, beneath a village, where this acreage begins and which overlooks the lake and wrote of the adventure in the currach and then fell asleep as the sun began working its way through the grey overlay. When I awoke the sun was fairly hot. A white mare clambered over the remainder of a wall about fifteen yards down to my left and passed in front of me at a pensive pace into the nearest green acre. She nibbled and gnawed at the tufts of grass that her lips were able to apprehend. I heard the barking of a dog coming down from the village and soon saw him, a soiled white collie, bent on his duty, barking and chiding the horse for its gentle but unlawful intrusion into the precious acre. The mare turned away from him, lifting its right forefoot in a gesture of non-aggressive frustration. The dog soon turned her and she trotted from the plot in the direction from which she had come, breaking to a walk as soon as she had entered the neutral and barren ground. The dog turned back to the village, its task performed, with an officious glance over his shoulder. Appearing from the same corner, a second, a brown horse came slowly up to meet the retreating mare. From the moment its foreparts appeared over the edge of the dune I recognized it as slightly more noble though no less gentle than the first. They met and their greeting was most tender, kissing on the lips slowly, standing side by side facing the sea, the brown stallion caressing the mare's neck with his nose and eyes. I thought of them as sharing that most intimate and patient kinship which comes of being lovers a long time.

I went back to have a swim before lunch. The water was very cold and a strong wind was blowing. The hooker from Connemara was being unloaded of its turf by a currach.

Last night I slept in a house by myself. I wrote the incident of the horses before falling asleep, promising myself to describe the arrival of the currachs on the strand at twilight. In the morning during my second sleep I dreamt of an old skill I had acquired long ago, that of flying. Even in the dream I reminded myself I had not flown in a long time. I was walking down a road with someone who said he remembered my doing it. It is a number of years since I dreamt of flying. It is done in the way and in similar surroundings as in the past. A road, telephone wires strung along it, a house and suburban scenery. I take off from the road, leaning against the air with head and shoulders, my legs rising from the ground behind me. Heavily at first and then with more ease I rise to a height of twenty or thirty feet, sweeping and turning with increasing skill. I make a flapping motion with my arms. I cannot seem to fly much higher than the height of a two storey house and I seem to be the only one in these dreams who is able to fly.

At twilight the currachs came into the strand. The bottom of the boats were strewn with the parallel bands of mackerel, lying athwartships and containing more light in their silver sides than the whole grey glow of the heavens. When a currach was unloaded three men hoisted it on their backs and an overturned currach went marching up the strand propelled by three pairs of human legs. All this in silhouette because of the hour, the sight was not without either humour or wonder.

I must have lunch now and bring this to the post office before the *Dun Aengus* arrives. I shall be in Galway on Monday to await your wire and, I hope, your arrival.

Richard

The wire was sent off to Galway, and I followed it by train on Monday evening. I was wearing a flame-red cotton dress, which I thought was very fetching. As I came off the train, Richard's first disapproving words were, "That's the colour the prostitutes in Amsterdam wear." I ignored the remark. It was good to be together again. We spent the night in the city at the Castle Hotel. Next morning we hitchhiked to the summer house of Ernie O'Malley, the erstwhile revolutionary, a leader in Ireland's war of Independence and Civil War, and author of the book *On Another Man's Wound*. He had invited both of us there when he and Richard met on Inishere. Cormac was with his father as he had been on the Aran Islands.

We supped by candlelight – no electricity in the house – and next morning Ernie's method of getting us up was rather original, I thought. Without saying anything he handed a supine Richard a glass of sherry. Then he came into my room and proceeded to beat me playfully with a toy tiger. All this in friendly silence too.

After breakfast Ernie took me down to see their boat. Richard was elsewhere at the time. I was surprised and pleased to hear later on that, not being able to locate me, Richard got decidedly worried and had gone out on to the road asking local people if they'd seen a young girl in jeans with long hair and a man in his fifties. It was wonderful to realize that he cared that much.

Our next port of call was Achill Island. Richard had been told about Major Freyer, a delightfully eccentric old gentleman who ran a guest house at the foot of a mountain on the island. There was instant rapport between us and this retired English army officer. In no time we were being hosted in his own private sitting room. While we sipped drinks the major read his poems to us.

We were both fresh-air fiends and spent most of that week out of doors. There was little sun and lots of mist and the inevitable gentle rain, but the inclement weather couldn't keep us in. We found a lovely little beach where we swam every day, even in the rain. We had it all to ourselves and used to race up and down it and, on calmer days, we'd skim stones in the water and shout and leap in the waves. We climbed the mountain. One evening we even went to the pictures. The local cinema consisted of a village hall with a corrugated iron roof with wooden benches for the patrons. That night we had great fun. Sometimes in the evening, if it was fine enough, we'd sit on the front steps (we were the only people staying in the guest house) and I'd sing my songs to him – especially all my latest Elizabethan ones.

As we were travelling back to Dublin, Richard announced

that he wished to meet my father. Father, home on leave from West Africa, was ill in a nursing home at the time. While I was in Edinburgh he'd been to a wedding where the celebrations had gone on and on for days and not surprisingly, he'd had some kind of a mysterious attack, and was admitted to hospital. On my return from Scotland, before catching the Galway train, I'd called in to see him to find out how he was, and to tell him I was joining Richard over in the west.

When Richard and I arrived, Father was sitting up in bed which was strewn with volumes of his much-loved late-Victorian poets. So they met and I was glad. A salutary side-effect of that illness was that Father gave up smoking for good. Shortly afterwards he also gave up drinking and has never looked back since.

Before he went back to England, we promised to keep in touch by letter, and Richard asked me if I'd consider coming over to visit him. Term would begin very shortly and that meant he would be confined to Oxford. If we were to go on seeing each other I would have to be the mobile one.

I sent off my telegram to Sir Compton and booked a flight to Edinburgh. There followed yet another exotic week with 27 Drummond Place as welcoming and brimful of celebrities as usual.

All the reviews of my performance during that first week of the Festival had been very favourable. Now there appeared a longish piece in *The Scotsman*. I wrote (my first) letter to Richard enclosing the clipping. His answer was immediate.

Magdalen College
Oxford
9th September 1955

Dear Mary,
To my delight I got your letter this morning and the clipping from *The Scotsman* of which I am very proud. I am happy to hear that you are comfortable at Sir Compton's and are able to rest after the rigours of our western travels. It is hot here, too, and clear mostly, and Oxford looks lovely under the September light. I am staying in college temporarily until my flat is ready. The Coal Board Conference moves in today so I may have to find somewhere else to stay. I hope not. College is very pleasant without the undergraduates around.

I spent most of the week writing what is for me a long poem and completed the first section of it yesterday, fifty-nine lines. I have begun to unravel somewhat, also. The first part, if not the whole thing, will be called '*The Coast*'.

However, *Beowulf* gurgles on my desk for translation. I will be dutiful and give him some attention today.

Listen, Mary, I think of you very often and miss your companionship keenly. And I want you to know that I am very fond of you and, knowing the sometimes ponderous fidelity of my own heart, will remain so. I'll send this letter special delivery for otherwise, this being Friday, you may not get it till Monday. Hoping to hear from you soon, I am,

> Your friend and affectionately,
> Richard

Later on when he sent me a finished copy of 'The Coast' I marvelled that I had lived through that same week with prosaic eyes and here was the whole experience transformed through poetry. Here is the first part of the poem.

THE COAST

Between two sheets, the one of heaven, the other land,
I am got and go down a sideless tunnel to the coast
Where space is and the narrow world breaks off
Thin as a snipe's cry. Where wind and ocean carry
The mind's message back to sunset, clouds, nothing
And that infinity the pulse denies, I watch
The weather, think of love, breathe and pace the sand.
All consolation, all disappointment end here.
Wind and sand that have gnawed castle and graveyard
Erase the vain commotions by which I know myself;
And I, equivalent to all the change about me,
Look at the world once more with neither fear nor longing,
Released from hope and yet not sad. I wait,
Still unable to hurl a human image to the stars,
Perceive the god in things or war or love holily;
Waiting without angels or any man-like creature
Greater or other than myself; without measure,
Order or metaphor with which to assure the blank air
My noise is important. I wait while the wind unsnarls
From around my shoulders and goes on a little diverted.

I wait while my shadow changes length and direction
Until it is gone. I wait, remembering myself,
So that I may last out the night with my eyes closed.

As surf against the rock explodes in white foam,
Invades, immerses but does not fuse, and then recedes;
As spray, blown back against the light, shatters
Glittering in tiny spheres that roll on the blind wind;
As ocean ascends and sky loops down nearly to touch
At eyes' level; as night confuses and the stars reach
Back into the brain making the skull its deep heaven;
As I stand on this shore alone as in a room,
I remember bone against bone, lip on lip, and heart
More desperate in its cage than brute thong fettered
To time and fear can bear or love can pacify.

Following the contours of this coast: cliff, island
And strand; watching the endless shift of color and form,
The belt of foam fraying and stretching, marking tide-end
And the sea's mood; watching the clouds dip or disperse;
And, for ease, tracing the solemn line of low
Rock-riddled hills; or, for God's sake, the birds
And slant columns of sunlight in the great cathedral air;
Seeing all this, storing it up in the mind's eye
With paintings, other coasts and friends long gone,
I take this scene as one more fragment of a world
I cannot piece together – death not sure, the chart lost –
And I, lonely as Jonas, swallow angrily my own words.

Not knowing what architect built these limbs or broke
This grass or scarred these stones: grey jagged stones,
Sere grass, young limbs, yet I record their presence
And that of shells, beige or white, always symmetrical
Except when broken; record, too, the heavy smell
Of rotting kelp, and the sound of, always pleasant, the sea;
And the ease of gulls constructed for the swoop of air
Beyond a ship, above waves, on headlands rising.

Beginning where silence and land leave off, I give
The vague, interminable longings that force these words
To the wind, where, at home in nothing human,
Among birds and clouds, sunlight and starlight,
They may echo and I, hearing, be answered.

Years later, when I was in the monastery, one particular line from the second part "The Epistle" appealed so strongly to me that I had a friend in the community scribe it for me on vellum. It was there daily before my eyes in my choir book. An impossible, yet perennial injunction, which one aspired to live each day. In the poem it was addressed directly to me: "Know that . . . the one riddle the one great enterprise in this world is to learn how to love and keep loving."

I did not know at the time, indeed I wasn't aware of the fact until I read about it in the press after his death in 1972, that Sir Compton had set the BBC wheels in motion where I was concerned.

A couple of days after my return to Edinburgh, the BBC TV people in Scotland phoned Sir Compton to ask me to appear on a programme which was to be done later in the week. He gave me the message and kindly offered to listen in on the extension in his room to ensure that all would go smoothly. He said, "When they get to the bit about fees, tell them you never get paid in anything other than guineas."

It was well after Richard's death that I came to hear that Sir Compton had wanted me to play the lead, opposite Donald Sinden, in the film version of his novel, *Rockets Galore*, which he wrote as a sequel to *Whisky Galore*. One evening, in Sir Compton's library, the subject of that film came up in conversation and Donald Sinden asked, "Tell me, I've always wondered why you made the heroine of *Rockets Galore* an Irish singer?" Quietly, Sir Compton pointed to me and said: "There's the reason."

Then he told me that the film company didn't want me because I wasn't "a name". Anyhow, I would certainly not have accepted the part, even if they had approached me – it was but a few months after Richard had died and I was in Arabia, planning a completely different future. Many years later, when I was in Stanbrook, someone reported to me that about a week before he died, Sir Compton was BBC's Radio 3 "Man of Action" and that one of the pieces of music he played was my recording of "Eibhlín a Rúin" and that he had spoken with affection of Richard and me.

I wanted to tell Richard the good news about the BBC television appearance and, since there was not enough time to write to him from Mackenzie's, I sent a telegram giving details and ended with the word, "Writing". I never did get down to writing that letter and the omission provoked the following splenetic letter from Richard.

15th September 1955
Dear Mary,
I woke up laughing this morning at the intensely absurd notion we by now have about each other. I think of you as a neurotic young female throwing her weight about not knowing what she wants but enjoying for all their worth her new found, though ephemeral, powers. And you probably think of me as a romantic and vulnerable young man, looking for the impossible, much too intense and all too easy to kick. I'm afraid it needed that letter you didn't write to disabuse me of the former. I suspect omission is your habitual way of getting out of things.

However, if you can muster courage this time and try explaining yourself – all well and good. Otherwise, according to a proverb I made up today: Give word. No keep. New friendship dies easy.

Richard

The "neurotic young female" was back in Dublin by then and deeply hurt by this letter. I think I was as much upset by *his* having been unintentionally hurt as by the well aimed barbs at myself. The injustice of being described as someone who "kicked" was the unkindest cut of all.

During my week in Edinburgh, following our days together in Achill I'd given our embryonic relationship some thought. While I undoubtedly wanted to be near him, I was wary. Nothing would have made me happier than to flit over to Oxford, but my pride would not allow me to do so. I would see him again, only if something else occasioned my being in his part of the world. Nothing would induce me to adopt the rôle of pursuer. Let him do the chasing, I thought. Part of it also was that I was like all human beings, vulnerable, and besides it was all so early in our friendship. What if he changed his mind?

He had everything going for him. He could have had virtually any woman he wanted. I was schooling myself not to get involved. Who was to say that the whole thing might not end as abruptly as it had begun? Already I had seen how he could "operate". People were drawn to him as to a magnet. He had only to enter a room and all attention was focused on him. His charm was immense and could be turned on and off at will like a tap. But his general impact on people was beyond his control.

Young and inexperienced as I was I could nevertheless see that Richard was a very special person. Naturally I was pleased that this twenty-five year old man so richly endowed, physically and intellectually, should be interested in me. As I grew to know him, I could see that he was, as Elizabeth Jennings the poet wrote to me in a letter after his death: "a rare and beautiful person".

He knew his considerable power over others and, as I was to discover as our time together went by, his integrity was to match – understanding all these things about himself he was unusually aware of his responsibility not to abuse those powers, and certainly while I knew him he never did.

Still smarting, and very much affected by Richard's obvious pain I wrote a longish letter and sent it by special delivery. That night he phoned me from Oxford, and the troubled waters were calmed. His letter arrived a couple of days later.

18th September 1955

Mary dear,
I received both your letters this morning and, of course, was very much cheered by them. It is so long since I met anyone who prefers my kindness and respect to my ferocity that I am overwhelmed by the change the possibility of such a person existing can produce in my character. Showing my teeth and expecting to be at war with people at the slightest provocation, has become a habit that is hard to break. I hope you will forgive my last letter in which I exceeded myself in lack of gallantry. The reason I called you last night, if I may take credit for some sense, is that I couldn't believe that I had been wrong about you. The one thing I am seldom wrong about is people's character.

Richard

The phone call and the letter restored me to my usual happy self. I was beginning to understand the contrasts in his character, the outer aggressive, competitive side – Theodore Roethke used the word "Barracuda" in his piece on Richard written after he died – and the gentler traits which he didn't advertise to the world in general.

One morning I had a phone call from someone who had seen me on that BBC television programme from Edinburgh. He'd also heard some of my recorded songs on a commercial radio programme from Radio Éireann. He asked me if I'd be prepared to make a test recording for the Decca Record Company in London. My fare and expenses would be paid for two to three days. I told them that I would be willing to have a go. Here was a golden opportunity of seeing Richard again, so this was the major news in that second of the two letters he referred to.

Along with your letter, I received permission from my draft board to stay overseas another year. I was rather worried about this since an American friend of mine, despite an appeal, has just been classified I-A, which means he can be called up any day. He is also at Magdalen doing English and expected to finish at the end of this year. I think I've set the record for academic deferments, this being my sixth year. I hope by the time I'm ready they will have changed the selective service law, leaving me high dry and a civilian. My deferment is until September 1956, which is quite generous and means I will have next summer in Europe if I want it.

I am delighted to hear that your father has recovered so quickly.

I do very much hope you get this recording try-out, both for your sake and for the selfish reason that I would like to see you. What with going about my studies, ordering fuel for the winter and working on a new poem, I am quite busy. I'm considering getting a record-player so that I will be less tempted to leave my flat for entertainment. Having some Bach, Scarlatti, Vivaldi, Da Falla, Mozart and Louis Armstrong around the house is my idea, or one of them, of pleasure.

On Sunday I am having a drink with one of the directors of Faber and Faber, the publisher, at All Soul's College. He seems interested in my work.

If I get enough done over the weekend I'll treat myself to a day in London. I want to see Sam Beckett's *Waiting for Godot*.

Yesterday I got a book bargain. A seventeenth-century edition of Sand's translation of Ovid's *Metamorphoses*. It is in fine condition, and a nice big old book.

   Love,
   Richard

In my insular fashion I knew nothing about draft boards till he mentioned it later on in this letter. As things developed, I am grateful to that institution for letting Richard stay on in Europe one more year.

Now he was settling peacefully into the new flat which I was soon to visit for the first time.

23rd September 1955

Dear Mary,

Thanks for your provincial letter.

I am writing this in the kitchen of my flat, a warm and most peaceful room. I moved in as scheduled two days ago on Wednesday. It is a more spacious place than I had remembered it, and I am already quite comfortable. (I was interrupted at this point by the arrival of my "house-boy", the man who will do menial work for me. He seems agreeable and has had experience cleaning this flat before.)

As I had promised myself, I went to London on Monday afternoon. I stayed, as I usually do, with Alan and Joan Woodin, my research bio-chemist and his American wife. We all three met one another on the *Queen Elizabeth* coming over to Europe in October 1953.

The next morning, I went to the embassy and had my passport renewed. Stephen Spender took me out to lunch at Wheelers. An excellent meal. Colchester oysters on the half shell. Then Scampi Walewska; scampi and slices of lobster in a creamy sauce. Accompanied by a good Hock. He had just arrived back from Milan after some lousy culture conference. We gossiped about things literary for about two hours over lunch and then parted. I am having two pages in *Encounter* in November, about seventy-six lines; poems which, if he pays me the usual rate, means £20. You can buy *Encounter* in Grafton Street, Dublin.

The Faber man is interested but considers me Spender's property.

I hope you will soon be able to get to bed at a reasonable hour.

Love,
Richard

Things were looking up for Richard. Top editors and publishers were showing interest in his poetry (at that time Stephen Spender was editor of *Encounter*), and there was a growing awareness of his gifts. When he'd first appeared at the Poetry Society in Oxford in 1953, the magnetism and the talent were at once evident. The guest of the evening, Lord David Cecil, was left in the corner while everyone fussed around this dynamic newcomer, Richard Selig, who sat cross-legged (his favourite position) in the middle of the floor reading his poetry.

28th September 1955

Dear Mary,

It is a poor substitute for being with you, and I hope that will be remedied soon, but I shall attempt to do with my pen what my presence could do a thousand times better. I am writing to you today despite not having received anything but your Sunday note because it occurs to me that you are again in need of some assurance of my continued affection for you. It seems the burden at present lies with me to assure you of my feelings, rather than with you to assure me of yours. There are good reasons for this but they are of little comfort to one addicted to impatience and the expectation that he will always get his own way. I am by habit, custom and experience much better fitted for competition than for wooing. I think it has never really occured to me that a well-balanced mixture of cruelty and tenderness, both administered with instinctive calculation, might be less effective than humility and forbearance. As you can see, though I talk of humility, the tone of this letter is one of pride. I speak of pride because I cannot repress the feelings that the tone of your letters has a certain flavour of a little girl's self-importance and of one who delights in the idea of a wooer but regards the fact in a slightly off-hand way.

I think I am being unduly critical because, having made the brave declaration of my feelings, I became frightened that it would not be given the respect and consideration my ego insists on. However, that is by the way. I am no longer particularly afraid one way or the other. Either you remember and know me well enough to continue to care, or you do not. All I can tell you is that I still like you very much and would be very pleased to see you again, and would appreciate it very much if you would let me know if you wish my interest in you to continue.

I am quite comfortably set up here in Oxford in a three-room flat. I live quietly and busily. If you care to visit me you will be very welcome.

Richard

Not only had I never had a personal relationship of this quality before, I was unaccustomed to having someone so alive to my needs and feelings as Richard was, care for me. His reference to the immature tone of my letters was fair. All of our life together, Richard, when he recognized the need to be so, was

69

cruel with the relentlessness of the surgeon: he cut away so as to heal. But I think he was motivated by love. This emotional insecurity he points to was still all too present in my make-up.

I'd warned Richard many a time that I was a poor letter-writer. He wrote resignedly to say that he enjoyed writing to me, and would continue to do so even though my letters to him were thin on the ground. And would I let him hear from me when I didn't feel it was too much of a chore to write. He admitted to sometimes restraining himself with difficulty from phoning me. One of his letters ended with the reminder that his birthday was on the October 29 and that though it would please him very much if I could get there around that time; if I couldn't he wouldn't be bitter, just sad.

An agent called Berlin had contacted me, and Richard's response to the news delighted me. He did indeed become my "chevalier" and shielded me from the slings and arrows of outrageous agents and entrepreneurs in the two years ahead. He was so right about the insensitive and shady ways of many people in show business. To this day I suffer from them; and alas I don't have Richard to act as the acutely necessary buffer.

A passage in the same letter illustrates his philosophy of life. And a further reference to the impending birthday.

8th October 1955

Sweetest Mary,
I've done my exams, fairly well I think, and am now lounging in my kitchen after having consumed a great fish, a corn on the cob and two bottles of ale.

Duly I am impressed with the promptness of your reply, a very pleasant one at that. Soon you will reach my standards of conscientiousness, I am sure. Anyway, thanks. I am pleased to hear the concert went so well and that it in turn has paid dividends in other engagements.

The term having begun, I will now be up to my teeth in work whereas before it was just up to my jaw.

I am being "idolized" by the local magazine so will have to have a photo taken next week. A friend of mine with, I am afraid, too good a sense of humour, is going to write the surrounding verbiage.

Apropos the letter from the agent and its ilk: not that I don't know you can take care of yourself; please allow, however, an elderly brotherly warning that there are a lot of unscrupulous people in show business. But, yours truly, "chevalier" lives only forty miles to the west in Oxford and would always welcome an opportunity to defend his lady.

While I think of it, write this down in your address book: 38 Norham Road, Oxford. Tel No. Oxford 57039.

As far as your getting "grip" is concerned, and growing into a finer, stronger, more disciplined being, I am all for it. That's what we're here for: to make the attempt and with luck, faith and some help to keep making it, success coming in part and pieces, the wonderful windfalls of daily living; doing what one can when one can as often as one can.

I am sure you have the strength and goodness to do what you feel you should and wish to do. As much as I may harbour reservations about you, as a young woman, having independence, I am also sure that you need and will make good use of that independence.

Since you asked me what I wanted for my birthday, I will be so bold as to tell you what I am in need of at present and you can choose between them. I need a long woollen scarf and I also need some underwear shorts (drawers to you). The ones I am wearing now acquire a new hole for every stride I take. You asked me!

Love,
Richard

The next few letters were as vivid and newsful as ever; one containing a lengthy dissertation on how to combat the common cold, to which I was too often prone in those days. Another included an acid dressing down for my use of red ink, exclamation marks and general bad taste in letter-writing. There was the news too of his myriad social activities: entertaining in his flat and dining out; and an account of the unintentional destruction of two squash rackets, one against his opponent's calves during the course of his usual fiercely energetic playing of the game. He had also been invited to address the Spectator Club on why he wrote poetry: "I will attempt not to be facetious. There are some serious reasons, besides the basic ones of pleasure and the desire to excel." His thoughts on praise and attention from others were revealing, and to me, very interesting. He wrote:

Thanks for your warning about the hazards of adulation, but it was not necessary. I have received insipid attentions for years but the only

71

effect they seemed to have had on my character was to awaken a mild humour and gentle contempt. I like to be admired, of course, but only for those characteristics and accomplishments in which I have laboured to improve and even to excel. Few people, I find, have been able to perceive these and to them I return my own admiration.

And there was the repeated question: when was I coming to visit him. A whole week went by without hearing from me:

. . . with difficulty I will restrain myself from telephoning you. I am worried, however and I hope your cold is better. If you haven't written already would you please answer this letter by return post?

Richard

23rd October 1955

Dear Mary,

While you were composing your answer to my splenetic letter of last Tuesday, I finished 'The Tiger and the Panther', a copy of which I am enclosing herewith. My tutor, a man very learned and grudging of compliments said: "Jolly good".

Thanks for using blue ink, refraining from the use of exclamation marks and from your usual clusters of nerve-wracking figures of speech. As for your ending your letters because they are so irritating, I can only suggest my ending mine if you find them too depressing.

I am at times a very irritable fellow indeed. It is an occupational hazard. Tacitus called artists the irascible tribe. I am also very often in rather expansive good humour, the reward for having no compunction about letting out my anger on others if they deserve it. You must forgive my annoyance at the fact that both your intention and your desire to see me have not at all been made clear by you. So far, all that I can gather from your plans is that a visit to me is contingent on a nebulous "call to London" and an orchestral harp. I am sorry but I am too egotistical to be at all pleased by your considering me a matter of convenience. I don't wish to offer prayers for your call to London. I would be willing, however, to contribute to the cost of a visit to me if you wished to visit me. I am thus much annoyed because, if you recall, you accepted an invitation to come to Oxford and then left me for five days with nothing but a telegram telling me you had written and that you were going to be on TV at such and such an hour. Forgiveness comes easy to me when that which I am to forgive is not reinforced by subsequent events. I never forget a wrong, however, and this will probably scare you so I suggest that you exercise some tolerance. As the result of a good memory for both favours and wrongs, if you knew me or my friends, you would discover that my dealings are usually very fair. It is the legalist in my blood.

I hope you like the poem.

My moods vary but not my love,

Richard

A call came to say that the plan to fly me to London and do the test recording was now complete. I phoned Richard from London Airport. When he heard my voice he seemed a bit stunned. After a pregnant pause he said, "My God – where are you?" I told him, and added that I'd try to get down for his birthday two days later.

All went well with the recording session and (foolishly as it turned out) I signed a contract with the Decca Record Company. My mistake lay in that I didn't have an expert read through the document.

Father had opted to travel over with me. Now, the business completed, he returned to Ireland with my harp and I trekked through London for a few hours seeking the perfect scarf.

In the end I found it: the longest, softest cashmere scarf ever.

4 Richard

the one riddle, the one great enterprise in this world is to learn how to love and keep loving.

From 'Epistle' in RICHARD SELIG'S poem 'The Coast'

Arriving in Oxford, there was no sign of Richard. There was no reply when I tried to phone him. Still in the kiosk, with the phone attached to my ear, someone tapped on the glass door behind me. It was he. Cool, and not exactly effusive, he said: 'Sorry I'm late. I was having an argument in the Bodleian with a friend of mine about prose styles.' In retrospect I wonder if it was an eye for an eye move: treating me in kind for my unpunctuality at the Bailey!

So started the first of my many visits to Oxford. Little detail stands out, but the overall memory is warm. Oxford and its ancientness I loved; and the long walks we took together through the meadows and by the river. Spring was even better. Anyone who has known Oxford in that season can never forget it. We punted and cycled a lot, I longed for spring and summer and the opportunity for tennis with Richard until one day in early summer we went out and bought tennis gear; from then on we played whenever we could. Out for a walk one winter's day (we were throwing a ball to one another) I said wistfully: "Richard, even if we don't get married, can I play tennis with you in the summer?" He thought for a few seconds and then said, "No". I didn't pursue the subject.

With each subsequent visit I met more of his friends, both English and American. Richard had told me quite a lot about himself during our time together in Ireland. Now I was regaled in greater detail. Excitement and success seemed to have attended him from childhood on. His happy nature and zest for life is apparent even in the snapshots of him as a small baby in his

74

pram. He had a radiant smile. Years after he'd left, he paid a casual visit to his old high school, and one of his former teachers said she recognized him instantly by his smile. An only child, he was born in New York City on Black Tuesday, the day of the stock market crash, an event which did not go un-noticed in his family since his father was a Wall Street lawyer. He grew up on Long Island, and in his teens his family moved to Washington, DC. He did exceptionally well at his schools in all subjects. After leaving high school he started wandering. He studied psychology at the Occidental College in Los Angeles. It was his least favourite city. He said one could sometimes smell the evil in it. He had a gift for painting and had a scholarship to the Museum of Modern Art in New York City.

Drama and Greek at the Catholic University of America in Washington, DC, brought him into contact with Roman Catholicism for the first time as far as I know. While there he studied comparative religion. By the time we met he was considerably more informed about the church, her history and her doctrine, than I, a cradle Catholic, was. He once described himself to me as being "fascinated by Christ". He spent a year studying French at the Sorbonne, a legacy of which was his elegant French accent sometimes commented on by his friends. He studied English at the University of Washington in Seattle from where he graduated in 1952. Later he held a teaching fellowship and taught English there for one year.

His peregrinations were not all on land; he'd slaved as a stoker on a merchant ship for at least one voyage (eight hours on, eight hours off). "My first and I hope my last glimpse of purgatory." He'd worked as an aeroplane mechanic, picture-frame maker and amateur actor – he'd been drawn to the stage at one point – so his background was both diffuse and extraordinary. He was an acutely aware man, benefitting in many ways from these diverse experiences. It was from the University of Washington in Seattle that he was awarded the Rhodes Scholarship in 1953. Vivid with life, he loved and relished its richness. People, arguing, art, literature, music, good food and wine were enjoyed to the full. He knew how to apply himself to hard work and how to play: how and when to relax the tension of his probing, keen mind. He could be arrogant and overbearing, but not unconsciously. He was often moody, but if he felt he acted harshly, he was big enough to say he was sorry. He was a man of intense passion and commensurate tenderness. One morning he got very angry with me about something – it must have been a trivial matter because I don't even remember what it was about. I tried to hide my hurt, but in spite of myself tears came to my eyes. Then he went off to school and left me in comparative misery all day. That evening, when he got back to the flat, he gave me this poem he had written for me:

> Why the minnows' flash or last night's moon
> should so deflect my thought I cannot say;
> because your tears this morning fell so soon
> to humble me, I fear they marred the day.

He had a perception of his own worth and gifts that seemed uncanny in one so young. The night I met him he told me that he had never met anyone more intelligent than himself. I was taken aback by what seemed to me to be gross conceit. Later I mentioned the remark to Sister Mary Angela, my singing teacher, a gentle, thoughtful, intelligent woman in whom there is no guile – a true Israelite. Her response was very unexpected. "It's probably true," she said. While being genuinely serious about things that mattered, he had a delicious sense of fun; and a childlike playfulness which, I think, he seldom showed others. Some of his close friends later expressed surprise at how playful he could sometimes be with me.

I left Oxford knowing that my attachment to this vibrant personality was deepening and that my burgeoning love was indeed reciprocated.

Almost as soon as I got back to Dublin I got news that I was to sing in Claridge's at an International Press Conference to be held there on December 12th. Richard was thrilled with the news. We both were. It meant we would see each other again. Richard wanted to know if I could go with him to Paris the week following the engagement to stay with the Jackson Matthews. He was working hard again and "missing you very strongly. This time we spent together is very precious to me. It was very good of you to come." The letters continued, with Richard bubbling with life and interest in it and his work. Term would end on December 4th and could I come to Oxford now *before* the 12th? From then on his letters to me were practically daily, and his deepening affection more evident and matching my own feelings for him.

In a moment of misguided humour I'd sent a cryptic note from Belfast where I'd been taking part in a concert. To my shame and contrition Richard had misconstrued the message and thought I was ill. Somehow he got hold of the telephone number of the private family I was staying with and phoned me. Confused by his unexpected concern all I could do to hide my embarrassment was laugh. This only compounded the situation. A very angry, hurt Richard wrote the next day.

Monday November 7th or Tuesday 8th

Mary,

When your laughing fit is over, do me a favour. I am enclosing a traveller's cheque for $10.00. Buy a white Ardan ganzie, like mine if possible, and send it as a gift to:

> John Leyerle
> Magdalen College
> Oxford.

He is a married friend of mine who needs to keep warm. If it isn't enough let me know, I'll reimburse you. *Also*, when you come to England next bring me tobacco, as much as customs allow: BALKAN SOBRANIE preferably, or THREE NUNS. Pipe tobacco.

Thanks. Richard

Then the next day.

8th November 1955

Dearest Mary,

I have been angry with you all day.

First because of the fright, now ridiculous, that your note from Belfast gave me; second because you addressed me with no form of endearment; and third because of your infuriating laughter over the phone. Even if it was deserved, it was very frustrating.

It is my too well developed, too sensitive pride that gives me the courage to be angry with you but it also prevents me from expressing a feeling that is much deeper to me and more important, that is that I love you.

I do not wish our relationship to become a game of pride. I wish to love you and to give you the best that is in me with all the tenderness and respect of which I am capable.

If the seriousness of my feelings offends or frightens you, please let me assure you that I require nothing more of you than that you obey the inclinations of your own heart.

Richard

Next day the storm had completely blown over:

9th November 1955

Dearest Mary,

I'm listening to flutes and harpsichord and what sounds like an oboe. I've just played a pleasantly strenuous game of squash and taken a hot bath and I am feeling more pure than usual.

No letter from you today but I suppose one will be coming soon. I read one of my long poems to the Poetry Society last night and it seemed to go over very well. Compliments from very grudging quarters were received.

I would appreciate your attending to the Ardan ganzie for John Leyerle. He has been admiring mine for weeks and finally gave me money to get him one. I hope you don't mind.

Of course, I miss you, please write.

All my love,
Richard

11th November 1955

Dearest Mary,

I hope you don't mind my writing to you so often, but I'm missing you extremely this week and have no other relief than to write to you. I wish you were nearer. . . .

This Sunday I speak to the Spectator Club to the accompaniment of clinking tea cups. It should be fun. I've become quite a lion on a small scale. Little girls tremble when they speak to me.

All my love,
Richard

I bought the Ardan ganzie for his friend. As a surprise I purchased the most spectacular one in the shop for Richard himself, plus a pair of socks. His exuberant gratitude was a tonic.

15th November 1955

Darling Mary,

Your gifts arrived this morning and are exceeding welcome. My ganzie is of a very superior ilk indeed! I like the design especially, the parallel paths of angles and arcs, diamonds and waves. I'm sure Mr Leyerle will be pleased with his: I won't show him mine. The stockings are a windfall, my feet having felt soggy, cold and wet for days now.

I don't think it at all strange that you should grow tired of certain of the songs you sing. I understand this very well: when one is young and/or of a romantic, emotional nature it is more for the sentiment that we love a thing than for its beauty and perfection as a work of art. Besides, most folk songs are extremely sentimental and in them there is little attempt to achieve the formalized sentiment of the art song, in which romantic convention plays so important a part. In the art song references to courtesy and to the pastoral life (shepherds, swains, etc.) abound and in this way the sentiment is objectified and refined, thus becoming *no more* important than the *way* it is stated and than the music to which it is set. I find that it is easier to become attached to an art song and remain faithful to it, regardless of the sentiment, because of its formal virtues, the verse, the melody etc. These virtues don't change and don't fatigue our emotions.

Both your letters, the one of the 11th and the one of the 12th, arrived on Monday so I was unable to hear the re-broadcast.

I hope to hear from you soon,

All my love,

Richard

PS If you take a flat don't sign a lease.

16th November 1955

Dearest Mary,

Thank you very much for your letter of Monday night.

I was pleased to hear of the success of your concert. I would love to meet your grandparents and the old Fenian, Mr Verdon.

On the Saturday night at the end of term, December 3rd, I've got tickets for Stratford and John Gielgud and Peggy Ashcroft. *Can you come?* I plan on going down to London on the following day.

I miss you, wish you weren't so far away, and pray that we can spend more time together soon.

All my love,

Richard

I did not agree with him about most folk songs being "extremely sentimental". At that time he was unfamiliar with the bulk of my repertoire and was later to change his mind when he came to see that many of the "big" traditional Gaelic songs are on a par with the best of *lied* and *chanson* and require considerable skill to sing them in a way that draws out the inherent beauty and excellence of the melodies.

Deciding now that I would be better off in a flat in the city I'd found one in Lower Leeson Street. Perhaps I should have been sharper and read between the lines. Richard's advice against signing a lease was because he had plans of his own regarding my future living arrangements.

17th November 1955

Dearest Mary,

It occurred to me, during this morning's labours, that I was harbouring selfish feelings concerning you. And they are these: I resent your being so far away and your wish to live independently in Dublin. Then, a stronger feeling rose up to spite these ignominious ones. That was: I want you to do what is best for you. That, ultimately, is what is best for me also.

However, I expect you to make every reasonable effort to spend as much time with me as you can reasonably afford.

It is difficult to love someone and not want to have them near. But since meeting you, I have discovered stores of patience I did not know I had. I have such faith in your good sense, Mary, that I no longer feel I need to exert pressure on you to make you demonstrate that you care.

The play I have tickets for at Stratford is one of my favourites: Shakespeare's *King Lear*. I do hope you can come. December 3rd.

During the week you have your engagements in London I shall be there also; if I may, I would like to be your chaperone at this "all male" press conference concert at Claridge's.

Let me hear from you soon,

All my love,
Richard

In the next day's letter Richard reported on the success of two Oxford enterprises:

I just finished and delivered an essay on Wordsworth which my tutor honoured with the exclamation: "extremely good". Rare praise from an Englishman. It was so conclusive that he had nothing to say so went out for coffee.

The long poem I read to the Poetry Society was described in the local paper as receiving a "great ovation".

If you love "hearing from me" you might encourage me by writing more often yourself. I'm at least as busy as you are so there's no excuse.

There followed "an internally stormy weekend" restraining himself from writing till he heard from me and recovering from "intense work and lack of sleep". More injunctions about bringing my passport and pipe tobacco. The former because of the vague arrangement about going to Paris which he still very much wanted us to do, and also a week in the sun somewhere South. But whatever other plans were made he wanted to spend Christmas with me.

 By now we had both declared our love and I knew that if Richard asked me to marry him I would say yes. And if he didn't ask me I would never marry anyone else. He was the one I'd been waiting for,

26th November 1955

Dearest Mary,

 Great quantities of thanks for your letter of Thursday night.

 I've had one of the stormiest of weeks this week which I'll tell you about anon. In a few minutes I'm going horseback riding on Port Meadow. It is a late November day of rich gold today and there are no clouds. Another poem is stirring in me and a strong desire to read nothing but jolly Chaucer. I want to write something very clear and full of all the possible radiance of humanity.

 I love you too, Mary, and admire you deeply. It is a rare happiness to me to meet a woman with your dignity. I want to show you my favorite Grivelli's and Rembrandt's in the National Gallery and also the Constable landscapes in the Tate.

 How was Segovia?

 I've got two sets of Graves mythology. I'll give you volume two. Rex Warner gave me one set.

All my love,
Richard

I was endlessly surprised at the way he could gauge his health needs – knowing which tonic to take and when; especially his own personal rhythm:

27th November 1955

Dearest Mary,

 I've just spent a lazy morning in bed and now that it is afternoon I feel lazier than ever. My coke fire is crackling and I am strongly inclined to fall asleep in my chair. I am surrounded by letters to answer and travel folders of Austria. Soon I shall go to tea at Prof. Trypanis's and, on the way, I shall take a walk and mail this letter to you.

My life alternates between periods of intense thought and activity and periods of relaxation. It is just about this time of year that I begin to relax again. I usually languish in the middle of summer, also. If I go against this rhythm I find I live too much off the spleen and all kinds of nervous discords are produced.

I explain this to you because, in my laziness today, there is a concomitant circumspection. I want you to know what to expect when you see me again. For my part I have pursued our relationship with a great deal of energy but, because of my belief in the possibility of its success, with little sense of strain. I feel now, however, that if my feelings continue at their present pitch without the renewal and confidence that only your presence can give they could easily burn themselves out. This is a harsh but I think accurate estimate of romantic emotion. Without each other's company on some kind of day-to-day basis and real physical contact calmly discovered, I think love would not be the correct word to apply to our relationship. You must understand this quite clearly of me, moreover: I am a man who lives in his senses first. What I see is what I believe. I have a sixth sense also and I have a faith in it, also, though it is like hearing sounds from a great depth. When I love, I love with my body, thoughts, speech and all my senses. I don't love ideals and possibilities. I love real things, present things, all the thousand particular characteristics that compose a person. And when that person is away, I love the *memory* of those things as *accurately* as I can.

I want you to know that I am keeping faithful to you with little reluctance.

I want you to write me often because I want you to keep me on your mind until we can be in one another's arms; talking, walking and eating together.

I love you,
Richard

28th November 1955

Darling Mary,

This weekend was an acutely lonely one for me, full of childish love-aches. I am over the aches.

I've just re-read your spate of green letters and want very, very much to be able to talk with you. My long dissertation on the senses was just another, if unfelicitious way of telling you I miss you and how nice it would be to have you in the vicinity. I am so unused to caring so much for someone else – being a veteran egotist – that it may make me a little uncomfortable at times. You will be patient, won't you?

I am just about to write to the tourist office of Obergurgel, a skiing village high up in the Austrian Alps. And also to Hochshölden for reservations. My budget won't allow plane travel. I hope you don't mind travelling third class by rail. When one is a student one must live as a student.

Write to me often, dearest, and if suddenly you wish to come on Saturday, I'll keep your ticket.

All my love,
Richard

The prospect of a holiday together in Austria was exciting, and when I got this letter I started consulting some of my friends about ski clothes. Radio Éireann had sent me a contract for a broadcast on Christmas Day, but I told them I wouldn't be in Ireland on December 25, and cancelled it.

30th November 1955

Good morning!

I have just read your letter of Tuesday in the GPO. It is profoundly appreciated.

Talking to you last night made me very happy.

In about an hour I shall go to see the surgeon. I hope something is done quickly. However, don't worry, I shall keep you posted as to all the details. You'll probably have to learn some anatomical terms so that I can explain things properly. Although I have never had an operation, I have seen many: your fear of them is unnecessary. The body is full of spare parts and can take a great deal of punishment.

Tonight, Stephen Spender will be the guest at the college Literary Society's dinner. It was I who persuaded him to come. In accepting the invitation, he took the opportunity to send back my poems. I tried to get out of asking him in the first place, but a sense of public duty and the other members of the society prevailed on me. Fortunately, the chairman has now taken full responsibility as host, so I am somewhat free to drink him under the table or at *least* to avoid sitting with him. It should be an interesting dinner. The menu includes: Sole Chaucer and pheasant.

Afternoon

I met the surgeon; a brisk, imperious man with large hands very bulbous at the joints, an extraordinarily long middle finger. He seems trustworthy enough. I underwent examination, blood test and X-rays and was out by lunchtime. I had a very pretty radiologist who took a cool delight in shifting me into all kinds of ludicrous positions. The doctor said something about my going into hospital today or tomorrow for further tests. So far no word. It is now nearly four o'clock.

No word has come from the surgeon yet and it is now 6.00 pm so I guess I won't hear anything until tomorrow.

I think it would be foolish for you to come up to Oxford for the weekend because it would only be a gloomy one for you and that would not make me happy. Why don't you come up a day or so before your concert just for the day? It would be a pleasanter visit that way. I would hate to think of you hanging around Oxford just to look at a drooping Richard. If you come up on a day *excursion* on Wednesday, 14th December, the day after Claridge's, it would only cost 8 shillings.

Spender has arrived, I must to dinner. I'll post this now and write to you tomorrow.

> All my love,
> Richard

In retrospect it seems curious that I have no memory of what it was that caused Richard to seek medical attention. Perhaps it's because he made very light of the pain or whatever it was, only mentioned it *en passant* in conversation, in his debonair way. There is certainly no reference to it in letters up to then. Treat the matter lightly – even humourously – in his letters he most certainly did. On the other hand, anyone who knew Richard then would understand that the idea of associating him with a fatal illness was preposterous. He was bursting with apparent good health, lively to a degree in spirit, mind and body; pulsating with life.

He was very wrong in thinking that I would not want to be there if I could, while the investigations were going on. I was able for a great deal more than he could have then guessed, and I didn't pare it down to a 'day excursion' but came for several days. Under this shadow which was to grow he continued to live life to the full, and his unending activities, social and academic, bubbled on unabated.

News followed about the imminent biopsy. He appeared unruffled. Due to uncertainty about the frequency of the tests and treatments, the plan for a holiday on the continent was cancelled. So I told Radio Éireann I would be available for the Christmas Day broadcast.

1st December 1955

Dearest Mary,

Infinite thanks for your letter of November 29. It was warmly received and appreciated.

Nothing to report about forthcoming operation. The surgeon managed to elude my GP all day. The surgeon has left me a message he will call tomorrow morning. The question at the moment is whether there is anything other than the jewel in the middle.

The dinner went splendidly. I managed to score my points without bruising anyone and S. now says he has arranged for my poems to be in the January issue, he also wants to see the 'T & P' and 'The Coast' again.

I have been keeping at work although somewhat desultorily. I'm going to see a French comedy now.

All my best, and every kind of love,

Richard

2nd December 1955

Dearest Mary,

I'm in the college library this morning. The surgeon is supposed to phone me about 10.00 a.m., in 10 minutes' time from now. I received a fine letter from my old friend, Wesley Wehr of Seattle: a composer and a young man growing wiser every day. He says: "Thank God for change and growth – and what a pity that it is to disappoint so many – as if there's time to stand still and be defined by the lazy."

Mary, I can't tell how much happiness your last letter gave me. It is wonderful to have one's feelings reciprocated.

The surgeon phoned to say I must go into hospital as a private patient for a day or so to have a biopsy. A bed has to be found. I won't hear from him again until one is found. This means I'll be able to see *King Lear*.

I just saw Sean White on the street and told him to call you when he gets back to Dublin to tell you how robust I look. I thought I'd discipline his propensity for gossip by requesting him to be a bearer of kind news. I hope you don't mind. I'll close this now and mail it. I hope '*Imaginary Conversation*' goes well.

If the timing is right, I may yet be able to meet you in London.

All my love,
Richard

85

Later that day:

2nd December 1955.

Dearest Mary,

I shall be going into the Ackland Nursing Home on Tuesday afternoon 6 December.

Going to two sherry parties this afternoon and *Lear* tomorrow.

Richard

3rd December 1955

Dearest Mary,

Thanks for your letter of the 1st. By now you will have received my letters. Mary, it is nice to have you worrying and praying, in so far as they are an expression of your care, but it would be much nicer still to know whether you would like to spend Christmas with me or me with you. I'm glad you got your Christmas engagement back. If I am on my feet I shall probably initiate yet another invasion of Ireland.

What do you want for Christmas?

All my love,
Richardus Seligonensus

4th December 1955

Darling Mary,

Today I went to the Magdalen College Chapel to hear a concert of carols. Mary, it was lovely and very peaceful. You must hear our choir some time. It is a treat.

Darling I love you and want to see you very much. Just to know you exist is a pleasure for me.

Richard

'*An Imaginary Conversation*' had been performed at the Arts Club in Dublin. I had written to Richard and was inordinately puffed up by my little success as an actress. His response tinged with sarcasm was appropriate to the occasion.

5th December 1955

Dearest Mary,

I haven't heard of a performance to produce such an effect since Sarah Bernhardt. You must have been good. Congratulations! I hope Dublin has recovered.

Thanks for writing.

All my love,
Richard

6th December 1955

Dearest Mary,
  Thank you for your letters dated December 2 and December 3.
  In one of your letters of last week, you said that you would be free to leave Dublin Wednesday, December 7. If this is still the case, then *come to Oxford forthwith*. I have no desire to be without you, either mobile or on my back, but merely suspected that you were a coward where illness is concerned and therefore suggested you should not come for any length of time.
  I received a reply from Hochshölden in Austria which I shall discuss with you when you come.
  I am in excellent spirits and am feeling very energetic, so the doctors can do their worst.
  I'd rather have you than your letters.

All my love,
Richard

  This was just what I wanted to hear: come to Oxford *quam primum*. He wanted me to be there with him as much as I did. The Austrian plan was apparently taking shape. His report about feeling on top of the world was very reassuring. He continued to convey this impression of well-being over the next twelve months, and doubtless this contributed towards my not grasping the gravity of the situation.
  He went into hospital and surgery was performed. That same day he got out of bed and phoned me, thus earning a severe reprimand from the surgeon. Since the operation was the removal of a lymph gland from his groin for analysis, this is understandable.

8th December 1955

Mary,
  I just saw the surgeon. The earliest he will let me out is Saturday. Therefore I cannot meet you in London as I had hoped. He was also very annoyed with my having walked about today.
  Please, please come to Oxford on arriving Saturday.

Richard.

  As usual I flew to London and took the train from Paddington. As soon as I reached Oxford I made straight for the Ackland

Nursing Home, expecting to find him still in bed. Not so. He'd discharged himself. I hurried down the road to his flat and rang the doorbell to no avail. Not having any idea where else he might be I just waited outside in the damp December twilight. Finally he turned up, looking his old self – and maybe a bit irritated that I'd not tried and discovered that the door was not locked. (Many were the times when Richard would throw up his hands and cry "Oh Mary you've got a head, use it!") It was very good being together again after another long lapse of about five weeks. Again, oddly enough, I have no recollection of any discussions between us concerning the biopsy. Perhaps they had told him nothing.

We travelled up to London together for the Claridge's engagement. I had with me my own very first evening dress, designed and made by a young Dublin dress designer, Sheila Russell. I knew exactly how I wanted it: material, colour, design. White broderie anglais, sleeveless, Princess line; buttons down the back (all the way to the floor) covered with broderie anglais; a scooped neckline in front forming a deep V at the back; a gentle bustle effect at the back of the skirt, achieved by the way the lavish underskirt was made. The making of it alone cost £20, which in those days was a sum to stop the breath.

This engagement was to be the first of many trips to London accompanied by my "chevalier". "Escorting me among the sharks" was Richard's expression. He revelled in it. He was more than a match for them. His strong, authoritative presence never failed to evoke either respect or fear among the wheelers and dealers. I think they sensed or recognized an all-perceiving shrewdness to match their own, in this handsome, cultured young man who was there with me at every meeting and consultation. He said little, but he always got things done.

That evening at Claridge's Richard wore his evening suit. There was something regal in the air that night. I felt decidedly fairy princessish as we wandered hand in hand through the elegant rooms adjoining the ballroom where I was to sing. We spoke hardly at all. I try to avoid talking before any kind of performance. I need the silence. Because of the nervousness and so as to concentrate. Few people understand this need; far too many, well-intentioned to be sure, chatter away and crack jokes endeavoring to be lighthearted and amusing. It only makes things more difficult for me. Not a few minsconstrue this quietness which I find essential and interpret it as moodiness. Richard never did. An artist himself, intuitively he just knew.

That night we were sitting on a couch together waiting for the signal telling me when I was to begin. It was to be an after dinner performance. As I was inwardly contending with my nervousness Richard leant tenderly towards me and said:

"Now you know what it's like when I don't get a letter from you."

Everyone seemed very happy with the singing. We left Claridge's and Richard took me to an exclusive French restaurant, where he'd booked a table. We dined sumptuously by candlelight. That evening had a special cachet about it. The beautiful dress, the successful performance, the ambrosial meal and the elegant, stunning young man with whom I was by now deeply and irrevocably in love and he with me. Almost perfect.

The diagnosis was Hodgkin's disease. It is a cancer of the lymph glands. They called it "the young man's disease". The victims are generally young males. In those days it was incurable, but, thank God, it is no longer so. Then it could be arrested by radiation. The researchers were experimenting with new drugs all the time.

When his GP broke the news Richard asked "How long have I got?"

"Well, you'll probably live to my age," was the reply. Losing no time, Richard sought out his tutor and asked him how old the GP was. "About forty-five," came the answer.

"Good, there's my essay for next week."

And Richard proceeded with the business of living at his usual intense, overflowing pace.

Who could presume to attempt or dare to say what was going on in Richard's mind when he got this news and during the weeks, the twenty-two months that lay ahead. When he did speak to me about it at the beginning, he seemed strangely matter of fact and objective concerning the disease. One of the things he said was "The sentence of death hangs over all of us." I returned to Dublin and prepared for my Christmas Day radio engagement.

21st December 1955

Dearest Mary,

Lunching with the president of Magdalen this morning. Trying to make some progress with *Sir Gawain and the Green Knight*. It's hard to get myself going again.

There is nobody in the library this morning but C.S. Lewis and me. I hope I will hear from you soon. Please let me know the dates and whereabouts of your engagements for the next month.

All my love,
Richard

P.S. As rare as my surname is, one bearer of it has just been elected to a Rhodes scholarship from the district of New England. I guess America will even take to mass-producing Seligs. His name is Edward J. Selig. What a blow.

R.J.S.

C.S. Lewis had been Richard's tutor during his first year at Oxford. He left for Cambridge the next year; an event which occasioned the following poem from Richard.

Valedictory poem for Mr C.S. Lewis

Now you go to Englands' other Eye
Take with you, Sir, your pupils love.
May th'other college of the tearful Mary
Be twin, in youths' love, to this you leave
Whose eye you opened year by year to see:
The Past can change but changeless is it's glory.
The hour when you departure take
Let Oxford weep and Cambridge wake.

When I was at boarding school I'd attempted to read C.S. Lewis' *Screwtape Letters*. Little if anything impinged. I wasn't ready for him. It was later that I discovered what a marvellous spiritual writer he was. He became one of my favourite and much-read authors.

22nd December 1955

Dearest Mary,

Thank you for the gigantic Xmas card but how about a letter.

I am writing to you every day not out of habit but because I miss you so much.

Spent the evening with the Mitchells and did my best to get

Maureen to laugh at herself or at something. Adrian appreciated the effort more than she did. It was a pleasant evening and I've been asked for a return engagement this evening.

All my love,
Richard

23rd December 1955

Dearest Mary,
Just got your letter of Tuesday. Delay is due to Christmas, I guess. I've sent you three letters c/o Dr R. Sorry to hear you are still stuck in 53. I wish I could go over and build a fire under Dr R. I know how to intimidate Dublin landlords.

George played me a lovely Haydn sonata (on the piano, not on a record-player) till the pubs opened; then we got thwacked on Irish whiskey and Guinness and finished the evening with a steak dinner. It was fine. Got up feeling slightly hung over but opened windows wide and did callisthenics.

Richard

Physical exercise is something I've always keenly enjoyed. In no time Richard became as enthusiastic as I about it. Each morning would find him doing his push-ups or whatever. Often we would do our callisthenics together during the day. When I was in Oxford I used to sleep in Adrian and Maureen Mitchell's spare room in their little flat round the corner from Richard. After I came to actually live in Oxford, before we were married, my usual routine was to cycle to St Aloysius for eight o'clock Mass, go to Richard's flat for breakfast together, and use it as a base for the rest of the day.

In the end, we didn't spend Christmas together but Richard came across for the New Year.

24th December 1955

Dearest Mary,
Many thanks for your telephone call last night. It was very welcome indeed. I shall make every effort to come to Dublin if I can.

Keep after Dr R. or the place won't be ready on the 31st either.

No letter from you this morning but am not surprised.

Mary, it is impossible, or at least very difficult, to tell you over the phone that I love you but please remember that I do whether I say so or not.

More than anything else at the moment I would like to march down Grafton Street with you.
>
> All my love,
> Richard

The business of moving into my flat had been dragging on and on. For one reason or another it was never quite ready on the day I was supposed to take up residence. Grafton Street was the most fashionable street in Dublin. It was a source of wonder and delight to Richard that so many people who passed up and down it seemed to know each other. In those days when we walked down it together I could be greeted possibly a dozen times in one journey. It was one of the more endearing characteristics of Dublin that the city was still small enough for an area like Grafton Street to become a meeting place for friends.

27th December 1955

Dearest Mary,

Three Christmas dinners in two days have left me surfeited of chicken and turkey. George's over-indulgence has given him a gastric attack. I've just left him with a cup of broth.

Christmas Eve in college was a very staid and elegant affair. The choir sang the first part of '*The Messiah*', then dainty refreshments were served along with mulled claret. The second part was a concert of carols which ended at midnight with the twelfth chime of the tower bell, "Gloria in Excelsis Deo", and the passing around of a loving cup.

The X-ray machine won't be repaired until January 2nd. I've lost my spectacles and must have a new pair made forthwith.

The radiation treatment to arrest the disease had begun. The "by-the-way" remark about the X-ray machine being out of commission was the only reference to his condition which appeared in any of his letters to me. He used spectacles only for reading and then not always.

I've got dozens of letters to answer and cards to acknowledge. I've been having a quiet, social and completely lazy time of it.

What did you sing on Christmas Day?

I resent your not being with me and hope that you will soon have your affairs sufficiently straightened out so that you can come and go without too much guess work, presumption and wishful thinking. Will the flat really be ready on the 31st?

Thank you very much for your fine letter of Wednesday and your message of Thursday. I love you, too.
                                                                                Richard

Richard flew over to Dublin a couple of days before the 1st and saw to it that, despite the flat's not being ready, I was installed in Lower Leeson Street. I didn't sign a lease as he'd advised me against it; this turned out to be good advice as, early in April I moved out of the flat and went to live in Oxford.

Although Richard hadn't asked me to marry him we both knew it was in the air and since I was a Catholic and he was not, with the possibility of children there arose the potential problem of their religious upbringing. I recall a long walk through the New Year rain talking about it. Richard's view was that children should grow up and make their own choice and not have a particular religion foisted on them from the cradle. But the ruling of the Catholic Church at that time was that all children of a mixed marriage should be brought up as Catholics. The non-Catholic party had to promise to agree to this and see that it was implemented. This ruling has since been modified.

Richard came from a completely non-religious background. Neither of his parents adhered to religious beliefs of any kind. In his late teens he'd examined the tenets of various faiths and found them all more or less wanting. But his attraction to Roman Catholicism was strong and became increasingly so the further he investigated. He was familiar with the writings of some of the great theologians and mystics, such as Thomas Aquinas, Augustine of Hippo and John of the Cross, before I became acquainted with the teachings of these and other spiritual giants.

It sometimes irritated him that I was so patently ill-informed about the history of my own church – the result of inattention during Church history classes. He soon gave up trying to provoke me with taunts about ecclesiastical scandals over the centuries. There was nothing I could say and, when I failed to rise to the challenge, in exasperation he would defend the Church himself, saying that it was members of the Church from the Pope downwards and not the Church herself who could be and often were corrupt and immoral. We never argued about religion. I have never been one for debate about my beliefs.

We'd been invited to a dance at the Arts Club on New Year's Eve. We seemed to be one of the very few couples who were not middle-aged or over and despite the fact that Richard was far from being a good dancer we enjoyed it all. He left for England on January 3rd.

3rd January 1956

Darling,

It is now 11.15 pm and I am sitting in the kitchen of my flat while the boiler is lighting and the third programme plays a piano sonata by Schumann dedicated to his then future wife. I have just done my exercises – the standing up ones at least – and have drunk from a sticky cup full of Bournvita. I must drink a glass of plain water.

I caught the plane at noon, the train from Birmingham at three and was in Oxford before five this afternoon.

Mary, come to Oxford on the fourteenth if possible. I suggest that you book your flight now since it is a Saturday. See if you can come by way of Birmingham. Have you written Mrs Rowlands about practising? I will make inquiries about practise rooms and harps.

Richard

Mrs Rowlands was the only person we could find in Oxford who had a concert harp and it was hoped I could be allowed to practise on it. An arrangement was made with her.

Geographical separation once again showed up my dilatoriness in letter writing. The number of letters I wrote was chronically insufficient to his demand.

(This (Jan 4) is a continuation of the letter started Jan 3.)

4th January 1956

This month's *Encounter* arrived this morning with one of my poems in it. I feel as you do after a performance – not satisfied.

Dearest, I do want you to be here on Saturday week.

A Christmas gift from my mother arrived, two pairs, one green, one blue, of American-type pyjamas.

According to her latest letter, her romantic life continues at full swing with various and sundry types of masculinity.

I am attending to my laundry now and afterwards I go to the library.

Is Dr R compliant with any of your requests? Did you find the gloves?

Being with you in Dublin was the profoundest of delights. I enjoy your company very, very much.

All and every kind of love,
Richard

5th January 1956

Dearest Mary,

Good morning from Magdalen College Library! It is below freezing in Oxford and the fog has crystallized into tiny spears, the better to penetrate the skin of pedestrians.

If you must sign a lease of a year with Dr R, make sure you have the right to sub-let. It would seem more practical to me that instead of spending so much of your money living in the grand manner you might better spend it on a decent wardrobe of which you are in great need. . . . In your trade, mobility is essential: are you sure you want to support a flat for a year?

I have been dutifully doing my exercises morning and night and am beginning to feel more like a prize fighter than a student.

I look forward to seeing you and before that to hearing from you.

All my love,
Richard

6th January 1956

Dearest Mary,

The gloves arrived this morning. Thank you for sending them. With the same post a cheque for £10 from *Encounter* arrived.

Is it pride or laziness that has kept you from writing? If it is pride, then you needn't be afraid: I love you and shall continue to do so. If it is laziness, please mend your ways.

Darling, please arrange to stay a longer time in Oxford than heretofore you have stayed. Let me know as soon as you've made your booking.

I love you,
Richard

7th January 1956

Dearest Mary,

No letter from you again this morning. I hope it is the fog that has delayed letters you *have* written rather than that under cover of some mental fog of your own you have omitted to write. I shall continue to write you as often as possible under the assumption (I hope it isn't a delusion) that you want to hear from me.

Last night I went to a Twelfth Night celebration at the Leyerle's. Mulled claret and all kinds of goodies were served. It was very pleasant. They did an excellent job of serving and of seeing that people got aquainted with one another.

I am working hard: writing letters, reading and school work; am doing my exercises; and am looking forward to seeing you again.

If nothing comes on the noon post I shall send you a wire,

All my love,
Richard

PS I just phoned the post office to find out whether there has been a delay in the mail from Dublin. There has been none. Mary, don't you believe in me or my love enough to write to me before you hear from me?

Richard.

The wire of consummate brevity arrived that evening. It said: Phone me now
Richard

During our last time in London together we'd been to see people at Decca, at their suggestion, regarding future recording possibilities. In this next letter Richard touches on Decca's concern with the commercial side of my singing. During my entire career the conflict, however unavoidable, between the music and the money nexus has been a constant irritant. My music and my performance of it are what matter to me; the box-office returns tend to outweigh other considerations in the minds of those on the organizing side.

10th January 1956

Most beloved Mary,

A windfall arrived this morning: two letters from you. Warmest thanks for them. I was deeply touched and delighted that you reserved your first phone call on your new phone for me. It was lovely to talk with you, Darling. I am more grateful for your love than for any of the favours that have ever been bestowed on me, and more honoured too.

As for S., an idea occurred to me, one of many, last night, that may be of use to you. I suspect that they are building up to do some popular recordings *comme ci*: "Joe Gooch and his Orchestra introducing Mary O'Hara on her Irish Harp". He will probably dazzle you with an introduction to Joe Gooch himself and to his famous vocalist, Marilyn Muck. You know, the girl who made a hit with "Stagnant Whirlpool" and "I loved you in Old Shoes". After meeting these bright stars, he will treat you to anything you want at a restaurant in Soho and expect you to be fawningly impressed and grateful. This is my idea for what it's worth. If you can get enthusiastic about some folk songs in English, some lively or poignant American ones, perhaps, to which you can give your own inimitable Irish flavour, you might turn the tables on him.

One of the reasons he is acting the way he is is that the first recording you made was rather effete and probably not very saleable. He is trying to get you to do something which is saleable in his own clumsy way. You feel that he wants you to go too far in the opposite direction, that to sing things like 'Groce de Oro' would be merely making a fool of yourself. You're probably right. Since you've been so passive about your repertoire, he is taking the initiative. Find some songs that are new and interesting to yourself before you see him and when you do see him: if you can, wax enthusiastic about them and ask to play them to him and Mr Lee. If you don't sell what sort of thing you want to do to them: they will try to make you do something in accordance with their own crude notions. Try Carl Sandberg's 'American Songbag' and some of Allen Lomax's collections. You may find them in the National Library.

All my love,
Richard

Richard was now into his third year and was beginning to chafe at the academic ethos.

11th January, 1956.

Dearest Mary,

Your letter of yesterday was happily received this morning.

The president [Tom Boase] finally got his copy of *Botteghe Oscure* [the international literary magazine] and found himself to be very "excited" by another American poet, also born in 1929, published in the same issue with me. It seems this other poet detracted somewhat from his interest and pleasure in mine. I went home to read him last night and I must say I, too, was quite impressed. This poet, by name of Calvin Thomas, has spent the past years in the American air force rather than at Oxford, with the result that his images have a much more contemporary and more attractive ring to them. Needless to say, the despair I have been feeling over my own work has deepened. I look forward to leaving this guilesome plot of antiquity where the past seems to sap one of any originality. I am very chastened but do not know what to do. I must find other artists for one thing.

All my love,
Richard

97

I've always liked beards – the smaller, neat variety. Although they were fairly rare in those days – the mid and late fifties – some of my friends sported them. To please me Richard grew one, and he looked even more strikingly handsome, if that were possible, than before. Being a six-footer already marked him out from most others. Like his head of brown hair, his beard was luxuriant, with reddish areas. There was one particular tie of a soft olive colour which he sometimes wore which emphasized his unusual green eyes. He had a black corduroy suit which the President of Magdalen used teasingly to refer to as his "Hamlet suit".

12th January 1956

Dearest Mary,

Your post-party letter just read, I am very pleased to hear it was a good one.

Hold your hat! I just got a wire from an American benefactor: "remitting Monday". Three hundred and fifty smackers, simoteons, dough, dough at last. $350.

If you're "full of love" I'm nearly overloaded. My bearded bristles and I emit involuntary sighs which sound very much like "Mary" or just m . . . m . . . m . . .

Richard

A few days later I arrived in England for an engagement. By now I'd started flying to Birmingham rather than to London. It was a shorter flight and Oxford lay conveniently mid-way between the two cities. Richard Afton, the BBC TV producer, was including me in his variety programme, 'More Contrary'. This time Richard didn't travel up with me – term had begun again, and he was confined to Oxford. Sydney MacEwan sent me a good-luck telegram. I was very pleased. Richard phoned me after the TV programme, which was live. Everyone was happy and I was signed on for the two remaining programmes.

Next day, after lunching with Decca people, I travelled back to Oxford and Richard.

We had a glorious two weeks together this time, having tea with friends, going to the Film Society, sometimes lunching or dining out, and going for long walks. And Richard was initiating me into the mysteries of the culinary art. He had an inate gift for cooking and he did it creatively. Over the years, and in different countries, he'd picked up some fairly simple but very appetising dishes to which he added his own inventive touches. Meals cooked by him were always succulent. Now I was to discover that cooking could be as exciting as the finished product was enjoyable.

Towards the end of that spell we travelled to London together. I'd had my eye on an elegant black coat I'd seen in the shop where I'd bought the evening dress for my first BBC 'More Contrary' programme. I emerged from the shop clad in the same coat but of a colour I would never have dreamt of choosing for myself, but which Richard had decided on. A very difficult colour to describe: a pinkish coral is the nearest I can get. It was the most successful purchase I'd ever made. People passed remarks about it's being a most flattering colour for me.

Next day, before leaving for Dublin, I bought some dresses in Oxford to team up with the new coat. Richard approved.

Together, we had a meeting with Richard Afton.

27th January 1956

Dearest Mel,

In case you don't know, your visit was a great delight for me. Also accompanying you among the "sharks" I find as adventurous as anything I have ever done.

It think it is wonderful that you are aquiring a decent wardrobe. I'm sure that I enjoy it as much as you do.

Well darling, I hope you receive this tomorrow instead of Monday, but in any case receive it with

All my love,
Richard

In between my visits to England for engagements and being with Richard, I was keeping up my singing lessons with Sister Angela and lessons on the concert harp with Mercedes. I continued attending Seán Óg's claisceadal classes, broadcasting from Radio Éireann, learning new songs and keeping in touch with friends.

Back in merry England Richard was not only immersed in his studies and the usual social whirl, but also finding time to

99

try to straighten out my career, and see to it that I would find the right agent "with good taste, integrity and who lacks the over-bearing attitude of self-aggrandisement which seems to possess many of them". A task which wasn't all that simple.

31st January 1956

Dearest Mary,

The second of your letters to be written "every single day" arrived this morning. Thank you. It was dated the 28th so I gather the weather in the Irish Sea is unpropitious for the postal services. I hope my yesterday's letter reaches you soon. I wish to keep you informed of professional matters. . . .

An incident with an acquaintance in Oxford prompted Richard to launch into the following reflections about indiscriminately bestowing and accepting friendships. He may also have had in mind the world of entertainment where people are so often "used" by others under the guise of helping them.

I think you can carry sympathy too far. Also I think you can overestimate your power to do good. There is an insidious element of pride in thinking that you can bestow love and affection on those weaker or more afflicted than yourself. It makes you feel very strong and generous when you make such a bestowal but beware that the cur that you honour with comfort and consolation does not repay you with laughter and destruction. You must be a saint, indeed, to bear the enmity of those to whom you are most kind. Those who need the most kindness are often the least capable of gratitude. Those who *ask* for your sympathy often have an insatiable hunger for which sympathy is insufficient food. They want more and more of you, more than mere sympathy can satisfy. It is noble to feel compassion. It is nobler still to know when and where love and affection will be gladly received and to be able to bestow them in a truly generous spirit. Compassion can also be an excuse to yourself. In its name you do for others what does them no good. In its name you do what you want to do anyway.

Darling, forgive this sermon but it has been stewing in me for a long time. I don't expect that you will agree with all of it or perhaps any of it. Please believe that it is not based on the distrust I have often accused myself of. I do not love people the less for what I have seen in their hearts or in my own heart for that matter, but rather I attempt to love more efficiently, with fewer delusions and self-deceptions, to

100

expect less and to give more. Human nature needs constant correction and attitudes toward it need constant revision.

Mary, I study to love you better and better, to love what is truly you, to love what is best in you because that increases my respect and admiration for you and to love what is at fault in you because in that, too, I know you – and knowing and loving you is what I desire and need to do more than anything else in the world.

Richard

31st January 1956

Darling Mary,

Your Sunday letter came on the noon post. Many thanks. Darling, I write you a second time today to tell you I love you: I love you.

I hope you will bear with me in my "complicated" moods. Sometimes I even try my own patience so I can imagine how you must feel.

I am hard at work. I am going to attempt a poem on the Antarctic today. The weather is appropriate. It is snowing. Last night 'The Tiger and the Panther' received very intelligent acclaim at the Florio Society. Tonight I will read 'The Coast' to the Poetry Society.

This week I have an essay to do on Shakespeare and am anxious to clear my desk early to get to it.

I have been exercising every morning. Yesterday I defeated an inchoate cold by imbibing great quantities of liquid and food. I don't feel so weepy today.

Dearest, I love you all the time.

Richard

My domestic arrangements in Dublin continued to cause Richard some small concern and he was as usual ever ready to come to my rescue and straighten things out.

1st February 1956

Dearest Mary,

Your letter of Monday the 30th is gratefully received. Remind me to buy you a gallon of blue or black ink. I do think it is rather a drain on one always to be writing in one's blood.

Dearest, I can't tell you how good it was for me to talk to you last night. As you have probably surmised I miss you very much.

As for signing a lease, if the question arises, explain that you cannot sign one until your next birthday. As for paying your rent you need not do so in person. Send him a cheque to the amount of a month's rent. Don't under any circumstances get yourself under obligation to him, keep the relationship business-like.

Though it is still contingent on a number of things, I think the best time for you to move to England would be during the spring, in early April. I could help you to move at that time. Also, even a short trip with you during my spring vacation, after moving you here, would be highly desirable. However, all of this must be discussed at greater length.

I look forward to hearing from you. I remain devoted to you with all my love,

Richard

2nd February 1956

Dearest Mary,

Darlingst Mary, I'm full of love for you this morning and wish with all my might I could be telling it to you in person.

There was no letter from you this morning but I am hoping for one on the noon post.

I'm down to my final revisions on my poem, a sonnet, on Antarctica. I finished reading Scott's last journal on Tuesday with tears in my eyes. It is the first time in a long time that a book has so affected me.

Yesterday evening I was with George Pitcher and Sir John Gielgud. Sir John is one of that rare, amazing ilk, the pure artist. I've known only two others to equal him, Mark Tobey, the painter, and Roethke. The surge of their thoughts is an experience I have long missed, especially in this effete, self-conscious and too-sophisticated community. And, darling, believe it or not, his intelligent simplicity reminded me of you.

I haven't told you this before. But I find the trueness of your reactions to things, and your clear, beautiful company most invaluable to me.

I'll wait to see if there's a letter from you before I mail this.

Sweetheart, I just got your letter of Tuesday. Infinite thanks! I love you, too, with all my heart.

Richard

Here the poem on Antarctica. He called it "On Reading *Scott's Last Expedition*" and it was published around this time in *The Listener*:

> The hazardous career meets death half way;
> Who chooses active dying must endure
> The thought of death much longer, see it lure
> Him past all hope and one by one betray

His chances until mercy is a brief delay
Before the ice immures the blood: make sure
They know ill luck, not fear, was cause of failure;
And silent, then, explore the last white day.

Richard asked Sir John for advice about "a friend of his" who was at a sort of crossroads in her career. He explained that several persons were trying to act as her agent and she needed friendly professional advice. Sir John recommended Joyce Grenfell. An introduction was arranged and she was subsequently to become my good friend.

Later I knew that Richard had battled with himself over the problem of his own prospects and mine. He wanted us to be together always but should he ask me to marry him or not? In those days the odds against a young man stricken with Hodgkin's disease living a normal life span were virtually nil.

3rd February 1956

Darling Mary,

I have a two-berth cabin, No. A7 on the *Queen Elizabeth* sailing from Southampton to New York on the 6th of September. Would you like to come along?

When you arrive in Birmingham eat lightly for I have two large steaks waiting for us.

With all my prayers that you will be able to come Sunday I remain
Your devoted
Richard

This was the first open acknowledgement that we should still be together when he had finished at Oxford. I felt that this meant he was now on the brink of actually asking me to marry him. This move was supreme Richard. A two-berth cabin on a ship to America with me, unconsulted, as the second passenger was sheer presumption. He, when he sent the letter and I when I received it, both knew I would want to accept.

Two days later I arrived in Oxford. On the morning of February 10, in the kitchen of his flat in Norham Road, Richard proposed to me. Without a moment's hesitation I said yes. After lunch we walked out into the cold February day and looked in the window of Davis the jewellers on the High Street. There was an antique ring there which caught our eyes, but when we got inside the shop we saw the perfect one. It was a late Victorian antique ring with four amethysts and one diamond surrounded by rose diamonds. It fitted me beautifully. On our way out Richard spied some lovely ear-rings and held them up against my ear. He paused, considered and then declared, "No, they don't suit you. Your face is too coarse."

I used to swell with secret pride when friends and strangers in shops remarked on my beautiful engagement ring.

5   Marriage

Fierce as the bursting seed
love taught her to unwind
Bright leaves to the light . . .
For growing is all her care –
By love her love is unbound.

(from "Song for the Bride" by Richard Selig)

We would have liked to have got married at once. But being a Rhodes scholar, Richard was not free to do so. In those days Rhodes scholars in residence were not allowed to marry. Some went ahead anyway and got married secretly. We toyed with the idea of marrying on the quiet during the Easter vacation, and in some obscure part of the Continent. But since it was to be a mixed marriage between a Catholic and a non-baptized person, we were going to need a whacking great dispensation for that alone. Marrying somewhere other than in my parish would have meant seeking yet another dispensation. So we decided not to complicate things, but wait until Richard's exams were over sometime in the summer.

At St Aloysius Presbytery Richard received the usual instruction meted out to the non-Catholic party. He learned nothing that he did not already know; and he spoke to me with gentle humour of the unnecessarily (for Richard) elementary nature and method of the teaching he received from the good parish priest. When the appropriate time came, he promised that any children of the marriage would be brought up as Catholics. It meant much to him that I grow in the Faith and be as diligently practising a Catholic as I could possibly be. It was never an issue with us. Countless times he opted to come to Mass with me on Sundays: never did I suggest or even hint that he might do so. He was a man who knew himself, and his own mind, and who acted with immense integrity.

At Mass he would sit sideways with his legs crossed, his arms folded with one hand under his chin and, in this informal attitude, listen attentively to the preacher. Outside the church after the service he would proceed to dissect the sermon with perspicacity and great good humour.

Thinking the coast would be clear by mid June and exams well out of the way, with the parish priest's concurrence we set the date for June 14. I was able to spend seven weeks in England: most of February and March. It was packed with happenings, great and small.

By now, Sydney Lipton was acting as my agent, although I'd not signed any contract. He procured a five-week tour for me with Harold Fielding's 'Music for the Millions'. Although it was a summer tour I did my first of these concerts at Eastbourne in April. Sometimes Rawitz and Landaur headed the bill; other times it was Terry Thomas or Eartha Kitt or Elsie and Doris Waters. I would be next on the bill, singing about half a dozen songs, with comedians following and occasionally two male dancers, Flak and Lucas, and a singing couple.

That February I had my first photographic session with Baron. Richard came with me to London on all these excursions, and excitement was never lacking. As arranged, I appeared on the last two 'More Contrary' TV shows. Maurice Wiggan of *The Sunday Times* wrote some unexpectedly kind things about my work after he'd seen me on 'More Contrary'. Almost at once I was offered a short series of TV programmes of my own. It was called The Starlight Series. Richard Afton was the producer of the first couple, and Frederick Kapman produced the remainder.

The performances went out live in March and April 1956. When it came to writing my TV scripts, Richard's help was invaluable. In February I had my first fifteen minutes on Children's Hour television. Sir John Gielgud had alerted Joyce Grenfell beforehand and she'd agreed to watch my perfomance on the children's programme, and invited me round to her flat in the King's Road for tea afterwards. She was gracious, kind and strongly encouraging. She was helpful in many ways – even about giving me tips as to what outfits looked better on television and what to avoid.

As best I could (it was rather complicated by then) I acquainted her with the situation regarding the agents who were approaching me. She advised me to opt for Sydney Lipton – the gentleman among the lot as far as we could judge.

More often than not, Richard and I lunched or dined in Wheelers during our London jaunts. Back in Oxford we lived our usual vigorous lives: the Rhodes Beer Party and later a Rhodes dance stand out in my memory.

I'd had to stop my harmony classes in the Royal Irish Academy of Music in Dublin because by now I was hardly ever there. An undergraduate friend of Richard's reading Music at Magdalen came to Richard's flat a couple of mornings each week to give me harmony lessons. We got on like a house on fire. His name was Dudley Moore. Years later when I was in Stanbrook I picked up *The Times* one day and read a fascinating profile of Dudley. I'd no idea that, in the meantime, he had become an international entertainer. He and Peter Cook had become household names. To my joy I saw him for the first time since those Oxford mornings on the Michael Parkinson television show in 1978. He hadn't changed an iota. Dudley Dorian Gray Moore. Since then we've had dinner together.

I flew back to Dublin for one week to see Seán Óg and learn some new songs, have singing lessons from Sister Angela, harp lessons from Mercedes, see people in Radio Éireann and contact friends. I returned to England for a Harold Fielding concert and the beginning of the television series.

It was the Easter vacation by now. Clad in jeans and duffle coats, Richard and I hitchhiked to Birmingham airport. We took the train from Dublin to our old haunt, Galway. There we hired bicycles and, for the next few days, rode through the Connemara rain enjoying every minute of it. Whenever the rain let up it was cause for celebration, but, rain or clear skies, the Connemara magic is potent. I know of nowhere else apart from the Aran Islands themselves to match the stark independent beauty of the treeless landscape. We both thought it was the most beautiful part of the world and later seriously thought of buying property there.

We returned the bikes to Galway and got a lift back to Dublin by car. Before we left for the airport I evacuated the Leeson Street flat.

The following Saturday, around 10.15 pm, I had my second programme of the television series, and again on the following two Saturdays. I did some more children's television and flew to Holland for a television appearance there. I sang two songs: "Eibhlín a Rúin", one of the most beautiful of our big Gaelic love songs, and "The Spanish Lady".

The repercussions of that appearance reverberate to this day. Holland continues to be one of the non-English speaking countries where my records have gone on selling steadily. During my years in the monastery, shielded from every vestige of publicity, the Dutch continued to buy my earlier albums and, in fact, had the first one 'Songs of Erin' re-processed for stereo in the early seventies. Indeed I was astonished to be told that during the folk boom of the sixties, without any publicity from the record companies, the sale of my albums all over the world soared. They were even being manufactured and distributed in Australia, New Zealand, South Africa and North America.

The contract I'd signed with Decca was for five years. There was no obligation on the part of the record company to release any material of mine. They were holding on to the four songs I'd sung for the test recording in October 1955 and showed no signs of bringing them out – hoping I would record "pop-folk" songs instead of the traditional songs I understood I had been contracted for. Little did they know that the sort of material I was singing was to become so popular in the sixties. I was not altogether unwilling to try the type of song they had in mind, but so far they had failed to introduce me to any song I felt comfortable with.

Richard had entered the fray and now proceeded to take measures to get things moving. A correspondence commenced between him and the record company which makes interesting reading. It was clear from his letters that while his objective was to persuade them to release the recordings I'd already made, he thoroughly enjoyed the sparring.

I was safely so far removed from this controlled warfare that I knew little about the detailed moves. Somehow, from somewhere, Richard sought expert advice which resulted in Decca's releasing the original material as an EP: two songs a side. Decca was stunned by the public's response. They called us to their office to tell us that in Holland alone they'd sold 2,000 copies in the first few days. Now they did a *volte face*. Would I record a long-playing album of songs of my own choosing?

My initial reaction was one of apprehension. Among other things, I thought I didn't have enough material. (In those days one recorded eighteen songs on an album.) This was also how I'd greeted the BBC's proposal that I have a series on my own, on television. On both occasions, Richard quietly but firmly banished that erroneous fear and very quickly let me find out for myself that I had more than enough songs. In fact, within fifteen months, I'd cut three 12-inch long-playing records: "Songs of Érin"; "Love Songs of Ireland" and "Songs of Ireland". A new recording contract with Decca was drawn up. An additional clause which Richard, his advisors and Sydney Lipton had Decca insert into the agreement, stated that my work must not be coupled with that of others on a recording without my express written permission.

Richard decided not to speak of his illness to anyone. Apart from the medical people and myself, only his tutor and the warden of Rhodes House knew about it. We didn't tell his mother or my father. Why? Richard was such a wise man that there didn't seem to me to be a need to question such a highly personal decision about himself. Compassionate towards others, he was also a man in whom there was no shred of self-pity.

At a party one spring evening in Oxford, in the midst of a light-hearted conversation, an undergraduate banteringly asked Richard if he was going bald on the chin. Richard laughed it off, but when we got back to his flat we examined his beard. Sure enough, there was an area underneath one side of his jaw where the hair was thinning. The lymph glands in his neck were acting up. Sadly, we said farewell to the beard.

Spring passed into summer and we were both fully occupied. Richard's final examinations were on the horizon. I was working on my first long-playing record and about to begin the summer tour. We spent what time we could on the tennis court or on the river. We got about on bicycles. There were end of term parties and picnic lunches on the lawn at Magdalen. I snatched five days in Dublin filled with the usual singing and harp lessons and sessions with Seán Óg. Then back to Oxford again.

For some reason not recorded, the date of our wedding had to be postponed. The new date was July 23. A few years ago I discovered that my birth which took place on May 12 was not entered in the appropriate archives until July 23 . . . While I toured, Richard stayed on in Oxford preparing for his *viva*, but he usually managed to come and join me on weekends, whether it was Llandudno, Bournemouth, Torquay or wherever. I did a week in Aberdeen and was grateful that the following week in Bristol was cancelled. This left me with eight days free before our wedding.

Together we'd shopped for the wedding dress and finally found just the thing in Knightsbridge. The shop assistants were horrified to discover that Richard was my fiancé. We'd never heard of the superstition that the groom ought not to see the bride's dress before the wedding. Richard and I laughed about it. The dress was very simple; ballet length and made of white lace. We bought the ring in Davis' in Oxford where we'd got the engagement ring. This, too, was antique; a thin band of gold with delicate tracery edged all around.

When Richard got the news that his *viva* was on July 24, he made every possible effort to have the date shifted. His attempts were futile. So the unheard of had to happen. We got married on July 23, and the exam was on the following day.

Richard's mother was in Washington, DC and my father in West Africa. Most of our other friends were on vacation. We'd planned a very small, quiet wedding anyway, and I was most anxious that it be kept out of the newspapers. No photographers were invited. Peter Levi, the poet, was to be Best Man; my brother-in-law was to give me away and my sister was to be the Matron of Honour. At the eleventh hour Frank got involved in a court case which necessitated his being in Dublin on the morning of the 23rd.

Alan and Joan Woodin had been invited, so Joan took my sister's place and Richard's tutor, Jack Bennett, gave me away. Jack and his wife, Gwyneth were very good friends of Richard's. I spent the night of the 22nd at their home in Ferry Hinksey and in the morning, Gwyneth drove me to eight o'clock Mass at St Aloysius. Back at their house we had straw-berries for breakfast. Then off again in the convertible for the wedding ceremony at 10.00am. I arrived to find that Richard's great friend, Peter Levi, was not after all to be our Best Man.

(Alan Woodin had stepped into the breach.)

Late that day I heard the story. Peter was a Jesuit scholastic at the time. It had been arranged well in advance that he would be Richard's Best Man and no dissenting voice was raised. But when Richard arrived at St Aloysius Church – about ten minutes before me – he was greeted by a very nervous parish priest who said he'd decided that Peter, being a Jesuit ought not to be involved in a mixed marriage ceremony. If that fact got bruited about it might look bad, and so on. "But," he hastily added "I've asked another Rhodes scholar to be Best Man instead." Cold with fury, in deadly quiet tones Richard pointed out that he had not invited any Rhodes scholar to his wedding. Who could he possibly mean? Taking him into the church, the poor parish priest, now all of a tremble, pointed to the Warden of Rhodes House himself, Bill Williams! Time has erased (if I ever did know) the memory of any further exchange between the irate groom and the Jesuit. We ended up with charming Alan Woodin being Best Man. It was indeed a mixed marriage. The non-Catholics outweighed the Catholics that sunny morning. Neither the groom, the Best Man, the Matron of Honour nor the Giver-Away were Catholics.

There was no nuptial Mass. There was no Mass at all. The ceremony was very simple. We both stood outside the sanctuary and exchanged vows. Peter acted as acolyte and handed the celebrant the ring. There were about a dozen people present. Afterwards we repaired to the New Rooms at Magdalen for our reception. Everyone drank champagne except the bride. Since we couldn't leave Oxford because of the *viva* the following morning, someone suggested we have lunch on the Isis. It was a brilliantly hot sunny day. We piled into some punts and for the next few hours lazed about on the river talking, eating and relaxing in the glorious sunshine.

In the late afternoon we left the punts and dispersed. Richard and I got a taxi back to Norham Road where he got on with his studies for the following morning while I slipped over to the Mitchells' place and did some ironing. That night we dined in our favourite restaurant outside Oxford, and spent the night in an hotel further down the road.

After the exams next day we flew to Dublin. We'd tried to book in at the Shelbourne, beautifully situated on Stephen's

Green, but it was full. We had to be content with the Gresham. Next morning after a gargantuan breakfast we headed for the west.

Hitchhiking as usual we spent the night in Galway intending to travel to the Aran Islands next day on the *Dun Aengus*. We discovered it was up for repairs. The locals told us that our best bet was to travel into Connemara and take a turf boat from there to the islands.

After breakfast we paid a visit to our friend Tomás O'Maille who owned a draper's shop in the town. We'd become acquainted during our last visit to Galway the previous spring. Tomás had taken a great liking to the pair of us and now he presented us with two handsome hawthorn sticks. We bought a supply of beautiful hand-woven tweed of various colours, which we left to be collected on our return journey. Later I had the different materials made up into suits, coats and skirts, before we left for North America. Richard had some suits made there.

On our way through Connemara we stopped at a pub out in the middle of nowhere so that Richard could buy a glass of beer. He stood at the counter ordering his drink while I sat by myself in a corner, incognito as I thought, in my duffle coat and jeans with my hair in plaits. The pub was filled with local men. To my consternation one of them asked me in Gaelic if I would sing for them. I did so. Here I was singing a Gaelic song at the source so to speak, so their response meant as much to me as would that of a sophisticated concert hall audience.

We got to Carraroe, but once more we were stymied. The mainlanders who rented the boat were on some sort of a strike. But it was thought that one man in the neighbourhood was going to break the strike and set off early in the morning. We booked in for the night in the only guest-house in the area.

Strolling down to the sea after supper, we clearly heard a piper playing. The thin, sweet sound filled the silent summer evening. We searched around but never found where the strange plaintive music was coming from.

Around midnight when we were both asleep the door suddenly opened and a man walked in holding a lighted lantern above his head, talking in a fairly loud voice. Leaping naked from the bed Richard grabbed hold of his hawthorn stick and with arm upraised advanced on the stunned invader. The latter backed out in terrified confusion. The explanation was simple. There was no double room vacant that night in the guest-house. The man's wife had put us up in the children's room and had forgotten to tell her husband. He'd looked in, as usual, to see if his children were safe and sound.

In the morning the rumour about the strike-breaker was confirmed, so after breakfast at eight o'clock, we presented ourselves on the quay. We came to a financial agreement with the owner of the "hooker" (the turf boat), climbed aboard and set off for Inishere. The sea was calm and the sun shone hotly down on us. At mid-morning the sailors shared their thick bread and jam and sweat tea with us and it was delicious.

Inishere is the smallest of the three Aran Islands and has no pier. The currachs come out to meet the boats, and the cargo, human or otherwise is transferred and rowed ashore. There were three men in our currach. I overheard their conversation, which was in Gaelic, and realized that they thought we were not married, so I displayed my rings and told them we were husband and wife. They looked a bit embarrassed and kept quiet after that.

Richard received a warm welcome from the Coneelys with whom he'd stayed the previous summer. When he was leaving they had expressed the hope that he would return another time, Richard's reply had been 'I'll be back this time next year with my wife' – some confidence! Once more our bedroom arrangements were not idyllic. Our double-bedded room led onto a single one which was occupied by another guest. To get in and out of his room he had to go through ours! Late that night he climbed upstairs, tramped through our room and proceeded noisily to attend to the necessities of nature. Richard swore in the darkness and wondered out loud why he couldn't have gone outside and done it.

Years later, when I'd started singing again, that same man, Richard Lyons, an architect in the north of England wrote to welcome me back. "You won't remember me but I remember you and Richard vividly!" I replied: "How could I forget you", and referred to the incident of the joint bedrooms. He wrote back: ". . . And please remember Mary, should you decide sometime to re-marry I hope you'll invite me to the honeymoon – because you know, it won't be quite the same without me!" Richard Lyon's friend Áine O'Malley who was staying there at the same time also wrote me after I'd resumed my career. She too had a clear memory of both of us.

★   ★   ★   ★

I remember you both so very well. I have a picture of Richard chasing you across the strand with a ribbon of wrack. You looked fulfilled that day and gloriously happy. Richard was a picture of handsome virility. I remember your arrival by boat from Connemara (that was the first thing that intrigued me because I'd liked to have done it myself). Then my rotten direct remark – blowing the gaffe on your lovely anonymity – and the demure, cheerful almost resigned way you answered. Me: "You're not – but of course you are – *the* Mary O'Hara?" And the lovely way you laughed. I remember you singing for us that night – and your Richard, too – some kind of rollicking western. I remember you both walking hand in hand towards the dunes – you were looking up at him and he was bending towards you, and I think you must have been singing something because when you had finished he flung his arms around you and gave you a mighty bear hug. Do I remember him swimming cleanly and strongly? I think so. I know he was a swimmer, and some time or other he must have done some underwater swimming or diving. He must have or he couldn't have written 'Among Silence' as he did.

It rained a lot that week and we were the only ones who ventured into the thrashing seas. Richard was a very strong swimmer. I am not. Too timid I think – I keep missing the reassurance of being able to touch the bottom. With Richard however I gained more and more confidence.

The day came for us to head off for Achill Island and our *sui generis* friend Major Freyer. We were rowed out to the *Dun Aengus* which was anchored in the bay. Soon after we'd climbed aboard, I was approached by a man who asked me if I'd sing something on tape for a German group who were in Ireland recording songs. I refused and the man persisted in his request. To silence him I explained that I was under contract to the Decca Record Company and was therefore not free to record for anyone else. I thought no more about the matter. The deck was thronged with people and some of the islanders prevailed upon me to sing for them before I left. So a few minutes before the boat weighed anchor a crowd of us went down below to the saloon. People seated themselves or stood around the edge of the room. One corner was partitioned off, hiding the bar from sight. When everyone had grown silent I began to sing. Richard sat next to me with a large mug of beer in his hand. As I neared the end of the first verse of 'Eibhlín a Rúin' out of the corner of my eye, I noticed a movement of something at the top of the partition. I nudged Richard and continued singing. Richard now saw the furtive micophone – and so did everyone else. By now I was beginning verse three. Richard rose from his seat and tiptoed noiselessly across to the partition. Reaching up, he coolly emptied the contents of his glass into the offending apparatus. No one budged, and I finished my song.

After my first Festival Hall concert twenty-one years later I was astonished and very pleased to receive the following letter:

Dear Mary,
Enclosed is the snap you so kindly allowed me to take of you and Richard on board the *Dun Aengus* steamer from Galway to Aran Islands, in 1956, I think.
I were thrilled that day when you let me take a photo and the press men were not.
I promised your husband a copy, but could not find out where you were.
I were a fan then and still am.
We were on holiday, my father was born on Inishere, you made that holiday for me and when you also sang for us it was great.
I am glad you are back and wish you all the best for your future.
Please write to say you got snap, I would like to know you received it after 21 years.
Yours sincerely, Mrs M. O'Neill

We sailed to Galway and from there headed for Achill Island and Major Freyer for a few days. Though we'd written to warn him of our coming, we had no way of knowing that he was expecting us. We'd heard it said that he never opened his letters – one of his charming but awkward eccentricities. Whether he expected us or not he welcomed us warmly. And our days there were lovely too.

Back in Dublin, I left the handwoven material we'd selected in Galway, to be made up into various outfits. We returned to England and I finished the tour with one week in Torquay.

Earlier that year I'd agreed to appear as guest artist in the official Edinburgh Festival production "Pleasure of Scotland" written by George Scott-Moncrieff. Before we went north I recorded in London "Songs of Érin" – my first LP for the Decca Record Company.

Calum Maclean with whom I'd kept up a correspondence, kindly offered us the use of his flat in Edinburgh for the two weeks we were to be in the city for the Festival. He was up in the Hebrides himself at that time. Just before we left he returned from the Islands and I was very happy at this opportunity for Richard to meet him and share my growing affection for Calum. They warmed to one another at once.

It was a lamentably cold and very wet fortnight. Alistair and Rena Maclean were all set to have us stay a few days with them on South Uist after the Festival engagement – I was longing to introduce Richard to the Hebrides – but the weather was too miserable and Richard had a cold so we opted to return to London earlier. It was a special joy introducing Richard to George Scott-Moncrieff and his family: Sir Monty and Chrissie; and all my other Scottish friends. We promised to be back again soon – hopefully the following summer.

September 10 was fast approaching and our excitement was mounting at the thought of our five day voyage aboard the QEII. We talked about it for weeks in advance. Richard would be returning to his homeland after a three years' absence, during which a multitude of things had happened to him. I would be arriving in the United States for the first time in my life.

We climbed aboard the ship with me carrying a celtic harp in each hand. One of the things we most looked forward to was playing deck tennis. After we'd deposited our things in our cabin we lost no time in seeking out the person in charge of games. It was a very windy day. I could hardly contain myself with delight – which was my undoing. The combination of excitement and the strong wind resulted in my tossing at least six rings into Southampton waters, in the space of half an hour. The man said: "Madame you may not have any more rings, nor

play this game again on the voyage." So we had to content ourselves from then on with shuffle-board. All very static, but
better than nothing.

There were two other Magdalen men on board, and we
knocked around together. The usual ship's photographer must
have been moving about. I don't recall being photographed but
we were. Twenty-one years later, the BBC did a profile on me
on the '*Tonight*' television programme and they flashed across
the screen a snapshot of Richard and me in deckchairs on board
the QEII. This was the first time I'd ever seen it. How on earth
did they get hold of it?

The BBC interviewer was David Lomax. He was a great
friend of Peter Hayworth's, one of the Magdalen men on the
ship with us. When David was told he would be interviewing
me he contacted Peter in Canada who told him about the snap
and where he would find it in a drawer of his summer house in
Oxford. The BBC also managed to root out our wedding
photograph from the archives of the *Oxford Mail*, which I'd not
seen before either.

In no time we were sailing up the Hudson River with
Richard showing me the Statue of Liberty. We were there.

6 Light and Shade

When God is on the thorn the rose is resplendent through eternity
(from 'Eight Proverbs' by Richard Selig . . .)

We were met at the docks by my mother-in-law Florence and her sister Elsie, both of whom I liked instantly. Richard used to say with amusement: "You get on better with my relatives than I do myself!" They drove us to the apartment they'd found for us as a stop-gap while we hunted for somewhere ourselves. It was out on Long Island and not far from Elsie's home.

Richard had decided while in England that he'd had enough of the academic world for a while and would try to get a job in industry. Through various contacts he had several interviews lined up. The morning after we arrived, as Richard was leaving for an interview, he handed me $15 and told me to buy food for the coming week. The only assistance he gave me was to explain that $3 was roughly the equivalent of £1 sterling. So there I was thrown in at the deep end. There was nothing for it but to accept the challenge and shop. I found the nearest supermarket (something I'd never seen before but only heard about), and started purchasing the necessary provisions, going round from item to item frantically dividing by three. Months later I was still able to buy our weekly groceries for $15 (it was the latter half of the fifties) with a little money to spare for wine, and Richard admitted his astonishment that I could do it. In fact I began to enjoy housekeeping. It was all new to me and I found budgeting quite exciting and satisfying. I would buy in the supermarkets only the "specials" that really interested me. As the weeks went by, I discovered particular small shopkeepers who sold certain items at a lower price than in the supermarkets. For instance I'd buy all my chickens from one butcher, all the lamb chops from another, and so on.

A young American couple at our wedding had scribed a delicious recipe for brown bread made with, among other ingredients, honey, buttermilk and sunflower oil. After a couple of abortive attempts (it tasted scrumptious but wouldn't rise and felt like lead), I succeeded in baking wholewheat bread and from then on I never bought a loaf.

At first we looked for a place in Greenwich Village but nothing suitable turned up. After some more searching, one day, out on Long Island, we saw a notice in a real estate agent's office window. It was unusual in that it was advertising for a *young* couple. Intrigued, we went to see the place and found that the apartment below the empty one was occupied by the landlord's young daughter and her medical student husband with two very small children. Below them again, on the ground floor and in the basement, lived the landlord and his wife. We were taken with the amount of light in the apartment – there were windows back and front – and decided to rent it. We both liked lots of light and air. So many of the places we'd seen up to then were dark, often with rooms within rooms. Decidedly depressing.

The apartment was unfurnished. Aunt Elsie was both very wealthy and extremely generous. In her beautiful house on Long Island she had a basement full of good furniture which she no longer used. She told us we could take all we wanted, which we did. We also discovered a cleaners where unclaimed carpets were sold at a very low price. The beds we bought from the Salvation Army. And Richard made a handsome dinner table with wrought iron legs, with a coffee table to match, and bookshelves.

We soon settled in and I felt very much at home. Richard had taken a job as a public relations consultant with the Western Electric Company and was enjoying his work. I was more than busy being an exceedingly happy housewife and practising my singing and playing each day, building up my repertoire, and both of us enjoying my growing skill at cooking. The only time during our life together that I was totally miserable was when Richard, exasperated with me about something or other, stalked out of the apartment without telling me where he was going. It was as though the bottom had dropped out of my world. I felt utterly devastated. Time passed and no sign of him. I walked over to Aunt Elsie's hoping he'd be there. She knew nothing. Even when I returned home he still hadn't come back. When he did, he told me he'd gone for a walk and then to a movie and "it was no good without you."

Shortly after we arrived in the States, the Decca people invited us out to lunch. We were taken to an excellent restaurant where I proceeded to concentrate on the food, leaving Richard to talk over business. A couple of days later Richard received a charming letter from the Decca representative, who ended his letter thus: "And I hope you'll come and have lunch again soon, if only to watch Mary eat."

Occasionally we went out to dinner to friends and also entertained in our apartment. At first I found the latter a strain, since as a child I'd had no experience of this – my parents' drinking and constant quarrelling precluded any socializing while I was growing up. But Richard was there to get me over the hurdles and I was learning. We sometimes wandered round Greenwich Village at weekends in the winter, visited galleries, went to the odd film, concert or play, and indulged our liking for Chinese food.

Frequently during the week after supper we would take a walk over to Aunt Elsie's, about three miles away. Her welcome was unfailingly warm and we often watched TV there. Syd Caesar was a big favourite of ours and we tried never to miss his hilarious programmes. On the way we had to pass a funeral parlour. The proprietor, an excessively fat man, habitually stood outside the doorway. One day Richard ventured his opinion that the owner ate the corpses, so from then on as we neared there, we crossed to the opposite side so as to keep a straight face!

In November 1956 we travelled to Washington, DC to spend Thanksgiving (Richard's favourite Festival) with my mother-in-law Florence. Before we'd left England, Richard's friend and tutor Professor Jack Bennett had given us an introduction to a friend of his, Anne Moray in Washington, DC. We had drinks with her and her Spanish husband one evening and she kindly brought us along the next day to meet Elmira Beer the procurator of the Phillips Gallery, with a view to arranging a recital some time later. She was enthusiastic and the date February 10 was set up. As this was our engagement anniversary, it augured well.

Richard was getting a lot of writing done in the evenings and at weekends. Shortly after we moved into the apartment on

Long Island he arrived home jubilant one day about his great purchase of a handsome roll-top desk. It was of such generous proportions that to get it up the stairs into the apartment we had to take the door off its hinges.

From about the time that Richard started earning we began to save. Like every young married couple we got enjoyment and satisfaction from this. I told Richard I didn't want to know how our savings were mounting up. Sometimes he would come home with a huge smile and say, "Guess how much I put in this month?" or "Guess how much we have in the bank *now*?" and I'd get all excited and say, "No, no don't tell me – keep it a surprise until the end of next year!"

Christmas came and Father flew from West Africa to spend two weeks with us. My mother-in-law travelled up from Washington, DC and he and she got on tremendously well together. Early in January he flew to Aden to take up his new appointment as a Technical Expert with the Food and Agricultural Organization of the United Nations.

It was my practice to go to daily Mass. We would set out together and at a certain point go separate ways: Richard to the city by subway and I to the local church. We would kiss each other good-bye at the corner, sometimes to the accompaniment of cat-calls from the passing garbage collectors. He'd whisper things to me like: "I wish I could take you with me in my briefcase." Since I took Communion at Mass, and in those days one had to be fasting from the previous midnight, this meant that on weekdays I didn't eat breakfast with Richard. (While he ate I prepared sandwiches for his lunch.) One day I decided that sharing this first meal of the day with him was important and consequently I forfeited going to Communion during the week. After a while, noticing this, Richard remarked, "Why aren't you going to Communion?" From the way he said it, I knew he wanted me to go on receiving the Eucharist during the week – so without any discussion I happily went back to the original routine.

Richard's doctor in England had referred him to a doctor in New York City. After the first couple of visits Richard became increasingly uneasy. This man kept boasting that the longest he'd ever kept a Hodgkin's disease patient alive was five years. He used the X-ray machine on Richard with appalling carelessness, not bothering to shield the rest of his body properly while the affected area was being treated. Richard told me that even the paintings in the Waiting Room were disturbing. When, through sheer negligence he gave Richard a third degree burn on his jaw, that was the last straw. As a result he had an ugly purple patch there for several weeks.

Richard had struck up a warm and humour-filled friendship with a splendid man called Michael O'Leary, who worked for the Bell Telephone Company. Michael was a Catholic, and one day Richard took him into his confidence and told him his medical history and that he was being treated by a very unbalanced New York doctor. Could he recommend someone else? At first Michael took it all as a huge joke. Here was this singularly healthy-looking young man bursting with vitality, spilling over with *joie de vivre*, his vigorous mind teeming with ideas telling him he was suffering from a killer disease. When Michael was finally convinced he was stunned and he wrote as follows in a letter to Peter Levi:

As to Richard's health, I must confess that I completely ignored the first oblique allusions that he made to this subject. I did not understand them and I put them down to a flair for self-dramatization perhaps. I just could not believe that this vital young man was anything but bursting with health.

Now and then he would remark to me, "O'Leary, I haven't got much time," to which I would not pay the slightest attention. I was always suspicious that he was ribbing me. Another time he said to me with a chuckle, "You know I have a strange affliction that seems to attack young men and kill them in their prime." I inquired acidly whether his was one of the commoner social diseases or one of the more odious afflictions found in the Orient. He chuckled as if over some secret joke and said, "You wouldn't believe me if I told you. But don't worry, I do not believe it's very catching."

Once the course of his conversation led to his posing this question to me. "Don't you think it's blind inefficiency on God's part to let a man of immense talent die before he has a chance to do anything with that talent?"

"Why? What does his talent have to do with it?"

"Well, if he writes a great play or a novel, why that's to the honor and glory of God."

One afternoon, when he seemed quite calm, he stopped by my

122

office and dropped into a chair. "O'Leary, I can't stand this progressive doctor I'm going to. Your brother-in-law is a doctor, isn't he?"

"Yes."

"Will you ask him for me if he can recommend a man who specializes in Hodgkin's Disease? Now, besides Mary and the warden at Oxford, you are the only person in the world who knows what's the matter with me." With that he got up and walked out.

In no time through his brother-in-law, a doctor, Michael introduced Richard to Dr Rottino, then head of the Research Department on Hodgkin's Disease at St Vincent's Hospital, New York City. When Richard told the first doctor that he was not coming again, the man behaved oddly and wrote a strange letter to him using military terms such as "come back onto the battlefield", and, among other things, accusing Richard of cowardice. Richard was considerably relieved at the changeover and said to me, "At least now I'm in Catholic hands." I don't know for sure what he meant by this, and it never occurred to me to ask him. But from other conversations we had, I presume he meant that Catholics are known to have a profound respect for life and for the living – an attitude of reverence towards the individual which this other physician seemed tragically to have lacked.

Joyce Grenfell had kindly written to Ed Sullivan telling him I was coming to New York. I did an audition for him at his apartment and he told me that he'd be delighted to have me on his programme on 17th March 1957. The William Morris Agency was acting on my behalf and they set up an audition for the Gary Moore TV Show. That, too, went well and I was booked for an appearance in February. When the time came I sang a couple of songs and they were well received.

Within a few days of the 'Gary Moore Show' we found ourselves once more in Washington, DC, for the recital at the Phillips Gallery. It was a great success. This was my first solo recital anywhere. Richard, as usual, wrote my script and helped me compile the programme of traditional Irish and Scottish songs. It was given from the room which has two paintings of St Peter just inside the entrance and which therefore I was facing as I sang. One picture is by Goya and the other one by El Greco. One of the reviewers, DC Frank Campbell of *The Washington*

Evening News, predicted that decades from then I would sound as fresh as I did that afternoon. Exactly one decade later to the very day I was singing the antiphons at my Solemn Profession in Stanbrook Abbey Church in England. But two decades later to the day, by an extraordinary coincidence, I was once more before the public giving a solo concert to a sold out house at the Royal Albert Hall in London . . .

When March 17 came round I was all set for the 'Ed Sullivan Show'. It was a Sunday. The night before, Sullivan phoned me to say that Bob Briscoe, the very popular Jewish Lord Mayor of Dublin, would also be appearing on the show. Would I, with my Irish harp, be prepared to be part of the background while the Lord Mayor was on stage? I had no objection to being on stage with Bob Briscoe, a man much loved in Ireland and especially in Dublin, my adopted home town. In fact he and my father were good friends, and later after I'd become a Benedictine and Bob Briscoe's daughter a Carmelite nun, our respective parents used to meet in Grafton Street and console one another that their entry into heaven was more or less guaranteed because of their daughters! But I objected to being part of any background, especially what I suspected might be an embarrassing stage-Irish one. But at this point there was nothing I could do but agree. Richard was seething about this. He instinctively felt that Sullivan had deliberately waited until Saturday night before asking me to do this – a time when it was impossible for me to consult with my agent.

We arrived for rehearsals and saw that I was advantageously positioned on the bill. That allayed Richard's fears somewhat. But as the afternoon wore on, they kept shifting me around on the programme. To my horror I saw them carrying on two giant cut-out shamrocks and placing them at the back of the stage. I was dumbfounded when I was asked to sit with my harp in one of them while Bob Briscoe was on stage. I envied the beautiful Irish wolfhound standing in the other shamrock, who seemed impervious to the indignity of it all. There's nothing wrong with the shamrock as such, but when it is perennially associated with leprechauns, shillelaghs, green beer and Delaney's donkeys, I feel it is prostituting the true image of our beautiful country and of its ancient culture. It smacks of stage-Irishism. It has echoes of *Punch*'s earlier racist caricatures of the

Irish as capering troglodites and simian-faced morons. Celtic Ireland has a wealth of art treasures of rare beauty and craftsmanship, much better suited for representing a nation than the kitsch emblems of pub-culture.

When the programme went on the air and I found myself perched up in the cardboard shamrock monstrosity, I was so incensed that instead of sitting facing out towards the cameras, at the last minute I deliberately sat as near to having my back to the audience as possible.

When the show was drawing to a close, the stage manager came to me in the wings and said, "Miss O'Hara, I'm afraid it looks as though there won't be time for your songs after all." It was supposed to be a St Patrick's Day, ergo, Irish programme. Apart from Mayor Briscoe – and the charming wolfhound – my songs were the only other contribution that was genuinely Irish.

After I was told there wouldn't be time for my singing I remained silent. Richard was by my side, livid, but powerless all day to alter the inexorable course of events. Suddenly a stagehand rushed up to me: "Quick, there's time." Unceremoniously I was shoved across the vast stage, had a stool pushed under me and was told, "You're on". Good accommodating Irishwoman that I was, I took a deep breath and launched into "O Danny Boy, the pipes, the pipes are calling . . ." It was Sullivan's own choice of song. But before I could even finish one verse, I felt his patronising hand descending on my head and heard him saying to the viewers something like: "That's it for tonight, folks". Off the air, he had the temerity to ask me to "sing a little song now for the studio audience . . ."

Richard and I had promised ourselves we'd sample Japanese food for the first time after the "Ed Sullivan Show". But by now Richard was so vexed that he wanted only to go home, which we did.

That winter and spring found us still living our lives in our customary top gear. But as summer approached, Richard became subject to more frequent attacks of the disease. These were characterized by severe exhaustion and accompanied by cold sweats. He would sometimes come home from work washed-out and deathly pale. His face was getting thinner but not his body. His appetite, which was always superlative, now waxed and waned. After these bouts he would be his old scintillating euphoric self, vivid with life.

Richard had read every book about Hodgkin's disease that he could lay his hands on. He knew every form it could take. The radiation treatment to arrest the disease continued at St Vincent's hospital and all the time they were trying out new drugs. He would phone me up some mornings and report that the most recent drug seemed to be showing good results. But our elation was always short-lived. They would find that it wasn't as effective as they'd thought it was, and start experimenting with something new again.

Although we were planning not to start our family before getting back to Ireland, sometime in the middle of that summer I thought I was pregnant. I don't recall having strong feelings about the business of child-bearing one way or another. We searched around for names. Richard asked me for my prayer book (the Missal) and read through the list of saints in the Canon of the Mass. We both liked the name Clement, and Charity was the girl's name we were happiest with. But it turned out to be a false alarm. I wasn't disappointed. With Richard I had everything; besides there was lots of time. Afterwards Richard said that he had sensed that I wasn't pregnant but had said nothing. And I'm certain that being the intuitive person he was, he would indeed have known if I was pregnant, even before I'd told him, perhaps even before I knew myself.

We were both realistic enough to appreciate the seriousness of the illness, but we lived, I'm sure like any other young couple in a similar situation would have done: full of hope. After Richard's death, many people assumed that we had married *knowing* that he had little time to live – that he was doomed to an early death. That's not the way it was. Such a thought was not something that influenced our lives or future plans. Richard's lifespan, as far as we were concerned, was going to be as normal as any other. We were going to grow old together. However, earlier that summer, Richard had taken the precaution of having our bank account in both our names.

From the time we got married I was concerned that his writing might stop. But I need not have worried. When he'd got settled in at his new job and in to the apartment, he began writing regularly. I am not a great reader of poetry. I was even less so when I first met Richard. There are still some early poems of his which I do not understand. But after our marriage I understood each new poem he wrote. That is to say, I saw meaning in his poems. He used to try out new ones on me and ask: "What do I mean?" I would say: "Well this is what *I* think you mean." One day he said: "Mary, I want to write poetry now for people like you" meaning, I suppose, the person of average intelligence who doesn't often read poetry. For instance, when he wrote 'A Small Request', I could tell him what I thought it was all about with ease. There is so much in that poem with echoes of our life together. The opening four lines clearly refer to my spirituality of that period when I had a strong sense of penance. The "suffering is a sign of grace" alludes to the occasions when we would talk about the mystery of suffering, especially in relation to Richard himself. I had been taught that suffering, far from being a sign of divine disapproval (a decidedly Old Testament view) is often in some mysterious way an indication of God's love. Scripture is dotted with such allusions. 'Gently falls the rain' is a reference to Ireland where we'd been so often together in the ubiquitous rain. The "small garden and a hearth" is about our decision to return to Ireland after about a year in the States, settle down there, preferably the Aran Islands or Connemara and raise a family. County Galway was the spot in the world we loved most. We would have supported ourselves by Richard's writing, my royalties and the occasional concert.

After Richard died, Stephen Spender read Richard's last poems and considered 'A Small Request' to be his best.

A Small Request

You who feel the instructive hand of God
Raise boils and welts upon your chosen skin,
Whose self-affliction quells the offended rod
And gets you up the hillside out of sin,

You whose suffering is a sign of grace
You whose privilege is to feel more pain
Whose hope is Heaven and to see God's face
Please recall how gently falls the rain;

> And when, if you remember me, you pray,
> Pray this for me: "Though he loves the earth
> Too much, do not send his soul away:
> Give him a small garden and a hearth."

'A Small Request' was written a few months before his death and was therefore in a sense his last request.

There are other of his last poems that appeal to me even more. The delicate loveliness of 'Reflection' unfailingly leaves me in a state of great inner stillness. It deals with the Greek myth of the beautiful youth Narcissus, who fell in love with his own image in the water. Here are some lines from it:

> Narcissus looking backward, saw the astonished
> Light. The morning air was full of it's surprise.
> The breezes trembled as if struck by bells
> Unheard by him, and yet so fair of tone
> The breezes chimed and grasses bent to them.

Sometimes he would write at breaks in his working hours. One poem 'From the 16th Floor' was actually composed from his 16th floor office in Western Electric, on Broadway. His eyrie afforded him a particular perspective of his surroundings, a perspective also affected, no doubt, by the knowledge of his own illness, which must have hung like the sword of Damocles over his life.

> Pardoning this borough for its evil,
> I look past the tops of buildings, to where
> The sky is. Remembering that man's malice,
> This man's fate: the former's cunning,
> The latter's jeopardy – seeing the sky,
> Placid in spite of soot and heartache,
> I am reminded to pray. Redemption,
> Like our janitor, comes as we go home:
> A stooped man turning out the lights.

These three poems were among his finest and last. One day in the summer of 1957, our second and last summer together, he phoned me to try out his latest prose poem. It was about a unicorn and he'd called it 'My Friends: *A Fable*'. I was enchanted by it, for I have an insatiable appetite for faerie and myth. Thus through Richard I was introduced to that mythological creature, a medieval symbol of Christ: the unicorn. Since then, my interest in this mythical beast has grown and whenever I can, I visit the Cloisters in New York to look at the Flemish Unicorn Tapestries there. I now have my own song about the unicorn. Peter Levi wrote the words for me and I set them to music. The chorus goes like this:

> Coat of snow Unicorn
> Horn of gold Unicorn
> Heart of fire Unicorn.

Late that summer of 1957 Richard sat down to go through his poems to see if he had enough to warrant setting about publishing them in book form. He rejected almost all of the earlier, that is, the pre-Oxford ones, and was quite rigorous in his selection of Oxford and current ones. He reworked some. He did me the honour of going through the list with me. In all honesty I told him which ones I didn't understand. He seemed annoyed by this. (Understanding these poems came slowly to me – some have not even yet yielded up their secrets to me.) The list he finally ended up with was, he decided, too short for a book. He never talked about it after that. About this time he was happily engaged in his first prose book. It grew out of the "fairy" story about the Rabbit People he'd told me in Oxford one lazy summer's day. He called the book *The Diary of a Balloonist*. He revelled in the research and in the writing of it. A satirical work, liberally laced with humour, it was to be in three sections; he completed the first part and had begun research for the second.

Ever since our friendship began and I was just visiting in Oxford, Richard took it upon himself to deal with all my business affairs. He took tremendous delight in this. Richard had no illusions about the piranha types that prey on unsuspecting neophyte performers in the world of entertainment and set out to protect me from these sharks.

After we'd become engaged Richard said to me: "One of the lovely things about our marriage will be watching you grow." Something of supreme importance had already begun to grow from the time Richard and I became friends: my faith.

Although it was never spoken in so many words, I knew that Richard wanted me to be a thinking, full-blooded Catholic or nothing. It was as though, with his uncanny insight into people's characters, he perceived that I would have to give myself fully when it came to any matter of lasting importance.

I'd had the usual convent education where the practice of one's religion was taken for granted. Up to the time I'd met Richard I'd felt no urge to delve any deeper into the beliefs I had inherited. It had never occurred to me not to go to Mass on Sundays; sometimes I went to daily Mass, too. But it could never be said that I was fired by my belief in God and by the truths of the Christian religion. I was what might be called a routine Catholic. My faith, as it were, lay dormant. With Richard's dynamic entry into my life it was awakened. I had never met anyone who probed like this before. He was instrumental in helping me examine and be ever more committed to Christianity. He was by my side shaping my perceptions and attitudes towards life.

There came a day when I saw with astonishing clarity that I was undergoing a conversion: the kind that I now believe every cradle Catholic must, at some time or another, experience. I had never heard or read about such a thing. It was happening to me and I was aware of it. And I was able to share it with Richard and tell him that it was taking place in me through our relationship. It was a realization that brought with it immense happiness and although Richard did not speak, he smiled and I knew he shared my joy.

It is common parlance today in the seventies to speak of "born-again" Christians. It is not news anymore. Charismatic groups experience it all the time. I myself have not felt drawn to participate in the movement as such, but I do appreciate the tremendous contribution it makes to the Churches today and how it has transformed the lives of many individuals. Perhaps I'm too much of a loner to become directly involved. I also discovered that the more I loved my husband the more I loved God and vice versa. I had come to perceive that love is one, yet many faceted. That too was a joyous discovery. And how grateful I was and am that I was aware of it at the time and not just in retrospect. So there was great light and shade in our life together; cause for rejoicing and celebration over against the distant threatening cloud of the illness touching the horizon of our daily lives. There were times in the midst of gaiety when we were arrested in our tracks by some casual word or insignificant happening: sobering reminders of the reality of Richard's incurable condition.

It was our ever deepening love for each other and the growing realization of the fatality of his illness that made us together more and more dependent on and rooted in God. We were also conscious of how singularly blessed we were in having each other and were deeply grateful. As things became more difficult, together we had learnt how to abandon ourselves to the Almighty. Different people have remarked on the pronounced element of playfulness discernible in our relationship, at a time when these people had no idea that Richard was mortally ill – in fact only weeks before he died. The situation was always bearable in the knowledge that we were in God's care and mysteriously upheld by Him. Like T.S. Eliot's "lady of silences" we were ". . . calm and distressed/torn and most whole".

There is one weekend that summer which stands out in my memory. Richard phoned me excitedly on the Friday to say he'd bought me a rucksack (a smaller version of his own), and sleeping bags and a tent for both of us: we were going to Fire Island for the weekend. I was thrilled. We started off on Saturday morning and all went well until we finally landed on the island and tramped happily across the sands for about a mile or two. By now it was evening and we decided to eat supper. Richard lit a fire on the beach and cooked some chops. After we'd finished eating Richard became violently ill. He was so bad I feared he would die. He recovered enough to prepare for bed. We got into our bags and lay half in and half out of our tent. Richard, as was his wont, mercifully fell promptly asleep. I lay there serenaded for hours by bullfrogs. They got so vocal and sounded so close that I was convinced we would be invaded at any moment. To add to the drama, lightning began to flash across the summer night sky. The storm didn't reach us and by morning Richard seemed restored.

Recalling this incident Michael O'Leary wrote:

Probably because of the foreknowledge he had of his inevitably early death, Richard seemed to take a kind of exulting pleasure from life and the people he met, even chanced to pass on the street. Once, in the late summer of 1957, he was completely taken with the idea of spending a night on the beach in the open. He had a tent and two sleeping bags, all stuffed into a surplus Army pack bag or rucksack. The outdoor clothes that he and Mary wore, while entirely appropriate in the Tyrol or any other part of the European outdoors, probably struck New York subway riders as somewhat eccentric. At any rate, at the outset of their journey, on the Queens subway, Richard felt himself stared at, particularly the enormous pack on his back. He smiled blandly and expansively at all who came and went and stared at him.

"It's a rucksack," he murmured, first to this one then to that one on the car. I recall very clearly, when he was telling me about it a few days later, that he pronounced it "rooksack".

Mary took her cue and nodded brightly at everyone. "Oh yes. It's a rucksack, of course." Only the experienced observer of the behaviour of New York subway riders would grasp the utter unconventionality of such conduct. One just never speaks to another subway rider.

They returned the following evening, rather late. As they emerged from the subway in Jackson Heights, where they lived, their odd aspect caught the attention of a few loiterers outside a neighborhood bar, who apparently remarked loudly on their passing.

"I just whirled on them with a savage roar and they dispersed," he reminisced with a chuckle.

Time and circumstance left my wife and I only one opportunity to have the Seligs to our home. It was quite a light-hearted affair. It was a hot summer night. There were no other guests about, only the children snoozing away on the upper floor. It was the first time I met Mary, who struck me as very pretty, skittery, and young. Richard was profoundly in love with her, it was plain to see, although his external manner was one of what you might call amiable and tolerant domination. Under any circumstances, these two would have been taken for honeymooners. The impression Richard made on my wife Jean, as she told me later, was that of a handsome, strong young man, wonderful company, bursting with health and vigor. Such things of course are the weight of irony in our affairs.

I was anxious to work, largely so that I could support Richard. He needed rest. Apart from the exhaustion brought on by the radiation treatment, the journey each day to and from work was taking its own toll. He came to dread that twice daily subway ride. He was beginning to look haggard and drawn, and suffered from a dry cough: he'd given up cigarettes for a

pipe after he met me, but with the advent of the cough, thinking it was due to the tobacco, he eventually gave that up, too.

As that summer wore on, the attacks of nausea and severe
sweats increased. There were nights when his side of the bed
(although it looked like one large double bed, there were
actually two separate mattresses) would get so soaked with perspiration that Richard would leave it and lie on the spare bed in
the study. When that in turn became uncomfortably wet he
would use the couch in the sitting room. Not having air-
conditioning didn't help. And being the top storey of the
house, by evening time the rooms often became uncomfortably hot.

One day, during the course of conversation Richard said: "If
anything happens to me, I want you to marry again. It's not
right for you to be alone." I remained silent. How could I tell
him that I could never marry anyone else, for I could not bear to
belong that totally to any other; that if he died my sole desire
would be to devote my life exclusively to God? The religious
life and monasticism in the Church was not something we ever
had occasion to discuss together. I wasn't sure that Richard
would understand this course of action for me. Perhaps I was
wrong? Anyway it was a very painful moment and didn't seem
to be the right time to bring it up just then. I let the opportunity
go – it never presented itself again. I still believed that Richard
would recover.

From time to time we prayed briefly and spontaneously
together. It was always a strengthening and peaceful experience. We knew ourselves to be in God's care. When at night,
before we went to sleep we said, "God bless you" to each other,
it was deeply meant. A favourite prayer of Richard's was
"Lord, give us the wisdom to know your divine will, the grace
to accept it and the strength to fulfil it."

People sometimes conclude that it was the knowledge of
Richard's fatal illness that made us turn in desperation to God
and commit ourselves and the situation to Him. That is not
wholly true. The process had begun long before Richard was
struck down by the disease. On the contrary, it could be said
that it was happiness that drew us to the Almighty; it was the
joy in our mutual love and the ever-deepening gratitude for the
gift of each other that quickened in us the awareness of the

Giver of life and all good things who is everywhere and whose right hand holds us fast. Some years later my Dominican friend Anselm Moynihan expressed this more eloquently when he wrote in a letter to me:

I think your experience has taught you a lesson which many people are slow to learn; it is that joy, received as God's gift, brings us closer to Him than suffering. Suffering, rightly borne, has the power to increase our capacity for happiness, but in itself it is happiness that lifts up the heart directly to Him.

So although it was in some ways a troubled summer it was nevertheless a happy one, with the odd weekend away at the homes of friends who lived in the country or near the beach.

Looking back I suspected later there were many times during weekdays throughout that summer when Richard was running a fever, knew it and kept the knowledge to himself, forcing himself to keep going. I recall weekends when he would ask me to give him alcohol rubs, and in a state of exhaustion he would sleep for hours. Sometimes the exhaustion was so extreme that he slept with his eyes open. At other times he was his usual energetic and happy self. We both felt that he needed more rest as the doctors had warned he must not get over-tired.

If I could become the bread-winner, it would considerably ease the situation. The William Morris Agency might not have existed as far as their getting work for me was concerned. So it was about that time that I wrote to Sydney MacEwan in Scotland, to enlist his help about getting some singing engagements. I made this approach on the strength of his having volunteered, back in 1954, to help me get work in America, if I so desired. At that time I was not interested. Now, whether I wanted to or not, I badly *needed* to work so that I could support both of us and so that Richard could have the rest which was so crucial. Father Sydney's reply was so unexpected and his interpretation of my request so wide of the mark that I was too disappointed and hurt to write back and explain. (And anyway, how could I since our policy was to keep the knowledge of Richard's illness strictly to ourselves.) Mistakenly, he'd thought that my wanting to work was motivated by ambition, and felt that I was putting my marriage in jeopardy. To reinforce his point, he described someone he knew whose work had taken priority over everything else in her life, thereby forfeiting her happiness as wife and mother, and who now bitterly regretted it all, wishing she had been pushing a pram down Broadway rather than seeing her name up in lights. No doubt Father Sydney had my best interests at heart when he wrote that letter. How was he to know the truth of the matter?

That avenue closed, we discussed the possibility of my taking a job locally as a doctor's or a dentist's receptionist. But first the new record had to be got out of the way.

Armed with the fat cheque my father had given Richard and me for a wedding present, we had gone out and bought a double action Erard concert harp from John Morley in London. He it was who put me in touch with Lucien Thompson, a harp teacher in New York City. That summer I had several lessons from him which I found enormously helpful. He was a good teacher and introduced me to a different finger-technique from the one I'd learned at the RIAM in Dublin and which I adopted and have used ever since. He kindly gave us what was to become our favourite LP 'The Art of Marcel Grandjany' (he'd been a pupil of the great French harpist). This incited us to buy our first record player and we played the Grandjany record till it was thoroughly worn out. But not before it had furnished us with numberless hours of untold pleasure.

July came and it was time to make my second album for the Decca Record Company. Much as we would have liked to go to London and record it there, the record company chose to send their man to the USA instead. I decided to record after 6pm so that Richard could be there, and chose the evening before our wedding anniversary and the one following it, hoping to get sixteen songs done in that time. We kept July 23 free to celebrate our anniversary. We didn't realize it but it was to be our only one together. Richard was far from well but insisted, despite my protestations, on our dining out as planned, so as to spare me. He gave me one perfect red rose which lasted for weeks as I put it nightly in the refrigerator.

The album was recorded in the Carl Fisher Hall and later entitled 'Love Songs of Ireland'. Like my first Decca long-playing record it was destined to be released in the UK, the United States, Australia and New Zealand, South Africa and Europe and became part of the sixties folk boom. But all that was in the future.

In those days the Clancy Brothers had not yet become famous. They had started their own record company: "Tradition" and wanted me to make a long-playing record for them. Being under contract to Decca, whose records in the USA were issued under the 'London' label, I felt I could not do so. But when they persisted, Richard approached Decca and persuaded them to allow me to make the one album for Tradition. By the time I came to make this record 'Songs of Ireland' Richard had been dead a few weeks. I intended it to be my last album as my interest in singing had died with him.

But I anticipate. That summer Paddy Clancy told us that Al Grossman was very interested in my work and wished to get in touch with me. Grossman was later to become wealthy as Bob Dylan's manager. Now he approached me with an offer of a season at the Gate of Horn in Chicago, soon to become a starting point for people like Odetta *et al*. I'd never met Grossman. Our conversations had always been over the telephone. At first this offer seemed like a good idea: an opportunity we'd been hoping for, so that I could support us both and allow Richard the sorely needed rest. However, to leave Richard alone in New York and go off by myself to Chicago was out of the question. The fee for the engagement was not sufficient to keep us both, so that was the end of the Gate of Horn. In fact I didn't get to meet Grossman for another four years, when I was returning to Europe via the USA after a concert tour of Australia and New Zealand.

August in New York City is a bad month: the merciless heat is oppressive. Weekend trips to Rockaway Beach and the anticipation of our impending holiday sustained us through those stifling four weeks. Earlier on we'd toyed with the idea of a trip to Seattle, a part of the United States which Richard thought very highly of and where he'd spent some of the most stimulating of his – always colourful – academic years and a place to which he was keen to introduce me. But it was a long and expensive trip away and we decided to postpone it until some later date. I've never yet got to Seattle. Instead we took a

flight to Nantucket Island for two weeks in early September.
We seemed unerringly drawn to islands.

As soon as we arrived we hired bicycles which were our
mode of conveyance to and from our seaside cottage, five miles
outside Nantucket. A few hundred yards from the cottage
there was a fresh-water lake and a boat for our use. The first
evening there we ventured forth equipped with Richard's
fishing gear recently purchased in New York. There followed a
dramatic episode out in the middle of the lake when one of the
rowlocks broke and Richard was hard put to get us ashore on
one oar, contending as he had to with a stiff wind. It was frightening for me, but Richard made light of the situation.
However, the ordeal was quickly forgotten in the excitement
of cooking a wholesome supper of our freshly caught fish.

We spent the next week lazing, reading and swimming,
cycling, and exploring the village and its fish restaurants. Some
days before we were due to leave, Richard's health worsened
and he slept a lot. By day, he slept outside, wrapped in a rug.
The night before we left Nantucket I found it well nigh impossible to sleep and the sight of hordes of mosquitoes pressing
blackly against the window attracted by the light inside added a
macabre touch to the night.

Time came for us to return to New York. We sauntered into
the airport on that Sunday morning with plenty of time to
spare. We hadn't known about the ruling that passengers must
re-confirm their booking twenty-four hours before departure.
This regulation had come into force while we were on holiday
so it was irritating to find that our seats had been given away.
The clerk, however, assured us that we would undoubtedly get
a seat on the next flight at 7.30pm. We resigned ourselves to a
long drawn-out delay of several hours. During the wait we
struck up a conversation with a charming American woman,
an official at the airport. It turned out that she was a keen radio
ham and was occasionally in communication with another
ardent ham radio operator in the west of Ireland with whom I
was slightly acquainted.

In the meantime the clerk approached us and volunteered the
information that we were certain of getting seats on the next
flight. From his experience he felt sure that as fog was forecast
at Boston Airport, where the plane was due to land first, some

137

passengers would cancel their booking and go by sea instead, to ensure their being back in time for work on Monday morning.

As the late afternoon wore on, we had ample time to observe the leisurely arrival of various passengers for the evening flight. Being such a very small airport (there weren't even facilities for refreshments) people could be studied at fairly close quarters. It was a motley little crowd. Because of what was about to happen I remember some of their faces to this day. An intense-looking bespectacled young man carrying paintings under his arm was in earnest conversation with a couple of middle-aged Eleanor Roosevelt-type ladies. Another couple were being ruled by their dog. There were family groups, and so on. Shortly before the first announcement about the flight was made a young man of compelling good-looks swept into the terminal accompanied by a middle-aged man and his daughter. The casual dress of the father and daughter implied that they were just seeing the young man off. He was a six-footer, darkly beautiful, quite flawlessly proportioned, deeply sun-tanned and with an air of great self-assurance about him. I noticed he had no socks on inside his 'Gene Kelly' shoes. While he talked with the man at the counter, he kept looking repeatedly in our direction. Now the fact that he was looking so directly and frequently at Richard was nothing unusual, but it seemed odd to me that he was looking at both of us. A few minutes later, at about 7.20pm the instruction to proceed to the gate for the flight departure came over the public-address system. After the announcement, the clerk called us over and said: "Mr Selig, I'm in the embarrassing position of being able to offer you only one seat. Because of the fog at the other end, they have had to take on extra fuel and so reduce the number of passengers. Which of you will travel?"

Leaving the decision to Richard I waited for him to answer. Naturally my preference was to stay with him on or off the plane. But he might deem it best to travel himself, so as to be home in time for work, leaving me to catch the next available flight. Or he might decide it wiser for me to go ahead of him. Whatever his decision I would go along with it. To my relief his unhesitating reply was that we would not be separated, but would leave together on a later plane. Naturally we were disappointed, and Richard was inwardly fuming over this further development. Could it be that this elegant young man, whoever he was, was known to the airline people and had somehow used his influence to obtain one of our seats? In any case there was nothing we could do about it. So once again we were left behind, while the last passenger boarded the aircraft and took off for Boston. The clerk, now displaying signs of nervousness at Richard's unspoken anger, timidly informed us that there was another small plane leaving Nantucket at 11pm. Another wait lay ahead of us.

About three-quarters of an hour later, our new-found radio ham acquaintance of that afternoon walked briskly into the terminal with a suprisingly business-like air about her for 8pm of a Sunday night. She headed straight for her office. When Richard made some comment to her about working so late, she kept on going and remarked that she had some work to catch up on, and left it at that. Minutes later, a local man came into the building, enquiring in a loud voice: "Has it caught fire yet?" In no time the horrific truth was out. Poor visibility due to fog had caused the 7.30pm plane to crash into a swamp close to Boston Airport and it had eventually caught fire. There were no survivors. Our ham radio enthusiast had, by chance, picked up the distress signal on her set and had come in at once to deal with the insurance papers.

Now of course there was no question of the 11pm flight taking off, so we were driven back to Nantucket for the night and given a meal, which we ate before the restaurant public TV set. The current programme was interrupted every now and then with news of further developments of the air disaster.

Next morning we flew back to New York City. During the flight Richard put his arm around me and said: "I wouldn't have minded if we'd both been on the flight together." I felt exactly the same way.

The air crash being a major one was front-page news on the Monday morning papers. Understandably Richard and I followed the accounts with unusual interest and concern. The news media gave information about dismembered bodies and other grisly details. The faces, if not the names of most of the ill-fated passengers were fresh in our memories. They were to be remembered in prayer for many months.

That was not the end of it. A couple of months later, after

Richard's death, I was discussing with Professor Jonathan and Mary Gray Hughes the possibility of setting up a poetry award in Richard's name at Oxford. This was something he once told me he would like to see happen. The Hugheses thought it a good idea and began to tell me about a talented young painter they'd heard a lot about from a mutual painter friend. His parents were very wealthy and had disowned their son when he decided to earn his living by painting. After he was killed in an air crash they were stricken with remorse and decided to establish a bursary for needy painters – all this to assuage their consciences and perpetuate his memory. The Hugheses went on to describe, among other things, his unusual good looks. Suddenly, something alerted my mind and, startled, I enquired further about the circumstances of his death. He was one of the victims of the recent Nantucket to Boston air crash in September. His name was Eli Schless. *He* must have been the young man who jumped the queue and ironically thereby saved our lives.

John Hughes had been a Rhodes scholar at Oxford with Richard and they were great friends. Mary Gray was up at Oxford at the same time. John and Mary Gray had got married clandestinely at Oxford just before Mary Gray left for the States one year ahead of John. The secrecy was because of the Cecil Rhodes' ridiculous regulations against married scholars. John later told me that Richard couldn't get over the celebate life that he, John, suddenly started to lead until eventually Richard was let in on the big secret.

A few nights after we'd returned from Nantucket, we had dinner with John and Mary Gray Hughes at their apartment in the city. This was to be our last social engagement together. During the meal Richard broke out into one of his enervating ice-cold sweats so badly that he was forced to leave the table. John, not knowing what the real trouble was, followed him out of the room and suggested a hot shower. After that Richard seemed to recover. They drove us back to Long Island and John recalls that Richard and I were restored to our usual high spirits, and on the way there was a certain amount of what John described as boisterous playfulness between us in the back seat. Stopping at one of the traffic lights, a car load of young hot rodders drew up alongside. In the late fifties hot-rodders were those who removed their silencers, and their thundering passage was a nuisance to every neighbourhood. Anyway this bunch of hot-rodders gunned their engines, challenging us to a race. John's convertible Chrysler had a defective muffler. It was only four years old but he'd bought it second-hand and it had already seen hard service, so they thought we had something special under the hood. Laughingly we declined their invitation.

Towards the end of that week (after we'd returned from Nantucket) Richard became so ill that Rottino had him admitted to St Vincent's Hospital in New York City. We travelled in by subway but by the time we reached the hospital Richard was so exhausted that they put him in a wheelchair. While we were together in the waiting room the gravity of the situation was borne in on us. We talked quietly together, our voices low and fully under control, but with tears streaming down our faces, oblivious of all the other people in the waiting-room. With my hand in his Richard said: "Mary, I'll come out of here either cured or dead."

From my heart I said: "Richard, I only want what God wants."

"So do I," he said.

Smiling through the tears I said: "Richard, you're a brick."

As if seeing ahead he warned: "It's easy enough to say that now, but things will get harder." Then we travelled in the lift up to his ward and joined the three other patients in his room.

At first Richard seemed to pick up wonderfully. By the time I reached the apartment on Long Island the phone was ringing. It was Richard on the line to tell me he was feeling *lots* better, had eaten some food, which he reassuringly described, and I was not to worry. He sounded very cheerful. More intensely than ever, I commended Richard and myself to God and slept soundly that night. It seems extraordinary to me that from then until Richard died I, who am a light sleeper, went to bed each evening and slept peacefully through the night until morning. Nor did my appetite wane.

During the final few days Paddy Clancy most kindly offered me a spare bed in their Greenwich Village apartment, a few blocks away from the hospital. My spirit knew such trust and calm that, one night, having come straight from hospital, as I was kneeling very still by my bed making some prayer, I noticed a disturbingly large insect scuttering across the pool of moonlight close to my feet. But I was totally unperturbed – I would normally have leapt to my feet and tried to get rid of it.

The visiting hours were very strict: one hour each evening. Whenever I tried to slip in unnoticed ahead of time I was invariably stopped. If I lingered on after the hour the attendant came and rooted me out. Except for the last few nights before Richard died. Then the attendant turned a kindly blind eye. The hospital authorities had by then waived the rules in my case and I was allowed to arrive and leave at any time.

Mine is in some ways a very simple faith. I do not argue with God. The certainty of the existence of a personal, infinitely loving Being who is omnipotent, omnipresent and omniscient has always been part of the very fabric of my mind. I like to have the knowledge that the science of theology provides. My intellect needs to be fed with truth; needs to know. But not my heart – in the sense that it does not question God's providence. I have always, despite the pain it sometimes involves, been content to let God go ahead and "write straight with crooked lines." I feel profoundly convinced that he is at the helm of the ship that is our life and that in the words of Julian of Norwich, the great English mystic: "all shall be well, and thou shalt see that all manner of things shall be well."

So at Mass every day for the three weeks while Richard was in hospital, I opened my heart and with all my being asked God to perform a miracle and cure Richard or else give him the grace of a happy death.

During those one-hour visits each day we talked quietly together. But not all that much. Richard seemed to be taken up with his own thoughts. He never again showed the insouciant side of his character. There was a gravity about him which I was careful to respect and it was enough to just sit there by his bedside, sometimes holding hands.

Shortly after Richard went into hospital, our nice Nantucket ham-radio acquaintance, who had asked me for our address, totally unaware that Richard was dying, wrote, and among other things made some kindly remarks about the relationship which she had observed between Richard and me. She wrote that with a love like ours, having each other was everything and nothing else really mattered. I simply didn't know how to answer her.

Richard's sense of humour had by no means deserted him in his illness. A few nights before he died, Michael O'Leary came on one of his visits. Richard's condition had greatly deteriorated. The curtains of his cubicle were drawn, to give him more privacy and hide the drip erected by his bed. Richard seemed to be asleep. Towards the end, whenever I arrived and Richard was lying there with his eyes closed, I could never be sure whether he was asleep or in a coma, and didn't like to disturb him. But hardly had Michael entered when Richard opened one eye, moved his head slightly in the direction of the bottle of glucose and said to Michael: "Tell the nurse to change the flavour!" The very night before he died when he was having blood tranfusions, Michael again called to see him. Minutes before his arrival the nurse had removed the blood and replaced it with a bottle of glucose. Once again Richard quipped at his own expense: "You've just missed the meat course."

It is not easy to watch someone you love suffering intensely and know that there is little or nothing you or the medical profession can do to alleviate things. Richard was rapidly losing weight. Somewhere I came across a powdered food rather like Complan which I would mix for him in the ward, hoping to give him extra nourishment. I used to bring him those delicious Italian tomatoes which I knew he liked so much, but either he couldn't eat them or, if he did, more often than not they came up again. Richard appreciated these pathetic efforts and generally made some kindly remark.

When he was admitted to hospital, the medical examination revealed that the persistent dry, hacking cough was caused by nodes all down his oesophagus. So the disease was spreading. Within a few days his spleen had also become affected. Preparations were being made to have the spleen removed and then without explanation the idea was abandoned. The only disfigurement was evident in his feet, which swelled up.

In the final days he had to have frequent recourse to an oxygen mask. It was very distressing to come on a visit and find him thus enmasked and unable to speak. One such day (on weekends the visiting hour was in the afternoon), feeling the need for the oxygen mask, Richard had put it on himself. He either indicated to me that he'd like the window by his bed opened, or else I decided myself that it should be. I called to a passing nurse to please get the long pole to open the window. This fat girl proceeded to walk off down the ward with such infuriating slowness that I couldn't stand it any longer. I dashed past her imparting a dirty look as I did so, and ran to the general cupboard to get the thing myself. At times they seemed to be short-staffed and there was a poignant comfort in being able to attend to Richard's bedpan needs. When he asked me to "campaign for an enema" I felt I was doing something positive. Richard was astonishingly calm about everything when he wasn't suffering acutely. There were times when he tossed incessantly from side to side and whispered: "Oh God, please help me."

He frequently asked me for a report on how the Tradition album was coming along. During that period while Richard was in hospital I spent most of each day working on the songs for the record. I think some of my best arrangements were done during those sad days. It is said that suffering is creative. I have often found this to be true in my own life. Richard was to have written the sleeve notes for the Tradition album when he came out of hospital. I wanted the album to start off with Richard reading the short poem by W.B. Yeats:

> I am of Ireland
> And the holy land of Ireland . . .
> And time runs on cried she
> Come out of charity,
> Come dance with me in Ireland."

But this was not to be. Eventually the poem appeared on the front cover of the album which came to be named "Songs of Ireland". Liam Clancy wrote the sleeve notes. Joan Baez has told me that she and her mother have been moved to tears listening to one of the songs on that album, It is Thomas Moore's poem 'Farewell But Whenever', also called '*The Scent of the Roses*,' from which this book gets its title. I was working on the song and writing the harp accompaniment for it during the days when Richard was dying.

144

Farewell but whenever you welcome the hour
That awakens the night song of mirth in your bower,
Then think of the friend who once welcomed it too
And forgot his own griefs to be happy with you.
His griefs may return, not a hope may remain
Of the few that have brightened his pathway of pain
But he ne'er will forget the short vision which threw
Its enchantment around him, while lingering with you.

And still on that evening when pleasure fills up
To the highest top sparkle each heart and each cup.
Where e'er my path lies, be it gloomy or bright
My soul happy friends shall be with you that night,
Shall join in your revels your sports and your wiles
And return to me beaming all o'er with your smiles
Too blest if it tells me that 'mid the gay cheer
Some kind voice had murmured: "I wish he were here".

Let fate do her worst, there are relics of joy,
Bright dreams of the past which she cannot destroy;
That come in the night-time of sorrow and care
And bring back the features that joy used to wear.
Long, long be my heart with such memories filled
As the vase in which roses have once been distilled.
You may break, you may shatter the vase if you will,
But the scent of the roses will hang round still.

Months before going into hospital Richard had spoken to me about his desire to talk things over with a "wise man." He said he didn't mean a priest or a psychiatrist – just some "wise man." With Richard's condition apparently not improving I phoned Michael O'Leary. Apart from the fact that he and Richard were such very good friends and Richard had confided in him about his illness, Michael was the only thinking, theologically informed and practising Catholic among our friends. Sadly, Michael, while understanding what sort of person it was that Richard was seeking, couldn't recommend anyone. All he could suggest was getting in touch with an old classmate of his who was a priest. This was unfortunate. I pointed out that Richard didn't want a priest. But Michael thought his friend would be better than nothing.

In the light of my own monastic experience later, I realise

145

more fully – though I did dimly even then – what sort of person it was that Richard wanted. Someone (preferably old) wise in the ways of God and human nature; a listener, a sifter, a gentle counsellor, a man of the Spirit. For his own best reasons God decided to deny Richard, and by extension, myself, this solace. Perhaps so that Richard would have to rely in faith, totally, without human intermediary, on God's infinite loving mercy.

Michael's friend was willing to come to the hospital, but had to officiate at a funeral. In his place he sent along a priest colleague. It was a disaster as far as I was concerned. The priest, for whatever reason, behaved throughout in a singularly unsympathetic and unpastoral manner. Without even showing the courtesy of having a preliminary conversation with me outside the ward, he presented himself by Richard's bedside, and in a voice audible to everyone in the room proceeded to cross-examine *me* about Richard's beliefs, his religious background, his prayer life, and even wanted to know whether we had been married in church. "Which church?" he spat out.

It seemed then and now incredible that his insensitivity was such that all this frightful and upsetting interrogation took place in Richard's presence. Richard just lay against his pillows, whether asleep or in a coma or listening to the whole charade I never found out. Stunned by this roughshod approach, I prayed that Richard couldn't hear the inquisition that was taking place. Though an amused remark he made to John Hughes during a later visit, "They're trying to make me a Catholic," makes me wonder whether he was having a good old listen in. If so I'm pretty certain there was some healthy chuckling going on in some corner of Richard's inner self.

When the situation became unbearable I made for the telephone and called Michael. I asked the priest to wait. As Michael's office was only a few blocks away, he was with me in a matter of minutes. Briefly I described the horror of my predicament and told him I simply could not handle the problem. This man was definitely not what Richard wanted. All he had succeeded in doing was to cause me deep distress. Leaving me, Michael took the man aside. Evntually the priest left.

Michael returned to me and said: "Everything is OK now. I explained all that was necessary and the priest said: 'From what you've told me, there was no need to come. This man has baptism of desire.'"

This statement was to be gratuitously made yet again. After enormous difficulty I succeeded in getting permission to spend the night by Richard's bed. It was to be his last night on earth. The nurse had come by and given him an injection (he seemed to be doing his level best not to allow it to work) and a large armchair had been wheeled in for me for the night. Suddenly one of the Sisters of Charity (they were in charge of the hospital), called to me from the doorway. When I got outside she said gently to me: "Mrs Selig, I thought you might like to know that the Chaplain says that your husband has baptism of desire." Words can't describe what her message meant to me. It was like manna from heaven.

One evening after I'd kissed Richard goodbye, I turned just as I was leaving his cubicle and said: "Richard, don't worry about anything."

Richard quietly said: "I don't worry. I'm completely in God's hands." I felt profoundly comforted.

These were not days for smiling. I must have given an impression of great gravity and quietness. One day I arrived to find a friend visiting Richard. He had brought a little portable radio as a gift and – one of his better days – Richard was smiling and enjoying getting the different stations on the set. He must have said something facetious, for I laughed and smiled, and in doing so happened to glance at the patient in the next bed, a middle-aged man. He had never addressed me before but now he called out. "What a beautiful smile you've got. I wish you'd use it more often!"

Regarding injections and analgesics, John Hughes has told me that Richard said to him: "I would rather feel pain than nothing." He took as little as possible. That night after the sister had quoted to me the chaplain's observation, I returned to Richard's bedside and he said to me: "Did she tell you I was resisting the injection?" I shook my head.

Seeing the armchair by his bed, with me settling into it for the night, Richard quietly told me that since he wanted me to have a proper sleep, I must go to Paddy's flat. Without demur I left the hospital that night. My personal desire was to remain by Richard's side. Only *his* wish that I go would budge me. I never questioned the wisdom of his decisions in my regard. They were made with love and I carried them out in the same spirit. It was the night before he died.

A couple of days before that a very moving incident had occurred. John and Mary Gray Hughes were at Richard's bedside. A patch of afternoon sunlight came through the window. Richard was very weak and exhausted and barely able to talk but he said: "I want to feel the sun."

John lifted Richard in his arms and helped him into a chair. "It was like lifting a child," John said later.

I was stilled by the unspoken affection evident between these two friends. Though he had lost so much weight Richard's mind remained unclouded and completely alert. Probably the reason why he kept drugs to a minimum was so as to be able to keep in touch with reality as long as possible. He was still able to see the funny side of dying to the extent of making rather macabre jokes to John about the moribund patient in the bed next to him.

About two or three days before Richard died, I asked him if he would like his mother to come and see him. He agreed that I should phone her. I did so and told her for the first time about the incurable disease. She took a train to New York and spent a couple of hours with her only son. We talked about the three of us going on a holiday together, somewhere in the sun, as soon as Richard got out of hospital. Florida maybe. Florence would treat us. She left shortly afterwards and returned to Washington, DC.

The problem of whether or not a doctor should tell his patient that he is dying is a perennially difficult one. Surely, it must depend on the patient. An experienced and intelligent medical practitioner should be able to tell whether a particular patient can "take" the truth about his being terminally ill or not.

The morning of his death Richard's doctor visited him. I was there. Minutes before, this same man had sent for me to tell me that it would be a miracle if Richard lived through the coming night. (He'd shyly informed me that there was a chapel in the hospital. I'd found it long before.) Now he was bending over Richard telling him that he had an ulcer in his stomach (to explain to Richard why he was passing blood) and "You are getting better Mr Selig." Richard received this information calmly, consciously, with closed lids. The doctor went away. Richard made no comment to me nor I to him.

As the morning wore on, Richard's mind wandered. He told me he longed to go for a walk. He struggled to get out of bed. I tried to reassure him that we'd go walking together after he'd had some more rest. Eventually he sank back on his pillows, mute with exhaustion. The early autumnal afternoon sun shone brightly across the bed and on his face. But Richard's senses were already fading. "It's getting very dark, Mary," he said.

"Yes," I whispered, "it's getting late," and I used our secret mutual pet name. This was it: the crisis Richard was destined not to get through. I could no longer hold back the tears. Soundlessly and openly I began to weep. It was like a fountain within. Just then the nurse came by to change, yet again, the soaking wet sheets. Together we lifted Richard and I helped her with her task. My voice steady as a rock, but with tears coursing down my face, I murmured tender comforting things to Richard as I held him momentarily in my arms – for the last time.

I phoned Michael. By the time he arrived I was on my knees praying aloud with great intensity of spirit. My whole being was concentrated in one burning desire: that Richard would see God face to face. It is truly a tremendous privilege to be physically with the one you love with all your heart, more than any other person on earth, at his or her moment of truth. To be near, when in death he reaches the remotest outposts of time and space; experiences with the totality of his being the mystery of God and makes his final and definitive decision about his eternal destiny.

Michael O'Leary wrote:

"If ever a man was now commended to God by the prayers of another, it was Richard Selig by his wife Mary, who continually for hours before and a long time after his death cannonaded the Gates of Heaven with strong and anguished prayer for the safe passage of Richard's soul. I have never heard anyone pray like that before. I do not particularly want to hear anybody pray like that again. It is a very awesome thing to listen to.

A young nurse spotted the end coming. She hurried out and fetched back a young interne who fussed over Richard with the oxygen mask. Two more young internes hurried in. There were muttered words, an injection. The last desperate measures to hold life. The medicos stopped muttering, stood there a moment. Two of them walked out quietly. The last, who had been the first to come in, stood, still holding Richard's wrist, feeling where the pulse had failed. I whispered to him.

"It's over?"

"It's over."

"He's dead?"

"Yes. He's dead."

The young doctor looked like a disappointed little boy as he walked out. He was not yet used to his job, I thought. Behind Mary, kneeling close to the head of Richard's bed, praying aloud oblivious to all about her, two nurses knelt for a moment and joined her. The patients in the other beds lay still and silent."

I had no wish to leave the cubicle. My instinct and desire was to stay on silently praying. Whereas clinical death can be recorded, no one can say for certain when relative death has occurred. But above all, the moment of absolute death cannot be determined. I deliberately refrain from using the expression "the separation of the soul from the body." This originally Platonic idea, later taken up by Thomas Aquinas, is an incomplete definition, and gives an inadequate explanation of what really takes place in the mysterious process of death. Can anyone really know? Medicine and metaphysics view death differently. So, I wanted to "stand by" and "help" Richard, if at all possible, at the impossible-to-pin-down moment when he would be swept into the splendour that is the unveiled presence of Almighty God, to make his final decision in a completely personal act, totally alone. Oh, the wisdom of the age-old practice of keeping prayerful vigil by the corpse for two to three days and nights. Later I was to take an active and joyous part in this beautiful tradition many times when I became a Benedictine. Side by side with the acute sorrow that bereavement can bring, there co-existed in me from the very beginning a sense of immeasurable gratitude to God, which somehow suffused the pain during the months and years that followed. I had been privileged to experience something of the meaning of love, both of man and of God during my time with Richard.

But now Michael was bending gently over me telling me that the doctor wanted to have a word with me. Very tenderly I kissed Richard's forehead. I knew it was no longer Richard, but his dead body, his remains. I turned and left the cubicle, drained, but at the same time charged with the indescribable conviction that Richard was safe.

Downstairs I signed a paper giving permission for an autopsy to be performed on the body in the cause of research into Hodgkin's disease. Richard once told me he wished to leave his body to medicine and had joked: "At least I'll make an interesting corpse!"

With Michael by my side I walked out into the fading light of the gentle autumn evening, wrapped up in the thought of the inconceivable bliss in which, with every fibre of my being I trusted Richard was now rejoicing, and in which in some inexplicable way, a part of me was somehow sharing.

> Who have gone before me,
> Stronger by the breath they give,
> I recall the men of my race,
> Grave ghosts in whom I live.
>
> I receive their many blessings
> For a journey from flesh and bone,
> Questioning their shadows, saying:
> Fathers, were you alone?

Richard Selig

7 Transit

You go out on a terrible wide sea
You go and you keep going, till there are storms
Where all except you get smashed up;
And in the morning of the next day the sun shines.

(from 'The Way I see you' by Richard Selig.)

It never occurred to me not to return to the apartment on Long Island, but as we left St Vincent's hospital Michael insisted that I spend the night with himself and Jean at their home in Westchester. From there I phoned my mother-in-law in Washington and sent telegrams to my father, Peter Levi and Sister Mary Angela, my Dominican friend and singing teacher. The O'Learys and I talked about Richard for hours and I confided in them my decision, crystalized that very evening, to go into a monastery. They were very startled and their immediate reaction was to tell me to wait and think it over. Surely, they argued, this was not the moment to make such a major decision. Perhaps, they said, it was a reaction to the traumatic experience I'd undergone. Best to let time pass and review things later on. I had made up my mind, but in deference to their evident, and very caring concern I said I'd not do anything immediately. Michael strongly advised me to go and visit my father in Arabia, and he volunteered to handle the entire business of the funeral.

Next morning I went shopping alone, in New York City, for a black dress. In the store where I bought it, the assistant asked me why on earth a young girl like me should be buying a *black* dress. When I told her my husband had died the evening before, she broke down and wept.

The night before the funeral, a few friends and some relatives of Richard's gathered at the funeral parlour. Now I have never been interested in the dead as non-living matter. To me, death is merely a doorway. The real, essential person I have known and loved in this life lives on, but now no longer visibly. That is why I could never be perturbed by seeing the dead body of someone dear to me. I know it to be but the discarded outer casing. The dragonfly, symbol of the resurrection has, so to speak, changed from its chrysalid state and, spreading its glorious wings, has flown out of our sight into eternity. It would never have entered my head to arrange this funeral parlour ritual myself, but Michael advised that it should be, so I went along with the convention for the sake of others. Moreover, he arranged everything, relieving me of yet another difficult chore, and I was grateful. Had Richard been a Catholic, the coffin would have rested in church the night before the burial. Instead here was the a-religious version of that meaningful vigil. The whole thing smacked of Evelyn Waugh's *The Loved One*. Artificiality and, in some instances, ersatz emotion were the keynotes. There was an unreal, 'padded', sort of hush-hush and airless atmosphere in the building. When I looked into the coffin marked 'Richard Selig' what lay there bore a very faint resemblance to my husband. The most ludicrous thing about it all was the way the face had been literally *painted*. After that initial glance, I ignored the coffin and greeted the people who had come along.

I think John Hughes was right when he later said to me that Richard would have relished the macabre confusion in the funeral parlour. There were several 'slumber' rooms connected by a long corridor, but there were no instructions saying which corpse was in which room. It was left to the mourners to find out for themselves. So John peered into coffin after coffin and was finally hailed by me in the correct room. John looked miserably at the open coffin and I said: "Don't bother about that, that is not Richard. It's only a painted shell." And the irony didn't end there. Next morning the cortège going to Ferncliff cemetery in Westchester travelled at a spanking 60 miles per hour! That too would have provoked chuckling from Richard. His grave is in a high and quiet spot marked by a simple brass name-plate on the ground.

Back on Long Island I continued working on the third album. Though I had no wish to go on singing, I felt strongly that Richard would want me to finish the work I'd begun. He'd always been like that. Anything worthwhile beginning was worthwhile finishing. I felt no need of human comfort. If

153

people came to see me I welcomed them, but I did not allow anyone to 'distract' me. I had my work to do, letters to write and to answer, packing to get on with and above all I needed to be alone for reflection. Now I reached for the books on theology and the spiritual writers on Richard's bookshelf. St Thomas Aquinas in an abbreviated form, St Teresa of Avila, of whom he'd spoken to me with admiration; St John of the Cross; St Augustine; Martin d'Arcy *et al*. I knew that he'd wanted to read Augustine's *City of God* and I had planned to buy it for his twenty-eighth birthday two weeks later, on October 29.

I cancelled a concert I was to give in Georgia and told the William Morris Agency that I didn't wish them to represent me as my agents any more. As the days following Richard's funeral went by, time and time again I was stirred to the depths by the letters of sympathy written to me by Richard's friends when they'd heard the news. His impact on the lives of other of his friends was as marked, if, for obvious reasons, not as profound, as it had been on mine and the affection, respect and admiration he'd engendered was fresh cause for yet further expressions of gratitude for his life. A couple of days after I'd sent the telegram to Peter Levi I sat down and wrote him a long letter from the heart. I knew no one who would better understand the depth and the glory, the pain and the peace of what I was experiencing. His letter in reply was perfect:

My dear Mary,
    I don't know even now after several days and many re-readings how to begin to thank you for your most honest and most treasured letter. It makes the world shrivel up, and it makes our lives into something far more seriously valuable – your very great loss and your peace. Many of us are praying for both of you, for you to be re-united and always united, by that same grace and pity of God which brought you together.
    Hard to express, at this moment of all, how very greatly I have valued yours and Richard's friendship (as being one thing) and been honoured by it. I loved Richard very much (and even so I didn't know how much until now) and valued his friendship and example, as others did too. I do mean this most seriously.
    It was only bit by bit one came to understand him: his kindness and patience in kindness, and his genuine seriousness. His love for you

gave him (did you know this?) a new dimension of personal tenderness and humility, and it made clear, what I know you understood, his real religion and his strong inward concern with right.

He was so delightful a man – his marriage to you made him very happy – it seemed to be giving him a secure possession of happiness he had never had before. One can imagine a little of how wonderful your life must have been, with your knowledge of Richard. Each of you was the instrument, under God's grace and mercy, of the other's salvation.

Mary, my dear, I am deeply sorry for your loss but penetrated by the consciousness of your being united with Richard in God's grace. I have told Richard's friends, particularly those you mentioned. I had never realised how much he was loved.

We ought, unless you don't wish to, collect Richard's best poems into a book. We could do that best in England, where most of his poems were published. If you wished, I would be very willing to see it done, if we can do it. Quentin Stevenson, Richard's friend and very fine poet, would be willing to help. There's no immediate hurry about this, but perhaps later you would think about it.

Magdalen, I think, would be very pleased and grateful to have Richard's books: a book-plate would be the usual thing. Would you let me take the list to the President and talk to him about it? (Jack Bennett said this was what to do). Richard's memory is very fresh at Magdalen. He was valued and loved there as he was by so many. I wish more people could understand the peace and goodness and greatness of the last few years of his life.

God bless you, Mary. *Anything* I can do, of course I should be very pleased and honoured to be allowed to do, for your sake as well as his. Let me know later what you will do.

Peter

Here are exerpts from Adrian Mitchel's letter. He and his wife Maureen had been so kind to me (we would have liked to have had them present at the wedding but they were away on holiday).

Dear Mary,

Peter told me about Richard, and although he told me how bravely you and he had come to terms with this thing, Maureen and I can't help feeling very sad. But he had achieved so much already, I admired him as a man and as a poet. He was honest and real in Oxford, a place which favours artificiality.

The others I have seen, people who knew Richard well, those who knew him a little, friends as well as sparring partners for arguments, are saddened too. Not only because they knew the excitement of Richard's poetry, a lasting, growing excitement, but because they knew him as a vital and wonderfully warm and generous person. Nobody ever felt he didn't care about them.

I'm not being 'fulsome when I say Maureen and I loved him. First I knew his writing and then him, getting to know him best perhaps through working with him on *Oxford Poetry* and learning so much from him that I never could have repayed it. I never knew him flippant, but he had that marvellous exuberance which sometimes burst out and then there was no one in the room but Richard. But about all the things that mattered he was in earnest.

If you come back to England, Mary, I hope you will come and stay with us.

> With our love,
> Adrian

Stephen Spender had done more than anyone else in England and America to have Richard's work published, and his poems appeared regularly in *Encounter* magazine. He wrote:

I have only just managed to get your address from Elizabeth Jennings, or I would have written before to say how deeply sorry and upset I was to learn of Richard's death.

He was a tremendously intelligent person, and he had great personal magnetism and beauty. In the past few days Peter Levi has sent me poems of his, which I want to publish, which seem to me far in advance of his earlier work. When his book is published I am sure it will stand as a real achievement. I cannot really add anything here, except that Richard is someone I think of very often and I am sure that I shall continue to do so.

Please accept my sympathy.

> Yours sincerely,
> Stephen Spender

One of the most eloquent and understanding letters came from the poetess, Elizabeth Jennings:

Dear Mary,

I don't know if you'll remember me, but I remember Richard and you so vividly and happily that I wanted to write at once when I heard about Richard's wonderful courage and death . . .

He was a beautiful person and I think the most startling thing about him was his deep innocence and childlike simplicity. Everything was direct and open with him. He was a very true person . . .

I am a Catholic and I feel, as I know you must, that all is very well with Richard. He was such a *naturally* religious person. I feel utterly inarticulate when I think about your great loss and yet there is joy, too, in a death like Richard's. To go to God when one is young and beautiful, and full of talent and honesty is something tremendous. . . .

"And yet there is joy, too, in a death like Richard's" – how I totally concurred with that sentiment. Elizabeth had expressed for me, as it were, a vital part of what I'd been feeling.

In his letter, Jonathan Bennett said:

. . . Oxford meant more to me than, I think, it does to most people; but there was not much there that meant more to me than those two years of friendship with Richard. People like me don't often get as near as that to true creativity and I shall always treasure the memory gratefully . . .

I just want to tell you that I was tremendously fond of Richard (and for two years, very much absorbed by him), that I am saddened beyond measure by his death and that you have the deep and steady sympathy of all those who knew Richard and loved him. . . .

Tom Boase, then president of his (Magdalen) college, who had known of the diagnosis from the beginning, recalled:

. . . he was so wonderfully courageous about it and I think often forgot all about it through strength of character: and you must know how very happy you made these last two years for him. We were all very fond of him, and, knowing the whole position as I did, I admired greatly the way he took it.

Both Jack (Richard's tutor and friend) and Gwyneth Bennett wrote separately. Gwyneth's letter contained the following memorable observation: "Happiness is not measurable in terms of time and Richard clearly found with you all that he had been seeking." Jack's letter said what a shock the news had been to them both. He'd heard through the president:

. . . But it was some solace to meet Peter Levi the next morning, to talk of you both, and to hear how you had written to him. Then came your letter; and I cannot say how grateful we are that you wrote so soon and in the way you did. It was as if you were giving us something out of your own rich store of happiness and faith; and it gave Richard's death a meaning we might have been slow to capture . . .

At Peter's insistence and because Richard and you were so well known and loved, I wrote forthwith a small notice for *The Times* . . .

We feel specially bound to you by the rare and abiding happiness of your wedding day, and all that day signified.

Here is the piece from *The Times*:

Mr Richard Selig

J.A.W.B. writes:

The many friends of the young American poet Richard Selig will be saddened by the announcement of his death in New York last week at the age of twenty-seven; none of them could have guessed from his recent poems or letters that he had known for two years that his life was likely to be brief. He was not the first Rhodes Scholar who has come to Oxford as a rebel only to leave it with filial affection; but few have transmuted such abounding vitality and such a rich love of miscellaneous experience – he had worked as cook, film extra, mechanic, and merchant seaman before he came to Magdalen – into poetry at once gentle and intense. Almost all of this verse was published in English magazines such as *The Listener* and *Encounter*, though some has appeared, and more is about to appear, in *Botteghe Oscure*. This last year of his life – the year of his marriage to the Irish singer and harpist Mary O'Hara – though it closed in weeks of pain, was certainly his happiest. "Cut is the branch that would have grown full straight." But his last poems, reflecting in their increasing mastery of form a hard-won serenity will be a meet memorial.

Peter's brother, Anthony Levi, wrote:

From my occasional meetings with Richard my strongest impression that remains is one of his enormous integrity . . . coupled with a really great simplicity . . .

You know, of course, how tremendously Richard was admired here and I think you would be touched and even grateful to know how deeply people have been affected by the sad news . . . Richard was one of the very few people who seem entirely worthy of our wholehearted admiration . . .

Brock Brower, the writer, a fellow American and Rhodes scholar, wrote:

. . . The shortness of (Richard's) life is appalling, but the fullness of it, when you measure it alongside the narrowness of the rest of us, was a triumph and I am shamed before it.

Perhaps what I am most ashamed by is the intensity he showed. Whenever we got together to make some assay of letters I was always the time-server, the one who wanted to work patiently in small steps towards a future goal. But he did not have time. None of us do. Time cannot be served. I realise that now, too late. We should have both rushed on against it . . .

The gift of life is always greater than the gift of any art. No art could ever have substituted for the passion he had in living . . .

George Scott-Moncrieff's empathy was exceeded by no one. (Our incipient friendship dating from the Edinburgh Festival days was to burgeon months later after my return from Arabia.)

My dear Mary,

It was a great shock to get your letter this morning. I am so terribly sorry. Only I am so glad that Richard and you feel as you do about death – only it is not just a feeling, but knowledge, knowledge with one's whole being. One is as it were cut in half by the death of a husband or wife although the other half is really a source of great strength. But I know how hard it is to be the one that is left behind in this world.

I liked Richard immensely from the moment I met him, and I had so looked forward to seeing him again, and talking with him. For I knew there was so much that he could say. His death is a shock, but, as you say, his life, of which you became the most real part possible to human creature, is something to be forever tremendously grateful to God for. And that gratitude and joy overcome all desolation. One does not have to be articulate to know it.

I have been praying for you both ever since I heard that Richard was ill, and of course I shall still be praying for you both now.

I remember a priest saying to me after Ann, my wife, died – "People will say this is the worst time for you. It isn't. In some ways it is your best time. For now you see things truly." I like to think that that vision has never really faded. As though the finest memorial one can make to

159

one's beloved is to keep and cherish and live by the vision that she – or he – bequeathed one at death. Some people hearing of Richard's death, express sympathy for you adding, "She is young, she will get over it." I don't reply because they obviously wouldn't understand, but I feel like saying 'She won't get over it. Mary doesn't want to get over it. It is part of her, something she loves and cherishes – as she loves Richard – a great growth unto grace.' Of course I know the pain too. But that is not the significant part.

The only thing I can add to what you already know – and this I can add because it is eighteen years this week since Ann died – is to reassure you (if you need such reassurance) that the vision, the "pure light" that Richard left you, does not fade. There is no need for it to fade. I am sure it is only our own fault if it ever should. Instead, it grows brighter and surer. Not consistently, because there is a kind of darkness that is a part of growth (all the mystical writers speak of it) but it is not the same darkness as we may have known before. Yet it is a darkness and we may feel very disconsolate in it. But if we wait – and pray – it lifts, and time and again we find that the brightness has grown brighter and even more sure. Even although we feel ourselves terribly bad at it, prayer does become our life now: prayer that is perfectly consistent with a life in this world, prayer that I suppose at last becomes a silent habit. For, after all, prayer is now the only true communion we have with our beloved partner in God. There is nothing sentimental or wishful about this communion, it is a perfectly real assured continuance of what we shared when the beloved was alive, and by it we grow on together. I suppose that what we have seen in the pure light is something of the real meaning of love, the way it is *rooted* in and part of God, and so continues to all eternity. Love is not possessiveness (and we have learnt how inessential possession is to love, for we have found our love only made mightier in dispossession) but God is love. What more is there to say! And you know it already, but you will still learn what wonderful things there are to find out about it.

God bless and keep you, dear Mary,

Scomo

Besides spending time with Michael and Jean O'Leary, I stayed on and off with John and Mary Gray Hughes. Michael and John had known Richard well in their own different ways and at different times in his life. It was an immense joy for me to talk with them about the Richard *they* knew. I think in the end John began to understand what I meant when I told him that far from seeing Richard's life as tragically short, I had a very definite

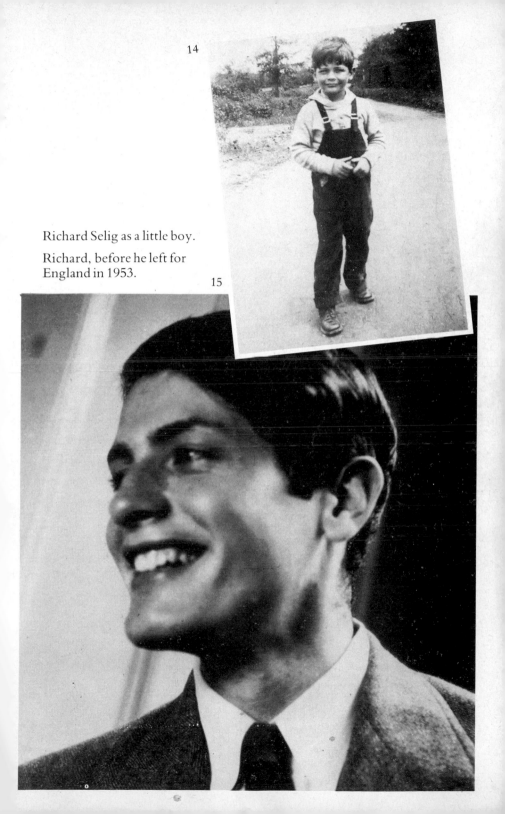

14

Richard Selig as a little boy.

Richard, before he left for
England in 1953.

15

Above: John Hughes with Richard outside Queen's College, Oxford, 1954.

Opposite page: (*Left to right*) Róisin O'Trama and her sister Másrín Ferriter, and Mary, March 1954, before going to England for St Patrick's Day concerts.

Mary, with Jean O'Leary and two of her children, John and Jeana, some days after Richard's death.

17

18

BBC television series 'Starlight', April 1956.

Mary, one year before she went to Stanbrook.

The Ed Sullivan Show, New York, 1961. Finale. Mary had bought her own dresses but was put into an Irish colleen outfit.

22

23

Scomo: George Scott-Moncrieff

Mary, taken during the Australian tour, 1959–60

sense of his life having come full circle. I had known something of his genuine, sincere inner searching. I knew that together we had found something irreplaceably precious in our spiritual lives which had welded us together, forged us in a common, shared reaching-out to God. And in my own case I had a sense of having lived *my* life. I felt there was a relatively fleeting interim period before my moment of truth would come and we would be together for all eternity.

It was about six months later, after I'd got back from Arabia, that I happened upon a prayer attributed by some to the Dominican Bede Jarett. It articulated so much that was in my heart and mind from the moment of Richard's death.

We seem to give them back to you O God, who gave them to us. Not as the world gives do you give, o lover of men. For what you give you take not away. And what is yours is ours also if we are yours. For love is eternal and life is immortal and death is only an horizon, and an horizon is nothing save the limit of our sight.

Lift us up strong Son of God that we may see further. Cleanse our eyes that we may see more clearly. Draw us closer to you that we may know ourselves to be close to those we love. And while you prepare a home for us, prepare us also for that happy place, where with you (and with them) we may live for ever and ever. Amen.

About a month after Richard's death, I was ready to leave the Long Island apartment. Before doing so I burnt all my letters to Richard.

It was more convenient for me to stay in the city while I was recording 'Songs of Ireland', and the Hugheses kindly invited me to use their place. Once the recording was finished my plans were to leave America, spend one week in Dublin and another week in Oxford before flying out, for an indefinite period, to my father who was with the FAO (Food and Agricultural Organization of the United Nations) in Aden.

It seemed only right that I should visit my mother-in-law before I left the States. Almost immediately after the recording was over, I took a train to Washington, DC. I was incredibly tired, emotionally and physically, and was looking forward to a very simple, ultra quiet couple of days alone with Florence. It wasn't until I got there that I discovered she had planned the first evening otherwise. When I arrived Florence told me she'd invited a couple of friends to dinner, who would "understand". My heart sank and I braced myself to be sociable.

I was lying down when the guests arrived, and was anything but attracted to the voice and attitude of whoever it was who was holding forth almost non-stop in the living room next door, from the moment she entered the apartment. I put in an appearance in time for supper. The voluble lady, who must have been in her seventies, later turned out to be a minister in some esoteric spiritualistic sect. I was prejudiced against her from the start. Firstly I wanted to be alone with my mother-in-law and the last thing I needed was to be burdened with an opinionated chatterbox, who behaved as if she had come to "cure" me of my bereavement. She was a tough hard-faced old girl, by no means endowed with a sympathetic nature. I think she sensed my dislike for her. I was reluctant to be drawn into the conversation, which mainly centred around herself and the importance she attached to her connections. She announced to me that a close relative had been the architect of some famous church or other known as 'The Church On The Corner'. Innocently I asked: "Which corner?" She took this to be flippancy on my part. Later on she took exception to some sharp retort I made and gave her the excuse to fly into a towering rage. Jumping up from the table she retreated to a corner of the room declaring that she'd been insulted and wouldn't stand for it. I've forgotten exactly what I said, but her next outburst touched a sensitive nerve: "Aha, now we know why Richard was taken." With that I burst out crying, left the table and ran out of the room into the night. As I was leaving I heard her shout: "Pay no attention to her, she's only acting."

For some time I kept running, still crying. I wandered forlornly along the suburban roads. It must have been up to an hour before I composed myself sufficiently to return to the apartment. It was now empty save for the leaflets judiciously sprinkled round the living room, for my benefit no doubt. Beneath her picture, in bold print, the leaflets declared that my erstwhile antagonist was, among other things, "in direct contact with the Divine". I could have guessed! Could it be that I had spoiled the opportunity for a good séance and lost for the Reverend X a potential client?

When Florence returned I apologized for upsetting the dinner party. Later I discovered that Florence herself had been going through a bad patch and had temporarily fallen into the clutches of this charlatan, who had guaranteed to put her into contact with her deceased relatives. The painful episode was never referred to again.

After all the business connected with the 'Songs of Ireland' album was finished, there was no further reason for me to linger on in America. John Hughes saw me off at the airport, and I arrived in Dublin on a cold and dull November day.

Up to that time my connection with Déirdre Flynn (as she then was) was fairly tenuous. She had written with typical warmth and concern when she'd heard from me the news of Richard's death. Now she came to meet me after my flight from New York. This meeting was to be the start of what was to develop into one of the deepest friendships of my life. Looking back I'm inclined to think that before Richard's entry into my life, I had many acquaintances and pals. But there were no real friendships as I now understand the word to mean. It was under the subtle tutelage of Richard's influence that the latent ability to form friendships began to grow. This is what Déirdre has written about that meeting:

My personal memory jumps back to meeting you at the Aer Lingus terminal when you came back to Dublin after Richard's death. We had always been in some contact, even though the lines of communication were sometimes long ones, and we had corresponded after Richard's death. You phoned from the airport to say you had just landed and your voice sounded the same. But grief had so changed your appearance that I did not, in fact, recognise you when you stepped off the airport bus. I had settled myself to wait for the next bus when I saw someone wearing a familiar heather-coloured tweed coat. Before you went to Sion Hill, I phoned Sister Angela to warn her that, though you had come to terms with what had happened, your personal grief was unbelievable – and all the more so for being so rigidly controlled.

I stayed in a hotel selected by Déirdre and from there visited my sister, Joan, and Sion Hill, where I spent quite a lot of time with Sister Angela and Mother Ambrose. The latter introduced me to the work of C. S. Lewis, one of her favourite writers, and urged me to try and find his book, *The Great Divorce*, but I was unsuccessful. From her I heard for the first time that wonderful Portuguese proverb: "God writes straight with crooked lines" which she inscribed in a little copy she gave me of Francis Thompson's *The Hound of Heaven*.

Dublin was followed by a week in Oxford staying with Jack and Gwyneth Bennett and their two very small sons, Edmund Piers and Charles Anselm from whose home on the outskirts of the city, I visited Peter Levi and other friends.

I flew to southern Arabia five days before Christmas. My father had advised me to fly to Aden via Cairo, and I booked my passage accordingly. His work in connection with irrigation and water resources took him to various areas all over the desert. So he had impressed upon me the importance of his knowing the date and hour of my arrival so as to give him a chance of getting back from the desert to meet me. Transport for him was varied and sometimes rather colourful, ranging from Land-Rover to camel, none of which tended to work to a predictable timetable, least of all the camel. At the last minute my plane had to be re-routed to Aden via Athens and Asmara, too late to let my father know of the change beforehand. It was a very long, tiring flight. We landed in Aden in the late afternoon and I recall the hilarity among the Arab customs officials when they read the description of my occupation as "housewife". I'm still not quite sure why they found it so funny, though if one takes the word literally, one can understand their being tickled by it.

There was no one to meet me. A high-ranking Arab official took me under his paternal wing and brought me off to lunch with himself and his daughter – my first experience of Arab hospitality. In the meantime my father had been contacted and a few hours later I was collected and was driven by a French woman to his quarters outside Aden. This friend of my father's invited us to a Christmas party at the European Club, but I was not anxious to go. My father was very understanding when I systematically declined all subsequent invitations to dine or attend parties that were forthcoming from his many friends and acquaintances. I had to make it clear to him from the beginning that for me all socializing was out. Mine was to be a retreat into the desert with time given over to reading, reflection and prayer.

I felt the need and desire to be alone as much as possible and in that quietness perhaps make out what was God's *specific* will for me for the future. Naturally I confided in my father my conviction that through the events of the past year or so God was calling me to serve him in some special way. As it happened, my father's lifestyle fitted the bill admirably for this Pauline-like sojourn.

When he was not away in the desert my father lived among the barren hills of Aden, in Marshag. The dwelling was pitched on the side of a hill well above a lighthouse. It was part of a complex formerly used as an artillery battery station and was situated six or seven miles from Steamer Point, the passenger entry port for Aden through the town of Crater. (Crater is actually built on the edge of an extinct volcano.) It commanded a magnificent view of the Indian Ocean, with almost no one to be seen apart from the occasional Arab fisherman, jogging down to the town with his early morning catch. This catch often consisted of a single fish, a tuna or a barracuda about ten feet long, cut in two and carried suspended from a stick across his shoulders.

The nearest church was a few miles away down in Crater. It was served by Italian Franciscans. In the mornings I was driven down by Land-Rover for six o'clock Mass and back again. More often than not I walked the distance there and back for Benediction in the evening. When my father was away in Yemen or elsewhere in the desert, I did both journeys by foot and enjoyed it. The walk along the coast road was bracing, with the Indian Ocean crashing against the low wall just a few yards away. Coming back in the pitch black could be quite awesome. With the sea turmoiling away on my left and the leaping fire-light of the crematorium stark against the forbidding hills on the right, if one were easily frightened, then scared one would assuredly be! From the look of incredulity on the faces of Europeans who, on stopping their cars and offering me a lift, found I preferred to go on walking alone, I gathered that it was not common practice in those parts. But I never felt unsafe – except for one night. Returning in the pitch dark (I never thought of carrying a light) – a night so black that I could barely see the light-coloured cotton dress I was wearing – I heard the unfamiliar patter of bare feet following me. I kept going. I could hear the steps quickening till they finally broke into a decided trot. My instinct was to bolt, but I refused to allow myself to alter my pace. I prayed passionately within for protection – making massive acts of trust in God. The sound of bare feet was almost beside me when suddenly the runner veered off to the right, obviously heading for the crematorium. . . . Relief, relief.

Another memory is of the strange, haunting singing of the Arab nightwatchman at the foot of Marshag, just after dawn. Was he recreating? Or perhaps worshipping? It sounded curiously like the traditional Gaelic singing one used to hear in places like Connemara in the west coast of Ireland.

Much to my joy and amazement, I was able to find in Aden a copy of C. S. Lewis' *The Great Divorce*. I became an instant devourer of as much C. S. Lewis as I could lay my hands on. A cliff-top house overlooking the Indian Ocean was as good a place as any to be introduced to his work.

In Aden in those days there was ample scope for doing charitable works. Although I'd never before felt attracted towards the active apostolate of alleviating the physical sufferings of the needy, now I regretted that Richard hadn't lived long enough for us to do something of that nature together. Here in Aden, every time I went into the town with my father to the market or to the library, I could not help but notice the cripples and beggars everywhere. People gave various reasons for this abundance of maimed humanity in a Moslem town, but the explanations were of little concern to me at the time. I felt a deep urge to be of some practical consolation to these people, but there was so little I could do. It was at this time that I started to visit the local hospital. I spoke no Arabic and the patients had no English, so we smiled quietly at one another and exchanged salutations. Whether or not the patients derived any benefit from my corporal works of mercy is hard to judge, but I have my doubts! They preferred the cigarettes to my Western-style sandwiches, however lovingly prepared. Nor was I ever sure that the ice-cream that they so graciously accepted was all that welcome to their palates. It was difficult to know how they regarded this Christian European girl wandering in their midst. I'll always remember the naked joy on the face of the little Arab boy when I gave him a toy racing car. He's probably driving a real *babur* by now. However, I gradually made friends in the men's and children's wards, and there were smiles of recognition whenever I appeared on the scene. I don't remember seeing a women's ward.

In Arabia some Biblical allusions took on new meaning. At home in Ireland no one mistakes a goat for a sheep. In Aden, however, what I took to be herds of goats turned out to be sheep. The animals looked so alike to me that I would have found it well-nigh impossible to "separate the sheep from the goats". Also I could imagine how the giving of a cup of cold water in anyone's name could be a most friendly act.

My stay in Arabia coincided with both the Christian Lent and the Moslem Ramadan, the penitential seasons of the two great religions. There is a basic difference between Moslem and Christian fasting. From sunrise to sunset the Moslem tastes neither food nor drink but can feast unrestrainedly after sunset. The Catholic fast was different. It consisted of one full meal and two tiny snacks per day. There was no food at night. It's hard to gauge which fast is more difficult, but I can still recall the voracity with which I fell upon that one full meal. I kept a very rigorous fast.

I was still deeply affected by Richard's death. Swimming and playing tennis and enjoying myself generally was something I had no mind for without Richard to share it with. I avoided the inviting tennis courts, swimming pools and even the sea. A wealthy Persian friend of my father's, who had a holiday house on Marshag, offered to teach me to ride on one of his many Arab horses. But that, too, I declined. I once overheard him remark to my father: "She's behaving just like my mother did when my father died. She spent all her time touring all the local mosques." When I eventually refused his invitation to go horse-riding his only remark was: "I thought you would." I was talked into attending dinner at his house (on one rare occasion) in honour of the young sultan of Lahej, but I was absolutely bored. The fault was probably mine. Apart from visiting the sick I limited my social contacts to the bare minimum. Only twice did I venture into the desert with my father in the Land Rover.

April's end came and my father and I decided it would be better for me to leave the Middle East before the dry season set in. I still held fast to my resolve to go into a monastery but where, or which order, was not yet clear to me. I didn't worry. I knew the way would be shown me. After Easter I left for Europe. I was physically underweight but spiritually buoyed up and charged with confident expectation.

8   Searching

Asylum of peace, prelude to violence
And the hazardous way up of the blest.
Because he walks on the world's roof and treads
The high ground where heavenly footfalls once
Passed lightly by, man can never rest.

From Richard Selig's poem Everest.

The United States, Arabia, England, Ireland. Places had lost
their significance for me at this stage of my life. I was not
unhappy but at the same time I felt I had no roots on earth any
more. I was a pilgrim. I remember remarking to Joyce Grenfell
some time later: "I am rootless."

"What!" she exclaimed in a horrified voice. She thought I'd
said "ruthless". She gently pointed out that I shouldn't think
that way; that Richard wouldn't want me to live out of a suit-
case for the rest of my life.

At any rate I was back in Dublin and had to anchor somewhere, however temporarily. Sion Hill, my old Alma Mater,
put me in touch with a person who had been recently widowed
and who had a room to spare. For the next three years I stayed
with the Morrison family as a paying guest. It was a happy
arrangement and without doubt what I needed at that time.

Having established a temporary base at the Morrisons, I set
about earning a living again. I contacted my former agent
Sydney Lipton in London, and informed him that I was available for work again and prepared to take on selective engagements. It seemed only right that while I waited for guidance
about my call to the monastic life I should carry on singing.

Finances, thank God, had never been a worry for me. I had a
steady income from my three albums. Two months before
Richard died I'd received my first royalty cheque from Decca.
It amounted to £8. Then the very day after his death a substan-

169

tial three-figure cheque arrived. It meant nothing to me then. All it evoked was a shadow of sadness that it had come, so to speak, too late. On the same day a fat cheque arrived for Richard. This was for poems of his that were to be published in *Botteghe Oscura*, edited at that time by Princess Caetani. From then on the amount in royalties kept progressively increasing, as the sales of my records multiplied. While the Tradition album, 'Songs of Ireland' was available only in the United States, the two Decca albums 'Songs of Érin' and 'Love Songs of Ireland', were being manufactured and released in half a dozen countries in Europe, as well as South Africa, Australia and New Zealand. What is surprising and encouraging is that to this day royalties from these records are still coming in. However, at that time I barely glanced at the cheques when they arrived.

Many of the songs on these albums are in Gaelic, a language not too widely known except in some Celtic countries and perhaps in parts of Eastern Canada. Yet there seems to be no relationship between the widespread sales of the records and the tiny minority who understand the language. There is the story of someone who purchased one of my records in France and was told by the salesgirl that the strange language was "old English"!

At that time I had not made any personal appearances in France, but I had appeared on Dutch television, and now they asked me back again to Holland to do more radio and television. On the way to Amsterdam I spent one night in London. That afternoon I called to see Sydney Lipton in the West End and from there took a taxi back to my hotel. As I wasn't the one paying for the taxi I was in my room before realizing, to my horror, that I'd left my small handbag in the taxi. Passport, travellers' cheques, airticket – all were lost. It was 6.30pm and as my plane was to take off at 9am it was impossible to find replacements. In a controlled panic I eventually got through to my agent who called the police for me. He also alerted all the radio cabs in London. The police sent out a call to all their stations. I tried to get through to the Dutch Embassy but got no further than the bureaucratic doorman. I rang the Irish ambassador at his home and could get little sense out of the au pair girl who answered. The family was out. When the hotel receptionist went off duty the switchboard extension to my room was left open, in case the police called with any information. At five o'clock the following morning the message came that the handbag had just been handed in to a police station somewhere on the outskirts of London. Sighs of relief all round. I got the handbag but precious little sleep. This didn't cure my propensity for losing things. No matter how hard I try I still manage to leave things behind me in friends' houses, public lavatories, aeroplanes and yes, London taxis. There's a marvellous rapport between myself and St Anthony, the Patron Saint of Things Lost. To date he's never let me down about things that matter. Only recently I left my handbag in another London taxi and a totally anonymous stranger posted it to me first-class the very next day with the following note enclosed:

Dear Mary,
 DON'T PANIC HERE IS YOUR HANDBAG BACK WITH ALL THE CONTENTS INTACT. I PICKED IT UP IN A CAB I USED ON FRIDAY AFTERNOON. I COULD HAVE DONE A LOT OF DAMAGE TO YOUR BANK ACCOUNT BUT I DIDN'T. HOWEVER AS A SMALL REWARD AND TO TEACH YOU A BIG LESSON IN BEING MORE CAREFUL IN FUTURE I AWARDED MYSELF £50 FROM YOUR ACCESS CARD. I FEEL THIS IS A NOMINAL CHARGE FOR RETURN-ING YOUR PROPERTY.
A WELL WISHER
XX

With plans for going into a monastery firmly established in my own mind, I decided to record a few more long-playing albums before finally giving up singing forever. My repertoire of songs in English and in Gaelic was comparatively large and I hoped, if possible, to make one album of Scottish songs because of my attachment to that country.

 By now a regular correspondence was underway between myself and George Scott-Moncrieff in Edinburgh. George was known to his friends as Scomo. This name was arrived at by combining the first three letters of "Scott" with the first two of "Moncrieff". His uncle, Sir Charles Scott-Moncrieff, the translator of Proust (who incidentally, like George himself, had also become a convert to Roman Catholicism), had "passed on" this nickname to his nephew.

171

Scomo's reiterated invitation to come and stay with him and his family in Edinburgh, eventually resulted in my bestirring myself and flying to Scotland. It was a happy reunion and the beginning of countless visits to stay with Scomo, who was to become, in that period of my life, my closest friend and confidant.

Scomo was a remarkably fine character. Endowed with a tremendous love of life, he had rare gifts of the heart. By nature a sort of bohemian, his income was forever slender and by some standards he was indeed poor, but the quality of life in that household was of a high order. I have never come across anyone so unswervingly kind. Open house, open heart. If ever there was anyone who gave the lie to the impression that religion is gloomy, it was Scomo. When I first knew him, Scomo's three children, Lesley, Michael and Gavin, were at boarding school and his wife was dead, so he lived alone in his flat most of the time. When the family was with him or when he had guests, food in the flat was plentiful, interesting and varied. He was a fine cook, but like many people who live for fairly long periods alone, there were times when he didn't bother to lay in a store for himself, and provender was low. He told me a story about one evening when he was walking back towards his flat in James Court in the company of a little-known acquaintance, who was accompanying him part of the way so they could finish a discussion they were having. During a lull in the conversation Scomo thought to himself: What's in the house for my supper? There's an egg and an onion. All I need now is a potato and I can have kromeskis. At that moment he spied a large friendly potato in the gutter. With enviable Scomic spontaneity he stooped down, picked it up and with a triumphant air pocketed the vegetable declaiming happily, "Ah, that's my supper settled!" His companion was so shocked that he insisted on treating Scomo to a gourmet meal at the Aperitif, the best restaurant in town.

After his first wife had died, about twenty years before I met him, Scomo had gone to live on the Hebridean island of Eigg. There single-handedly, with insight and energy, he combined the difficult rôle of father and mother, and successfully reared his three small children. Some time after his marriage, he and his wife had become Roman Catholics. Scomo was my first close contact with a convert and I found in him a commitment and a spiritual fire that I had not so far encountered in anyone else. His intellect, and not just his heart, was totally involved in striving to live the Christian life. He had taken the trouble to inform himself theologically about his convictions and up to that time he was one of the few lay people with whom I could discuss religion comfortably. Those next three years of intermittent visits to Edinburgh, during which our incipient friendship budded and blossomed, were an education for me.

I have always maintained that he was a man of whom not only I, but countless others could say: "He was my closest friend." Not physically handsome, but of a noble and endearing countenance, he had immense charm and one of the things that distinguished him from others was his unabated gaiety. Later, when I first read Hugo Rahner's *Man at Play* where he writes at length and with acuity about the grave-merry man, I immediately thought of Scomo and I wrote to tell him so. Scomo was good and thus "diffusive of himself" – his playfulness marked him out indeed as one enjoying the freedom of the children of God which, of course, is a participation in the very freedom of the Almighty Himself. His work and play (was he not after all, a *play* writer?) never entirely lost contact with one another.

The duration of my visits got longer and longer. I would arrive intending to stay for one or two weeks but Scomo would press me to stay on. This frequently led to urgent requests to my father in Dublin to go to my wardrobe and send necessary items of clothing. For instance, late summer sojourns would imperceptibly drift into autumn and I'd need an overcoat and so on. One such occasion resulted in a customs declaration form being hurriedly filled in by my father. I'd asked for a specific fine wool black sweater that my mother-in-law had bought for me. It was a bit on the small side. The little green customs form completed in my father's handwriting stated: "Old black woollen lady's vest". Beside the word "value" appeared not the usual "no commercial value" but "useless." On receipt of the garment we all fell about the place laughing at the idea of an old black woollen lady.

While no one could accuse Scomo of being musical, he had a great appreciation of the arts in general with a keen awareness of and high regard for beauty in any form whether visual or aural. He agreed that it would be a splendid idea for me to make a long-playing record of traditional Scottish songs. His encouragement and help in research on individual lowland Scottish songs was prodigious. He introduced me to David Murison, then editor of the Scottish National Dictionary. I regularly visited David in his rooms at the School of Scottish Studies in George Square in Edinburgh, where together we painstakingly went over every syllable of each word. David would pronounce the word and whenever I had an initial difficulty I would write it down phonetically. It was astonishing how this gentle, learned man could say with authority how a particular word was pronounced in such and such a century and in a particular district.

For the Scots Gaelic songs I turned to my very dear friend Calum Maclean, also based at the School of Scottish Studies. After he'd heard of Richard's death he'd typewritten a very affectionate letter to me with a PS at the end: "I'm recovering from the loss of my arm." Cancer had struck. A year or two before that he'd had a kidney removed. He died, peacefully, in his mid-forties in South Uist very shortly before I entered the monastery and before I could implement my plan to visit him in a Hebridean nursing home. Calum had become a Roman Catholic some time before I'd met him. His family was staunchily Presbyterian and once, in his flat in Edinburgh when he was teaching me some Gaelic songs on a Sunday morning, his mother kept trying to dissuade him from doing so. Finally, in her beautiful Hebridean accent, she threatened: "If you don't stop singing, I'll hit you with the poker." I believe she meant it, too.

The fine singer Joan Mackenzie from the Island of Lewis was also a generous mentor. Scomo and I used to visit her and her growing family on and off in Edinburgh.

It was while I was staying with Scomo that I met his great friend Father Jock Dalrymple the well-known spiritual writer who came to dinner a few times while I was there. He was to play a most important rôle in my life years later. Scomo's friends were legion.

From the beginning I felt in tune with Scomo's philosophy of life. The notion of self-abandonment was central to his spirituality and from the moment he first spoke of it, I knew it was meant for me, too. He had been practising this "way" himself for a long while and fed daily on a book called *Self-Abandonment to Divine Providence* by J.P. de Caussade, the seventeenth-century French Jesuit. Scomo and myself had endless conversations about the book's teaching. The book was not readily available at the time and it was two years before I acquired my own copy, mailed to me in Australia by Scomo. I treasured this book and made use of it daily in the same way I was later to use the Psalter and that great medieval classic of English mysticism, *The Cloud of Unknowing*. Each day I extracted from this book some phrase or idea which I found practically helpful or inspiring and "lived" with it throughout the day, savouring it, like "dissolving a lozenge on the tongue" to use one of Jock Dalrymple's images.

It was Scomo who also introduced me to the writings of Julian of Norwich. Her *Revelations of Divine Love* afforded me untold sustenance and her optimistic vision of life reinforced my own philosophy and had a benign influence on my own attitude to living from day to day. "All shall be well and thou shalt see that all manner of things shall be well."

Besides being a playwright Scomo was also the author of a number of novels and prose-works including some dealing with spiritual matters. In one of these works he wrote that "happiness is a duty" and no one discharged that duty more incessantly and whole-heartedly than Scomo did.

I think he was a sage – the sort of wise man that Richard was looking for – and I feel deeply grateful that I received the benefit of his happy wisdom. There were times when I learned as much from his behaviour as from his words. What he was, was as eloquent as what he did or said.

Once while staying with Scomo in Edinburgh, I undertook to babysit for his friends, Patrick and Biddy Nuttyens. It was my regular practice to go to evening Mass and I always stayed on afterwards in church to engage in various devotional exercises of my own. This particular evening I was obviously going to be late for my babysitting appointment, and as I walked back to the flat I met Scomo. He had seen I was going to be late and was on his way to babysit in my place. He told me to go and have my supper, which he'd kept warm for me, before joining him at the Nuttyens', which I did.

As the evening wore on, we talked about various things. At some stage the conversation turned to Richelieu and his times, and especially to that extraordinary power behind Richelieu known to history as the *Eminence Gris*. He was a Dominican friar who was reputed to be a man of prayer and yet who seemed to deliberately close his eyes to the many evil things that were happening around him. He had it in his power to prevent these happenings, but neglected to do so. Scomo pointed out that in spite of his apparent prayerfulness the *Eminence Gris* was guilty of grave sins of omission. I got the message. I had undertaken to babysit. Yet I had thoughtlessly put the "saying of prayers" before my commitment to the Nuttyens. It was a salutary lesson which has stayed with me ever since. There was another time when I felt chastened by something Scomo said to me. He was telling me an amusing story about his sister Joanna's daily woman. The latter was describing to Joanna someone she knew and commented, "She's a bit of an abrupt like yourself, Ma'am." While I was laughing at this (and thinking yes, Joanna *is* a bit of an abrupt), Scomo said, "You're like that, Mary." That soon stopped the chortling.

Me: "What do you mean, Scomo? I'm nice to everyone, ain't I?"

"When you feel like it," Scomo said.

A sobering glimpse of myself as others see me. I've been working on that one ever since!

Back in Ireland once more, my agent Sydney Lipton telephoned me about an eight-week concert tour of Australia. It was to be a charity tour to raise money for the homes and hospitals run by the Vincentian Fathers and Sisters of Charity. The prospect didn't enthuse me, as my primary concern at this stage was to seek for guidance about a monastic future. However, as I was still unable to see my way ahead very clearly, I consented to do the tour. Talking to my father on the telephone he happened to mention that he was going to Australia and had in fact already booked a passage by sea to Sydney. It was to be a business-cum-holiday trip. "What a happy coincidence," I said. "I'll probably see you there." We decided that the sensible thing would be to travel together, so my agent arranged a passage for my father on the ship I was to travel on.

The Australian tour was to start in early July 1959 so we set sail from Southampton on the *Southern Cross* at the end of May. Scomo was in London and came to see me off at the station. He was fully aware of my reluctance to undertake this tour, and in his own inimitable way he did everything possible to encourage and cheer me up. I can still see him standing on the platform in his bright blue corduroy jacket and suede shoes (startlingly dyed to match) his wild hair flying in the breeze, waving his hat in the air and – with a total absence of self-consciousness – shouting after me: "Abandonne! Abandonne!"

The voyage took five weeks and I thought the rest would do me good. However, despite the comforts of first-class travel, I found five weeks cooped up in the one place a bit much. We went ashore at Las Palmas in the Canary Islands and again in Cape Town and Durban, South Africa and these were welcome respites. But generally I was to find the voyage tedious. I was in no mood for joining in the social activities on board ship. I played some deck-tennis and tombola and saw a few films. But what I enjoyed most was playing table-tennis and reading. There were two Cistercian monks from Mount Mellery Abbey, in Ireland, on their way to New Zealand to start a foundation there. They were both "late vocations" to the religious life: one had been a civil servant and the younger, more taciturn one, a scientist and, as I soon found out, a superlative table-tennis player. I looked forward to a game with him whenever it was possible. Years later, when a New Zealander came to my monastery, she brought kind messages from the older one who was then Head of the new foundation. He had succeeded the Table-Tennis Monk (for want of a better name), as Prior when he had been killed in a tractor accident on their farm.

Twenty-seven days out of Southampton we docked in Cape Town. Sion Hill must have sent word that I was coming because the Dominican sisters waylaid me and brought me to their convent. They gave me a very warm welcome. I remember we laughed a lot. They were a very happy group of people in that place, a fact which struck me about every Dominican priory and convent I had ever had occasion to visit. That evening in Cape Town I tried to sing a certain humorous Irish song, but with all the laughing we were doing I don't believe I ever finished it.

From Cape Town we sailed on to Durban. For a time I had been corresponding with a retired colonel who lived in Natal, outside Durban. When I was eighteen the *Irish Digest* magazine had featured me on its cover. This colonel in Natal had written to the magazine for a copy of the photograph and my address, and periodically wrote me charming letters telling me about his own history and about his family. It was a warm correspondence that developed between the teenager and the eighty-six year-old colonel. He bought my albums as they came out and even sent me a wedding present. Before setting out for Australia, I wrote to tell him I'd be stopping off at Durban. When we docked there, his grandson was there to meet us and take us to visit his mother. But strangely no sign of his grandfather. He was somewhere inland and sent his apologies. The grandson was my own age, and I remembered that after Richard's death the colonel's letters made frequent mention of the virtues of this particular grandson. It didn't require a high IQ to realize that the kindly colonel was playing the matchmaker. Anyhow, it didn't work, (I most certainly wasn't interested) and I never heard from the colonel again, though I remember him with fondness.

About an hour before our arrival in Sydney I got word that I was to give a press reception in my cabin as soon as we docked. "Impossible," said my father. "You couldn't swing a cat in that place." Though I was moved into a larger cabin, the reception eventually took place in the ship's lounge.

Just after dawn (or so it seemed to me) a representative from the promoter's office came aboard with the pilot. She briefed me about the day's events and every moment seemed to have been accounted for. I was to start with TV, radio and press interviews, which I found difficult enough, but what I was not prepared for was the giant green shamrock that confronted me at the foot of the gangway. Shades of the "Ed Sullivan Show"... This is, my least favourite representation of Ireland. It was supported by two little girls dressed in matching green and gold Irish dancing costumes. Smiling as warmly as I could, I descended the steps to pose for the cameras in the shade of the towering shamrock. I discovered later that all this was being televised for a "News of the Day" programme. Mercifully I was quickly plucked away and taken to meet Cardinal

Gilroy, who was patron of the charitable organization for which the concert tour was being organized.

From there I was whisked off to the Town Hall to lunch and a civic reception given by the Lord Mayor of Sydney. The packed day ended with an appearance on a popular, live TV programme where I sang a couple of songs on my own. But I simply *could not* bring myself to join in the dancing to the song "If you're Irish come into the parlour" which concluded the programme.

The eight-week concert tour opened with one week at the Assembly Hall in Sydney. The critics were unanimously kind, and the audiences very warm, all of which contributed towards sending me on my way for the next seven weeks full of encouragement. The promoters were not altogether sure how a diet of voice and harp alone would go down with the Australian audiences, so they added a dash of Irish tenor in the person of a young man with a pleasing voice called Terence Finnegan, who was accompanied on the piano. He started off the concert with a group of songs for about twenty minutes, after which I took over for the rest of the evening. As far as I know, attendance at the Sydney concerts was good, but at that time I preferred not to ask. Even to this day I prefer not to know how a concert is selling until after the event.

As this tour was in aid of charity, I was receiving a fixed fee per week and the rest of the proceeds went to the charity. The organizers were amateurs and as time went on I could see that they relied too heavily on the support of the local clergy throughout Australia. Somewhere along the ecclesiastical line communications broke down, and I recall going to some smaller towns where even the parish clergy did not know of the concert until my arrival there. Publicity was virtually nil. There were no posters or flyers to announce the concerts.

When I first arrived in Sydney, Joyce Grenfell was in the midst of a season at the Phillips Street Gallery. (Needless to say she was a thundering success.) She came to one of my concerts and was very enthusiastic about the concert but concerned about the way things were being handled. I remember how, backstage afterwards, she complimented me lovingly, and then graciously but firmly – in a way that could offend no one – she made some remark to the organizers of my concert to the effect that she felt I wasn't being looked after properly. It was a genuine caring on her part. All through the subsequent phases of my career we kept in touch.

After the opening week in Sydney, I recorded a series of seven fifteen-minute programmes for ABC Radio, and then I began to travel throughout New South Wales giving concerts in different towns. Joyce invited me to spend one free weekend with her in her flat at Maclay Regis overlooking Sydney Harbour. She told me that she closed her eyes to the decor and furniture, but selected the flat because of the breath-stopping view it commanded. She was an unfussy hostess and her patience unruffable. One night, knowing I'd be back later than she from the theatre, Joyce had given me a key. Coming up in the lift at about 3am I clumsily dropped the key down the lift shaft. Nothing for it but to ring her door-bell. A sleepy but exceptionally sweet-tempered Joyce came to the door, her long brown hair in a plait down her back. My profuse apologies were all received with a dreamy, genuinely kindly smile and a reassuring shake of the head which meant "It's nothing, don't worry." Not a word of disapproval was forthcoming.

Australian winters in New South Wales can be bitterly cold. Sometimes the theatres and concert halls were badly heated (backstage at any rate) and the lavatories like refrigerators. There was one place that didn't have a loo at all. At least I never found it. I recall opening the only door in sight to find nothing but some steps leading directly onto a huge mound of coal. My need must have been particularly dire, for it was there, on that pole-axingly cold antipodean night, that I attended to the necessities of nature.

After the bitter cold of New South Wales the warmth of the weather in Queensland was heavenly and welcome. The night I sang in Brisbane coincided with a public visit by Princess Alexandra. Just down the road from the theatre where I was performing someone was playing the bagpipes loudly – and I'm sure devotedly – in the Princess' honour, out on the street, as part of a ceremonial welcome. After my road manager heard the cacophonic non-duet between the offending bagpipes and an unaccompanied song of mine, he promptly scampered down the road and paid the piper handsomely to stop, at least until the concert ended. I doubt if the Princess ever noticed.

By now the organizers were happy the way the concerts were going, so they extended the tour to a further six weeks in New Zealand. Early in September, with no break, I flew to Auckland. I was exhausted. I was about the first person to disembark and I noticed quite a sizeable group of people waiting behind the barrier with an air of expectancy. A few of them carried flowers. I immediately assumed that they were waiting to welcome *me* and summoning my best smile I walked confidently towards them hoping they wouldn't notice my weariness. But to my growing puzzlement there was no sign of recognition. It was only when I came up close to them that it dawned on me that they weren't waiting for me at all but for members of the Russian Ballet who had travelled on the same plane.

The New Zealand tour was more skilfully organized than the Australian one. Here, too, the reviews were favourable and the audiences enthusiastic and appreciative. It was in Auckland that I met Father David Sheerin, a Dominican of the Irish Province, a brilliant young man, who was then chaplain at Auckland University. He came backstage after the first concert in the Town Hall (I gave two concerts in each of the major cities in both the North Island and South Island) and introduced himself. Father David and I visited the zoo together next day. It was there that I confided in him about wanting to enter a monastery. He was very sympathetic and said he knew the person: his former novice master Father Anselm Moynihan, now Prior of St Dominic's in Drogheda, Ireland. David felt sure that Father Anselm would be the right person for me. He was sensitive, wise and discerning.

When the six-weeks' tour was over I flew back to Sydney. My agent had offers of television work for me in Melbourne, so I decided to stay on in Australia for a while longer. Within days of my arrival I was contacted by Dr Percy Jones, a Catholic priest and head of the Faculty of Music at Melbourne University; he was also one of the foremost liturgists in the English-speaking world. Dr Jones is an Australian who had studied in Rome and in Ireland and while a student in Dublin had acquired a love for Irish music and culture. He was eager to organize a concert for me. Eventually I did give a concert – in a hall where the temperature was 95° – which was so successful that I was prevailed upon to give another one a couple of weeks later. I say prevailed upon because I was expected to present a completely different programme and I wasn't sure if I could do justice to it at such short notice, especially as I already had ample work in hand in connection with the TV programmes. Soon after that the seven live weekly TV programmes which had brought me to Melbourne in the first place had finished, so I decided to return to Sydney.

With the help of friends my father and I rented a bungalow on the beach outside Sydney where we spent Christmas. It was my first experience of eating Christmas turkey with the sun blazing down.

When I got back from Melbourne my agent had another offer of a recorded series of thirteen fifteen-minute television programmes. So I was to remain on in Australia for a further few months, preparing for and recording the series. Another person who entered my life then was Mother Angela Quill. She was principal of one of the Sacred Heart schools outside Sydney. She phoned me one day to ask if I would go and sing for the children. She sounded stuffy, but she put the request in such a way that I couldn't refuse. Her friend, Agatha Devine, came to pick me up and the evening was an enjoyable one for all of us.

Mother Angela turned out in fact to be anything but stuffy and our friendship is still going strong. With Agatha, too, I became good friends and in no time she had me moved out of the hotel and staying as her guest in her attractive home in Wallaringa Avenue where her garden ends in a swimming pool and the waters of Sydney Harbour.

May came and I felt it was time to close the Australian chapter. I turned down the offer of more concerts in Sydney. I had worked hard and made lots of new friends and now it was time to return to Europe by air and sort out the monastic business.

I returned to Dublin after an absence of a year with one thing uppermost in my mind: to find a monastery. Following up David Sheerin's advice I wrote to Father Anselm Moynihan explaining who I was and why I wanted to see him. He sent a cautious reply, graciously inviting me to Drogheda to meet him at my convenience. So in late summer 1960 I set off on the two hour bus journey to Drogheda. I found him to be a man of great spiritual strength and matching gentleness. He was in his fifties. At times he had about him an air of severity, but his delicious sense of fun and humour was ever ready to break through to the surface. He had a flexibility of spirit that combined, in a happy blend, respect for tradition and openness of mind and was forever hearkening to what the Holy Spirit is saying to the Church today. His reputation as a sound theologian meant that he was in great demand as a giver of retreats. He was knowledgeable about the ways of contemplative communities and was the official *visitor* appointed by the Vatican to the Contemplative Houses of women in Ireland.

From the start I trusted him wholeheartedly and spoke very freely to him about myself, my failings and my aspirations. I felt that, guided by him, I would, sooner or later, be shown what I must do. He had to see me a number of times in order to assess whether or not I had a real vocation to the contemplative life – which I believed I had.

After many visits and prayerful reflection on both sides Father Anselm concluded that I did indeed have a genuine call to the monastic life. We drew up a list of the major Contemplative Orders for women in the Church and systematically set out to examine what differentiates one Order from another, something that Father Anselm was well versed in. It was his estimation that we should look for an Order where there was some emphasis on study. He felt that I was the type of person whose mind needed to be nurtured on a substantive diet of theology if I was to lead a balanced spiritual life. This eliminated some Orders. When I mentioned that it was in the Poor Clares' favour that they did not sing the liturgy but spoke it, he dismissed the remark with a wry "that would be an easy way out". And that was that. I was strongly attracted to the Cistercians because of their perpetual silence and austere way of life, though Father Anselm was doubtful about my ability to endure such physical hardship. He also made the observation that my inclination was to practise charity vertically rather than horizontally and that living in a community which did not include in its timetable regular verbal communication with others might only accentuate that tendency.

The next step was to visit the individual establishments of

the various Religious Orders. Travelling in connection with my work facilitated this part of my quest. Whenever I had occasion to be in England or Scotland I made a point of visiting whatever monastery in that area we had singled out. It sometimes involved lengthy train journeys. I always wrote beforehand asking for permission to come and talk to the Superior and over a period of nine months I had visited six monasteries. Even after one visit a warm bond was established between me and the Superiors of four of these Houses – a bond that lasted for many years after I entered Stanbrook Abbey. They showed genuine concern for my well-being and in a couple of cases only my Solemn Profession as a Benedictine at Stanbrook ended our correspondence.

The first House I visited was in Ireland, where I was quite well known to the community. But since what I sought was relative obscurity, for that reason it was unsuitable. My meeting with the Prioress there led to a friendship which has lasted to this day. The next place was in Scotland. Like most of the other Superiors I came into contact with, the Prioress of this House was a remarkable woman. She struck me as having a single, shining passion – the service and love of the Lord. She explained to me the particular way the enclosed life was lived in her community and I came away feeling encouraged and impressed by the warmth and evident happiness of this dedicated woman.

The next two visits were not so successful. In one place I was put off by the fact that the Abbess resembled an aunt of mine. Also she took notes while I was talking and when she discovered I was a professional singer she spoke with a certain measure of awe about the fact that a member of her community had at one time sung with a famous international orchestra. This sign of being impressed by worldly acclaim disappointed me. That ended the visit and I didn't even wait for tea. She was nice, but when an Abbess looks like your aunt, what can you do?

The other monastery was quite forbidding. The Superior here was the only one who didn't answer my letter. And when I telephoned, the voice on the other end did not seem over-enthusiastic. However, I went there by train. The Abbess here was wearing those convex spectacles that magnified the eyes in an alarming manner. She, too, used the pen and paper technique and questioned me in a rather critical fashion. "Do you smoke? Do you drink?" All very clinical. She then handed me over to the Novice Mistress, but the damage was already done.

The next encounter was an experience I still look back on with affection. The setting was a most attractive medieval house in a picturesque part of rural England. I warmed immediately to the Bavarian-born Prioress who welcomed me – a stranger – like an old friend. She had a vivacity of spirit that belied her years and she radiated joy and love. She seemed genuinely disappointed that I wasn't staying overnight and personally showed me around. Because this was an historic building the community was in receipt of a government grant which obliged them to open the house to tourists during the summer months. This effected a modification of the strict rule of enclosure and wouldn't do for me. I wanted the whole or nothing; I couldn't be content with half measures.

These ventures into the unknown took place at intervals during my engagements. I was doing a series of thirteen programmes for Scottish Television which kept me in Scotland for a few months. I divided my time between Edinburgh and Glasgow. In Edinburgh I stayed with the Scott-Moncrieffs, but I spent one day in Glasgow each week working in the STV studios.

Scomo helped me with the STV scripts. I taped the programmes in the morning for transmission that evening and by next day I was back in Edinburgh.

Scomo was the only one who knew that this might possibly be my last appearance ever on TV. Therefore he was very angry when he discovered that STV had erased the tapes after each programme went out.

It's not difficult to find Irish and Scottish traditional songs that contain a reference to God, however obliquely, and I made a point of including one such song in each programme. The make-up girl told me that during one of the programmes someone in the control room was overheard remarking: "What the hell does she think this is, the Vatican Radio?"

Because of my interest in the Cistercians I visited Nunraw, the Cistercian monastery outside Edinburgh, to talk to the Abbot, Father Columban Mulcahy. He was away when I called so he came to see me later at Scomo's. A small man, he had a huge presence. I was told that in his youth he had a stammer and that his father went to great expense and trouble to have this speech impediment remedied, only to have his son enter a Cistercian monastery, where the monks observed virtually perpetual silence.

One afternoon Father Columban arrived for tea at Scomo's flat bringing along a book on the Cistercians called *La Trappe* in English. After we'd spoken for some time he suddenly leaned forward urgently in his chair and said: "I know the place for you – Stanbrook." Puzzled, I asked, "Where and what is Stanbrook?" He explained that it was a Benedictine monastery in the Midlands. When I asked him why he was enthusiastic about the Benedictines and not his own Order, he said, "It's a hunch." He added that it seemed to him that the singing gift I had was such that if I didn't use it an important part of me would not go on developing. When he said that there was a strong tradition of Plainchant at this Stanbrook Abbey I threw my eyes up to heaven, thinking: "Here we go again!" While I enjoy listening to singing when it's properly done, I have never been attracted to the Gregorian Chant, sometimes called plainsong, plainchant or simply the Chant. Mary Gray Hughes had given me an album of Plainsong by the monks of Gethsemani Abbey in Kentucky, which had left me quite unmoved, even rather bored. It is too much of a coincidence to expect that a group of disparate individuals called to live together in monastic community should each be endowed with the gift of song. I suspected that Father Columban had not much of an ear for music. And listening to him later singing the Divine Office confirmed my suspicions. He was quite tone deaf.

I became friendly with the monks of Nunraw, Abbot Columban and Father John, the Guest Master, in particular. One day I sang for a few of them in a small parlour. They couldn't speak but there was nothing wrong with their hearing.

When the TV series was over, I stayed on in Edinburgh continuing work on the material for the three long-playing records that I hoped to make before entering the monastery. I read *In A Great Tradition*, the book about Stanbrook Abbey which Father Columban had lent me. The book was no great help but on Father Columban's advice I visited Stanbrook. There I spoke to the Abbess, who later on was to become not only my Superior, but also a close friend and confidant. The Novice Mistress joined us after a while and then departed. As in the other monasteries I visited, I was separated from the nuns by a wooden counter, on top of which was a double iron grille reaching to the ceiling. There was also a black veil which obscured everything beyond the grille and to see Lady Abbess I had to open this curtain. All this seclusion appealed greatly to me. As I was leaving the Abbess extended her hand through the grille and gave me one of her transformingly lovely smiles. It was about 3pm and the community was in church reciting *None*, so on the Abbess's suggestion I stopped in the Extern Chapel to listen on my way out. My feelings about monastic choirs remained unchanged.

Some time after I got back to Ireland at the completion of the STV series, I went to see Father Anselm to discuss with him my monastic peregrinations. I had a strong feeling either for or against each place I had visited, except Stanbrook. We discussed this at length and went our separate ways to pray about it; and eventually we both agreed that Stanbrook should be the place for me. I then wrote to each of the five other monasteries I had visited to tell them of my decision in favour of Stanbrook. Interestingly enough, the three who answered wrote to say how happy they were and that they felt my choice had been a wise one.

Stanbrook sent me a questionnaire. My father happened to be in the room when I was completing it. I was absent-mindedly reading the questions aloud and when I came to "Reasons for wanting to enter the monastery" my father piped up, "Trouble at home!"

The year before, when Father Anselm was first sure I had a monastic vocation he gave me what he called a small test. He asked me not to wear mascara (which was the only make-up I used) between then and the time I would enter a monastery. That was no small test for me, because ever since I'd finished school I'd darkened my eyebrows and eyelashes with mascara. I am very fair and without mascara I feel quite naked. When I asked if I could continue to keep my eyebrows tidy, plucking them to give them shape, after some hesitation, he said yes, as that was like "brushing one's hair." Yes, of course, I could wear mascara and other eye make-up in connection with my work. Denying myself these female vanities was quite a trial, especially as I had to travel so much during those days. I must admit that I gave the dispensation "in connection with my work" a wide interpretation. During this period my sister Joan often remarked: "Oh Mel, why don't you go back to wearing mascara? It's so depressing when you don't." But she was not party to my secret plan.

In the autumn of 1961 I took my father for a holiday to the Hebridean island of Barra. I thought it would be the last holiday, for I expected to be in the monastery before the following summer. I'd written to a friend on Barra who arranged accommodation for us in one of the local houses. We flew from Glasgow in a very small plane which landed on the beach. For some reason it circled the strand for ages before it touched down and I felt exceedingly air-sick. As I staggered from the plane the friend who was meeting us remarked: "There is no doubt about which country you come from – your face is green."

The holiday was quiet, as it was meant to be, and there were plenty of lovely long, windswept walks. Walking has always been a favourite exercise of mine and I still manage to get a few miles in most days even when I'm staying in a city. Indeed, often if I've been too busy during the day, I enjoy walking through the fields alone at night; and many visiting friends have sometimes found themselves press-ganged into wellingtons and marched out into the darkness. They learn to enjoy it – at least our friendships don't seem to have suffered.

Barra was also ideal for cycling, so I hired a bike and cycled contentedly along the island roads. It was October and there was very little sun, but one day I braved the elements and went for a swim in Seal Bay. It was not a misnomer. My father was sitting on a sandbank reading a book while I disported myself in a large sheltered natural swimming pool. Suddenly I heard my father shout – I turned around and there looking into my eyes a few yards away was a large inquisitive brown seal. I'm sure it meant no harm, but I didn't wait to find out.

Another time I had cycled out alone to a different part of Seal Bay and, walking along the deserted strand, I was thinking about a story I'd read of someone who had attracted seals with her singing. I had a good look first to ensure that no one was watching and think I was dotty. Standing at the edge of the sea I began to sing "Bella Signora" – a vocal exercise which consists of a rising arpeggio on the first four syllables with a descending scale on the last syllable. The phrase is repeated a note higher each time. After the first phrase I waited expectantly. After a few seconds a head appeared in the water. I tried a note higher. Another head bobbed up. I continued until I could go no higher and counted in all twelve pairs of eyes staring soulfully at me. So the singing worked. I think a seal has a beautiful head. If I was to have a fishy pet it would be a seal.

Back in Dublin I recorded a number of programmes for Radio Éireann. Since my return from Australia I had had numerous concert offers but I declined them.

I did travel to New York once to make an appearance on the 'Ed Sullivan Show', arranged by Al Grossman. My friends the Clancy Brothers were appearing on the programme, too, as was Brendan O'Dowda, whom I was meeting for the first time. Mr Grossman was attentive and took me to different folk clubs of note in Greenwich Village. He had a large collection of interesting records in his apartment and it was there that I heard for the first time the glorious voice and artistry of Joan Baez. It was her first album, just out, and she was nineteen. I'd never heard anything to match it and I was instantly hooked. Magic. For years afterwards, I raved about her to everyone I met. It wasn't until December 1977, after one of her sell-out concerts in London, that I met her briefly backstage. Later, in the ITV programme, 'This is Your Life', with Éamonn Andrews, I was honoured by her presence on the screen in a tele-recorded tribute to my own work.

During that visit to Mr Grossman's apartment Odetta walked in, very surprised to find me there. She said: "Oh . . . oh . . . oh you're beautiful . . . er, I mean your *record* is beautiful." She was referring to "Songs of Ireland" which had become well known in the United States by then.

Mr Grossman was disappointed in what seemed to him to be my lack of ambition. I just wasn't interested in getting further work. After seeing me sprint up the steps to his apartment he remarked wistfully: "Won't you even let me make you into a star *athlete*?" I just laughed. All this combined with occasional remarks I made in conversation, must have led him to believe that I was planning something special or "taking that last mystical step" as he referred to it in the taxi on the way to the airport.

Towards the end of 1961 Ireland was preparing to set up its own television station. It opened for the New Year on 31 December. I was asked to take part in the opening night, which I did, doing a number of songs accompanying myself on the harp. I never saw that programme as I was in Africa that night visiting my brother Dermot and his family. He lived in Apapa with Colette and their two sons John and Mark. My father was travelling with me and we had planned to stop off in Rome for a couple of days. The Prior at the Irish Dominican House of San Clemente knew we were coming and had arranged a surprise private audience for us with Pope John XXIII. Unfortunately, because our plane was late we missed the audience. Eventually we reached Lagos.

It was a pleasant few weeks in West Africa. I hadn't told my brother anything about my future plans, and didn't see him again until 1978 when he walked into the television studio for Eamonn Andrews' programme 'This is Your Life'. By then he was living in Alberta, Canada.

The material for the albums was now ready to be recorded. Once the recording was over I could enter Stanbrook as soon as they gave the green light. I thought it would be appropriate to enter sometime in Lent, since penance was a sizeable ingredient in my vocation. But I was told that some time in Easter week, in April, would be more convenient for the Benedictines. In March I recorded forty-four songs, eighteen of them Scottish and the remainder Irish, for what were eventually to be released as 'Mary O'Hara's Ireland'; 'Mary O'Hara's Scotland' and 'Mary O'Hara's Monday, Tuesday – Songs for Children'. Material for the latter album was chosen with children in mind, but the songs are by no means children's songs. The recording took place in the basement of a house in Lower Mount Street in a small studio owned by Prionsias MacAonghusa, a well-known Dublin journalist and broadcaster. The whole operation took a matter of days – at a cost of £183. Since there was no immediate plan for making records from these tapes, I left them in the care of MacAonghusa, a decision which later led to untold confusion when the studio changed hands.

My last public performance before entering the monastery was on St Patrick's Day March 17 1962, when I appeared as soloist with the Radio Eireann Symphony Orchestra, singing three songs: 'My Lagan Love', 'Roisin Dubh' and 'Cucúín a Chuaichin'.

I entered Stanbrook on April 23 1962 to begin the final chapter in my life – or so I thought at the time. It was at the same time the definitive end of a singing career and I had absolutely no regrets; in fact I was relieved. The only unfinished business was lying in the basement of a Dublin studio gathering dust, and this proved to be more of a headache than anyone could possibly have anticipated. At the time my agent had failed to interest any of the major record companies in England, and I was too busy with all the physical preparations for entering the monastery to be bothered with it. I had far more important things to occupy me. I arranged for my father to look after all my business affairs including my income from royalties until such time as I could officially sign everything over to him at my Solemn Profession. In the meantime all my income was to go to him to do with it as he wished, and I considered it to be no longer mine.

Over the next few years, beyond the walls of my sequestered world, the saga of the "Mount Street tapes" dragged quietly on, punctuated by long intervals of silence. Eventually, it was decided at Stanbrook that I had to listen to these tapes and judge for myself. As they could not be played at the monastery I had to go to London to hear them under proper studio conditions. Sister Raphael accompanied me and the result of the trip was that in 1972 I signed a contract with Emerald Records of Belfast, whose records were manufactured and distributed by Decca. All the songs on the original "Mount Street" master tapes have been included on three albums, now available in many countries.

9   Stanbrook

The spirit entered at all doors,
• awake and fresh.

From the poem by
RICHARD SELIG
"Meditation in Lent"

Don't talk to me about packing. Even the anticipation of it, trying to decide what to put in and what to leave behind, wearies me; I generally end up taking more than is necessary and leaving some essential things behind. In packing for Stanbrook I was spared all this. I'd been sent a list – not unlike the boarding-school list of my childhood. So it was just a question of ticking off the various items: one black dress, two pairs of black shoes, long black stockings, and so on. For laundry purposes each person was allotted a number, and mine, which was number five, had to be stitched on all my belongings. This took some time.

Neither my sister, Joan, nor my brother, Dermot, knew then about my decision. I felt that they would not have understood. In Dublin, apart from my father, Sister Angela and Mother Ambrose at Sion Hill were the only ones I confided in. The last thing I wanted was publicity; and so the fewer who knew the better. Those who did know about my plans accepted my decision, though I suspected that some of them did so with reluctance. Up to this time my father was staying in lodgings in Dublin. Thinking it would be better for him to have a place of his own after I had gone away, the two of us moved into a flat out in Monkstown on the outskirts of Dublin. It was from there that I left for Stanbrook.

Some days before I travelled to England, I telephoned my good friend, Seán Óg O'Tuama (whose claisceadal music sessions I'd been attending on and off since my return from Australia), to see if he would give me a lift to the airport. I could have got a taxi, but I wanted to see Seán Óg and tell him what I was doing. When he arrived and saw the trunk full of black clothes, he was puzzled. "Where on earth are you going?" he asked. When I told him, he was stunned. He and my father saw me off at Dublin airport and I left Ireland, as I thought then, forever. I wasn't to meet Seán Óg again or hear from him, until one day twelve years later he turned up unexpectedly at Stanbrook to see me. (It was exactly two months before I was to leave the monastery, though at the time I did not know that I would be leaving.)

As the plane took off over the Irish Sea towards England, I settled back in my seat and thought to myself that this was to be my last plane journey. It was the first step of a spiritual journey for which I had been consciously preparing for over four years. I felt a deep peace.

I stayed overnight in the Manchester area to attend to some family business and was joined the next day by my father on the final lap of my journey. They were expecting me at the monastery by late afternoon, but whatever happened en route I did not reach Stanbrook until about 9pm, after Compline, when the community was about to retire for the night. Not for nothing was I subsequently referred to as "the late Sister Miriam".

My father deposited my luggage in the front hall and, after a few words with the Abbess in the parlour, I gave him a quick embrace and said good-bye. "I'll see you in the morning," he said and went off to stay overnight in the village.

Then I did what countless people who aspired to live the Benedictine life have done down the centuries – I knocked on the enclosure door for formal admittance.

Lady Abbess asked: "What have you come for?"

And I replied: "To give myself as completely as possible to God."

I then stepped across the threshold into the monastic enclosure. From there Lady Abbess led me to the church where the community was assembled and chanting psalms. After a few moments of silent prayer kneeling at the altar steps Lady Abbess put me into the charge of the Novice Mistress who, over the next few years, was to initiate me into the ways of Benedictine monasticism. Afterwards, each member of the community in turn gave me the welcoming kiss of peace and Lady Abbess bestowed on me the name Sister Miriam.

The Assistant Novice Mistress, or Zealatrix as she is called, brought me to my cell in the novitiate, a building separate from the main part of the monastery. My cell was a small room about ten by twelve feet with a high window from which trees were visible. It was adequately if plainly furnished – a bed, a table, a chair, a priedieu, a small cupboard and a bookshelf on the wall. Above the priedieu hung a wooden crucifix. The curtains were dark green, the walls off-white and the bare floor of polished wood. My luggage was brought to the cell door by a couple of smiling novices. Neither of them spoke, nor did they enter my cell. Soon all was beautifully quiet except for the sound of an odd bird trying to settle down for the night. Before long I followed suit and did not hear another thing until I was called at six o'clock the next morning.

Having dressed in my black outfit with a short black veil trimmed with white covering my long reddish-brown hair (pinned up), I was taken down to church by a fellow postulant, a tall, quiet girl. (What a relief from then on never to have to ask myself each morning, "What shall I wear today?") After Mass I was led to the refectory. There I was struck by the beautiful adzed oak tables which ran the length of the room. At the west end of the refectory sat the Abbess, and on either side of her the Prioress and Subprioress. At the opposite end of the room stood the reader's pulpit.

After breakfast I went with Lady Abbess to the parlour to see my father. Clearly, it was a shock to him that I was already well and truly 'inside' with a double grille dividing us. I think he'd been expecting me to be able to stroll outside in the garden with him. For a while the three of us chatted briefly and cheerfully together, which I think helped him. Soon it was time for him to go. We exchanged good-byes through the grille and he departed, making a valiant effort to hide his emotions. He had known from the time he got news from me of Richard's death that I'd wanted and intended to enter a monastery, but he didn't

194

believe I ever would. He was very lonely at my going away, but wanted only my happiness. For the next twelve years he was to visit me occasionally as the Rule allowed, looking forward eagerly to coming to Stanbrook. He used to refer to those trips as his journeys to the 'Happy Valley.'

My recollection of the rest of that first day in Stanbrook and indeed of the ensuing weeks is scant. It is much more difficult to get into a monastery such as Stanbrook than it is to get out of it. A person is admitted only after the authorities are satisfied about the person's suitability and motivation. At that time, it was customary for those who wished to join the community to make several visits to the monastery beforehand. They were given the opportunity to discuss their aspirations with certain members of the community delegated by the Abbess. On admission the person became a postulant; after about six months she became a novice, a year later a Junior and, after three more years, she was solemnly professed as a Benedictine nun. Of course things did not always work out that smoothly. One or other of the parties may have had second thoughts and the various stages would be lengthened or, as happened in very many cases, the candidate left or was asked to do so. "They comes and they goes, but they mostly goes," as someone once put it.

The sixties was a period of change throughout the entire Catholic Church, and the spirit of Vatican Council II affected many aspects of monastic life. Some time after I first entered and while I was still in the novitiate, changes were gradually being introduced, especially with regard to the vernacular in the Liturgy and the daily timetable. The day began at 5am with personal prayer and spiritual reading until 6.25 when the community assembled in church to recite together the Morning Office. Then work between 9.15 and 12.25. All came together in Church for the recitation of the Midday Office. Dinner was in the refectory at 1pm. This was the main meal of the day, and it was followed by a period of relaxation when the community met and chatted with one another about matters of common interest. There was a rule of silence – not a vow – and this was the only time during the day that we talked, except if one's work or charity required one to speak.

The afternoon was divided between work, prayer and study.

195

On some days of the week a half hour out of the work period was devoted to either choir practice or a conference given by the Abbess. There was sung Vespers at 6pm followed by spiritual reading or prayer and then supper at 7.30pm. Compline was sung at 8.15.

The Stanbrook community at the time of my entry numbered about seventy people, including those in the novitiate: myself, another postulant, one novice and about three Juniors. New people were coming and going all the time. In the morning the novitiate had various conferences which dealt with the Rule of St Benedict, theology, the scriptures, the monastic spiritual writers, church and monastic history. Philosophy was added later. We were also trained in the ways of prayer, in the customs and traditions of the house, and in Gregorian Chant. Every moment was accounted for and when the end of the day came I was tired out, but I felt it was a fruitful tiredness. This is what I had expected and indeed wanted.

I believed that I had a call to the monastic life, but I was fully prepared to leave this to the judgement of my superiors. I was also aware that my first five years in the monastery must be a period of probation. Richard's death and the circumstances surrounding it had made me detached from earthly things. It had caused me to realize with unusual clarity how brief and fleeting this life is – whether one lives to be twenty-seven (as Richard did) or ninety-seven. If you are a Christian, then the death of someone you love more than life itself can be a tremendous eye-opener, if you have been with them through their dying. You see things and events in their proper perspective, as they really are. Only essentials matter – all the rest falls away. You stop being preoccupied with ephemeral things and you think a lot about death, especially your own death. And strange as it may seem you can become more alive and sensitive to the enduring things of the spirit. As Ladislaus Boros writes:

But to be forgetful of death is to be forgetful of life, whereas thinking of one's death is an act in which life begins once more to appear as a source of light. A man who knows death also knows life. The converse is true, too: the man who is forgetful of death, is forgetful of life also.

I went into Stanbrook to prepare for death. Once, in conversation with my brother-in-law, Frank, I must have said something about my desire to get to heaven as soon as possible. Gently he asked me if I had a death-wish. I hadn't thought of it in those terms. Frank did not know at that time, or indeed until after I had entered Stanbrook, of my intention to go into a monastery.

How often one hears a vocation to the monastic life described, nay decried in negative terms such as "turning one's back on" or "running away from" something, anything, even life itself. A vocation is a call – derived from the Latin *vocare* – and one responds to or answers a call by turning and moving towards the caller. St Benedict even talks about running towards God and eternal life. To the eyes of non-faith this desire for eternal life may seem very like a death-wish, but to those who believe, it is in fact a life-wish.

Though I had an independent nature, I yet had a strong desire to be under obedience. I saw my future monastic superiors as God's agents and the monastic life an unparalleled means of being sure – as sure as one can be – that at every hour of each day and night I was doing His will. It was for this reason alone that I'd looked forward to going to Stanbrook. Ever since Richard's death, through all the ups and downs, I'd maintained an imperturbable inner calm (which is not to say that many a time I did not give way to impatience), for I knew that soon, very soon, all the fuss and scramble of everyday life outside would be put behind me forever. I would then try to concentrate on *the one thing necessary*. I was prepared to put up with anything and everything however difficult. Monastic life, as I see it, is a means of jettisoning bit by painful bit unnecessary 'baggage', so that, getting progressively lighter, one's pace becomes correspondingly swifter. In themselves the monastic life and its traditions held no attraction for me. That they were all a means to an end was something of which I was keenly aware. Going into the monastery was also my way of saying thank you to God for all the good things he had showered on me. He had given me a measure of rare happiness that I had no right to expect.

That first summer came and went. I prayed and I studied and I worked in the fields, learning new things all the time. I grew accustomed to the monastic way of life, though I never got attached to it, nor did it ever become easy or routine. Soon the initial six months were up and it was time to take the next step. For my part I was prepared to continue, but the decision of accepting me as a novice remained with the Abbess and the community. It was plain to me that I had made the right decision in coming to Stanbrook, but if my superiors had told me, as they had countless others, that I must leave, I would not have been upset. Perhaps Richard's death had schooled me to bear any disappointment. 'There's nothing more the sea can do to me now,' the mother lamented in Synge's *Riders to the Sea*.

I didn't in any way look forward to my 'Clothing', the word used to signify the putting on of the religious habit by the novice. This entitled the novice to live like the rest of the community but in no way obliged her to stay or to take vows. A white veil distinguished the novice from the nuns who wore black.

A day came when the Abbess and her council met to decide whether I should be allowed to take the next step and become a novice. As was the custom I waited in church while they deliberated and, after some time, I was summoned into their presence, to be informed that I had been accepted. I did not expect to be emotional about it, but I was. I found myself weeping with gratitude. As I was hurrying back to the novitiate after I'd been given the news, I met one of the older nuns on the stairs. Misconstruing my tears she put her arms around me to console me, saying: 'Poor Sister Miriam, have you not been accepted?' Giving her a quick hug, I whispered that all was well.

The Clothing was an important milestone on the journey towards becoming a fully-fledged Benedictine. Much was made of it in the community and it was a day of general rejoicing. The would-be novice was allowed to invite her family and a few close friends to be present. December 8, the Feast of the Immaculate Conception, which was a major feast in the Roman Catholic Church, was the date chosen for the ceremony. It was a bitterly cold day. The land had been covered with snow for weeks and a great stillness had settled on everything outside. I did not invite many people. My father, my sister, Joan, and her husband, Lesley Scott-Moncrieff, John and Mary Gray Hughes all watched the ceremony from the extern chapel. They were amused when in the homily, the officiating Abbot reminded me that I had come to an 'approved' school. He was referring to a phrase of St Benedict's about a monastery being a school of the Lord's service, but to my uninitiated guests the term was synonymous with a school for delinquents.

After the Clothing the guests had tea in the parlour, where I joined them for a while, the double grille dividing us. It was a rather awkward get-together, since few of my guests knew one another and when I joined them it was not possible to converse with everybody at once. The bell summoning the community to prayer put an end to the visit, which had lasted about an hour, and as the visitors went off into the night I got ready for my first Vespers as a novice. I was to be a novice for one year. The monastic habit now replaced the black dress which I'd worn daily for the previous eight months. It had been specially made for me in Dublin, (my 'little black number') and I'd never got such satisfaction and wear out of a garment before. It had become quite diaphanous in parts.

In a monastery time seems to fly more quickly than it does elsewhere. My daily routine as a novice was substantially the same as it had been when I was a postulant. I've always disliked having things on my head for any length of time and for that reason the headgear one had to wear as a novice was something I was never wholly comfortable with. It was a complicated pin-up job which I never seemed to get quite right, and the absence of mirrors in the monastery didn't help matters. After a while, I thought I'd got the hang of it, but obviously not, for one day the novice mistress was asked by the Abbess to "see what you can do with Sister Miriam's veil to make her look less like a skinned rabbit." So I must have looked a lot less fetching than I thought. I was still not used to doing without mascara and lipstick. Of course, I didn't mind while among the community but later, when on the occasions I had to see visitors in the parlour, I felt exposed. Vanity dies hard. Visits were restricted in number, something for which I was very grateful, and I believe that most members of the community felt the same way; they were also generally of short duration, as indeed they had to be, as they tended to disrupt monastic routine.

In one of her letters to me before I went to Stanbrook, Lady

Abbess asked me to bring my harp. It hadn't been my intention to do so, but since it seemed to be the Abbess's wish, I looked on it as a sort of first step in obedience. A few months after I'd arrived was Lady Abbess's Feast Day, and I was asked if I would sing for the community. I was in a quandary. There was little or no time for the amount of practice I felt was necessary to give a proper performance. Besides, the life was very tiring and one of Sister Angela's great maxims was: don't sing when you're tired. I'd been encouraged by the Novice Mistress to get out the harp and practise, but I'd never felt comfortable about it. There were other things I preferred to do. Besides, had I not made the studied decision to give up singing and playing completely? My present way of life took up all my time and energy. I did perform for the community on Lady Abbess's Feast Day, but after that I was not to sing for them for several years. In the novitiate I was prevailed upon by my fellow novices and Juniors to sing for them on a few occasions, but when they realized how reluctant I was, they soon stopped asking, and the harp was put away safely in the attic.

My presence at Stanbrook received no publicity whatsoever, a wish of mine that was also in keeping with the monastery's policy. Even regular visitors to the Abbey and people like John McEvoy, whose work on behalf of the monastery brought him daily into the enclosure, did not get to know that I was there. I did not then know John McEvoy or his wife, Connie, but they had a record of mine from the early days. They have since become my good friends and only recently did John tell me of an incident that happened during my first year inside. One day in summer when he was passing the novitiate, he heard coming through an open upstairs window the sound of the harp, and recognized the voice of Mary O'Hara, familiar to him from his record. Somewhat surprised at hearing a record being played in the novitiate, he went home and mentioned to Connie: "Some clot in the novitiate has a record of Mary O'Hara. Whoever she is keeps starting and stopping. That's certainly not going to do the record any good." What he'd heard, of course, was Sister Miriam Selig practising. It was a long time after that before he found out that I was in the monastery – though he must have seen me around often enough.

After a year as a novice I was asked whether I wished to take the important step of Simple Profession, to become a Junior. The Junior makes vows for three years: stability, conversion of manners and obedience – *stabilitas, conversio morum et obedientia*. Implicit in those are vows of chastity and poverty. Stability commits the person to living the rest of her life in a particular monastery; conversion of manners means that the person turns away from worldly attitudes to embrace the Benedictine Rule and to concentrate on the single-minded search for God. At the time of Simple Profession the Junior receives a black veil in place of the white one. After I'd made known my desire to take vows, the Abbess convened the council to discuss my suitability; having ascertained the approval of the rest of the community, the verdict was communicated to me. Lady Abbess chose February 10 to be my Profession Day. What she did not know was that February 10 was the anniversary of my engagement to Richard, seven years earlier. The happy coincidence I interpreted as a divine endorsement of what I was doing, and I was deeply moved.

After making my Simple Profession, I experienced a completely unexpected sense of inner freedom. This may seem odd since I was, after all, binding myself more firmly to a singularly disciplined and regular way of life. I viewed it in the way I had viewed my marriage. It imposed restrictions but it granted freedom – freedom to love one person totally and in return to be likewise loved. Freedom, in order to be enjoyed, must be somehow circumscribed.

My three years as a Junior passed quickly and were outwardly as uneventful as my novice year. In the life of a nun the adventure is within. The ordinary everyday happenings in a monastery don't make for exciting reading, but beneath the seemingly even tenor and sometimes even dullness of daily living can occur spiritual revolutions and personal discoveries. As a cradle Catholic I had been brought up with an emphasis on what are sometimes referred to as devotions, such as the recitations of the Rosary, the stations of the cross and other time-honoured extra-liturgical practices. There is nothing wrong with this type of spirituality, but it is not the Benedictine one, which emphasizes worship, especially through the liturgy, which is the Church's corporate prayer. One day I happened upon a book in the novitiate library which made me see that I was practically ignorant of the deeper meaning of the Mass, the Eucharistic celebration which is the heart of Catholic worship. This realization prompted me to explore the mystery in greater depth, under the guidance of the Novice Mistress. My studies soon led me to the 'discovery' of the Resurrection, the overwhelming significance of which had escaped me until then, and with this a spiritual joy I had never known before entered my life. Previously, my general approach to things religious had a somewhat sombre flavour about it. This could well be attributed to the Jansenism which permeated Irish Catholicism, dating from the days when the Irish clergy had perforce to receive their training in a Jansenistic environment on the continent of Europe. When for political reasons (to stem the flow of revolutionary ideas from continental seminaries), the Irish Church was eventually permitted to establish a national seminary of its own at Maynooth, the Jansenistic tendency was confirmed. Whatever the explanation, I certainly had a strong puritanical streak in me, and I am grateful to Stanbrook for rinsing it out of my system.

I remember my mild irritation during the first conference Lady Abbess gave in Easter Week on the day after my arrival. She talked a lot about joy. I recall sitting there in the Chapter House with the rest of the community thinking to myself: "What is she going on and on about joy for?" In those early days, mine was very much a cross-orientated spirituality: I seemed to have got stuck at Good Friday. The Easter Liturgy meant nothing to me. I'd never even attended the Easter Vigil before I'd entered.

It was during my third year or so in Stanbrook, when my whole outlook was becoming increasingly coloured by my new-found understanding of the Resurrection, that I started to re-read Richard's poems. A selection, edited by Peter Levi, had just been published in Ireland. There were some early poems which I didn't understand. One morning, as I was sweeping the stairs, some lines from one such hitherto impenetrable poem called 'Eros' kept going through my head. Suddenly I saw meaning in them. For me the whole poem, every line of it, was all about the death and resurrection of the God-man Christ, though the author may not have in any way intended it

as such. Some years later I set it to music, and have since recorded it on an album.

> *Eros*
> His heart held a hundred roses,
> Roses red as thundering Mars:
> His heart was a city full of love,
> Assaulted city, sieging stars.
>
> The rain that fell all day
> From heaven, down from heaven falling,
> Could not melt his heart away
> Nor flood, that red vine killing.
>
> Green stones, dark earth, O love!
> The lips of all the world foretelling,
> Red lips foretell that city's fall
> And darkness falling over all.
>
> With falling dark the milky stars,
> Cold white stars encircled him:
> Around the city heaven's wars
> Did rend him limb from limb.
>
> But limb by limb revived, O love!
> The single sun came up once more.
> A strange explosion in the heart
> Did, in her arms, that vine restore.

All through the novitiate years, the emphasis was on training.
After five years, the candidate will have had ample opportunity
to satisfy herself that she wants to spend the rest of her life in
that one monastery. The authorities, too, and the community
as a whole had to be satisfied about her suitability. Fitting in
with the others was obviously important, and the community
wasn't likely to vote for someone who was self-centred and
incurably introverted.

From the start I threw myself into the life of the novitiate,
shrinking from nothing, but having one of my biggest strug-
gles with 'joining in' with the other postulants, novices and
Juniors. During the hour or so of relaxation, conversation did
not come at all easily. There were times when the Novice

Mistress had occasion to point out to me that I should be making more of an effort to participate. One was expected to contribute to the general conversation even if one didn't feel like it or found the subject of no interest. Somebody once made the remark: "Mention the subject of music and Sister Miriam will clam up." I also never talked about Richard or my marriage, though he occupied my mind constantly. People seemed willing to talk about their families and books being read in the refectory and so on. There was neither radio or television and I for one didn't miss them for a moment. Occasionally a newcomer to the novitiate brought odd scraps of information. For instance, one day it was mentioned that Marilyn Monroe had committed suicide. Conversation lingered briefly on the subject, but the Novice Mistress had never even heard of her. The first time I heard about the Beatles was when a postulant gave us a bar or two of 'Eleanor Rigby'. I thought the words were weird, but poignantly intriguing. I wasn't to hear mention of them again for over ten years until I left Stanbrook, when I was lent one of their records. A song of theirs is on an album of mine now.

It's not until one has been away for some time that changes in style become noticeable. The first long-haired young man I saw was in the enclosure doing some brick-laying. He fractured the silence of the monastery with blaring music from his transistor; we were all relieved when the work was completed.

Around that time I had been mending a cloche in the garden, filling in the broken bit with old newspaper to keep out the snow. My eye caught sight of a large photograph of what must have been a pop group. The figures had long very fuzzy hair, and I couldn't believe they were men until I read the names. This shouldn't have caused any astonishment because some of my more bohemian acquaintances in the late fifties tended to wear their hair longish.

With monastic silence, I was in my element. No strain or struggle. I used to contend that my silence was more eloquent than my words. I think that like the plants I did my growing in silence. I still love it – I am one of those people who find it easier to pray in an ambience of silence. Not the negative, sterile silence referred to in Paul Simon's song "The Sound of Silence", which is a wall preventing communication between people, but the positive fruitful silence so beloved of the Desert Fathers and their descendants, one of whom celebrates it as follows:

Behold my beloved I have shown you the power of silence
How thoroughly it heals and how fully pleasing it is to God
Wherefore I have written you to show yourself strong in
this work you have undertaken
So that you may know that it is
By silence that the saints grow
By silence the power of God dwelt in them
And because of silence that the mysteries of God were made
known to them . . .

In the *Philokalia* one of the Greek Fathers says: "I see that you, too, have been wounded by the arrow of the love of silence." Silence is rather like prayer: the more you practise it, the easier it becomes. From the moment I was introduced to the writings of the Desert Fathers I felt at home. The asceticism and emphasis on silence and inner solitude which characterized their spirituality had a strong appeal for me. I used sometimes jocosely to refer to myself as a Desert Widow.

People often equate monastic living with austerity and penance, and it is true that self-abnegation plays an important rôle in the disciplined life of a monk or nun. One can do penance to make amends for past misdeeds, but the asceticism practised in a monastery is primarily aimed at setting the spirit free – establishing the power of mind over matter so that the individual can more easily concentrate on seeking God. The right motivation is important when it comes to the practice of penance, which should always be undertaken for the love of God. Thomas Merton wrote that in a monastery an austere discipline is required so as to preserve the spiritual leisure, the *otium sanctum* which is the only legitimate business, *negotium*, of the monk:

Hence . . . the chief obligation of a monk is to preserve for himself a dimension of awareness which cannot be authentic without a certain depth of silence and interior solitude.

*   *   *   *

The daily living out of the Rule of St Benedict was in itself penitential. At certain times of the year such as Lent and Advent, we
fasted. In those days I had a very large, healthy appetite and
wholeheartedly enjoyed my meals. However, I threw myself
into the fasting with relish but, extremist that I am, tended at
times to overdo things. Already I was setting myself a regime
which in the end I could not sustain. From the beginning I
tended to tax my strength too much. Not for me the Golden
Mean. The hours for sleep were adequate for the normal adult,
but being so highly strung I have always needed more than the
average amount. Before I entered I realized that in the monastery I might not be able to get enough sleep, but I gladly welcomed the opportunity for further self-denial. I declined the
extra hours of rest that I could legitimately have availed myself
of. The result was that, over the years, the lack of sufficient
sleep was taking its toll. I was developing migraines, fibrositis
and sinusitis, but I kept it all to myself. I presumed other
members of the community suffered similar ailments, and I did
not want to appear a softy by reporting mine.

A very important subject for study during the novitiate was
Gregorian Chant. As I mentioned earlier, I was never en-
amoured of the Chant, nor did I grow any fonder of it with the
passage of time. It seemed to me that it never quite got off the
ground, perhaps because the mystique surrounding its interpretation prevented the voice taking wing. Singing the
Chant in choir was, for me, a bit like dragging heavy chains.
Surely it should be possible to *sing* the Chant in a detached and
objective way without depriving it of life? It is a vehicle of
prayer. I approached the Chant as I did all the other exercises:
determined to do things the way I was told. I found that there
was an unspoken assumption that there were two kinds of
vocal music: song and the Chant – that they occupied different
worlds and therefore the Chant should not be treated as a song
would be. I willingly subordinated my singing instincts and
used my voice as the collective body was directed to do. It was a
strain. Whenever the choir mistress during choir practice
rebuked the community for bad singing, I always took it personally, though I never betrayed my true feelings.

The difficulties did not decrease as time went by, but in those earlier days I had the resilience not to let choir practice and other irritations get me down. Having said all that, and acknowledging the unavoidable strain associated with choir, my time as a novice and a Junior was one of contentment and fulfilment, shot through with joy.

Members of Enclosed Orders often have wide-ranging interests, and appropriate hobbies were encouraged. People took up carpentry, botany, bird-watching, painting, flower-arranging and, above all, gardening. Each novice was given a flower garden to tend. I was not a successful gardener. One day a particular nun watched from a distance in horrified silence as I sedulously uprooted an entire bed of lily-of-the-valley believing they were weeds. To add insult to injury, it was she who had caringly planted those flowers there some time previously. Another time I was so anxious to be *seen* to have flowers blossoming in my garden that, unable to wait, I went off and found some fully grown foxgloves which were flourishing by the roots of an acacia tree, and transplanted them in my patch. I did not realize that others consider them weeds. But then again what are weeds but flowers in the wrong place?

A number of us grew interested in the night sky. I suppose one could call it astronomy. We shared books on the subject, and it was all very fascinating. It was a study in accord with the spirit of silence and very conducive to prayer. On the one occasion we were lent a telescope, we went out with the Novice Mistress into the garden to observe the sky. It was a beautiful, unclouded night with a full moon. I had the first go with the telescope, but try as I might I was unable to locate the moon. By the time we'd got over our fit of laughing our limited time was up and we had to return the telescope, and we still hadn't found the moon. I continued my star-gazing, but from then on using the naked eye.

My discovery of the Resurrection led to an all-consuming preoccupation with the mystery of the Parousia (Christ's Coming in Glory), of which the rising sun is a powerful analogy. My interest, therefore, was not confined merely to the heavens at night, but extended also to the sky at dawn. No words can describe the spiritual thrill and feeling of expectancy and longing which the beauty of a rose-coloured sky at dawn can provoke. Advent, my favourite liturgical season, produces some spectacular sunrises.

My father once asked me what I would do if I wasn't finally accepted in Stanbrook. "I would look for a place where they accepted rejected nuns," I replied. I meant it, too. After Richard died, it was as if all doors were closed except one, my own door, the only door for me – and the name on that door was monastery. I did not attempt to try the other doors because they held no interest for me. From the moment I walked into Stanbrook there was no doubt in my mind but that this was what God wanted of me. This was how I was meant to seek and hopefully go on finding Him. "You would not seek me if you had not already found me." Therefore as my novitiate ended and the time for my permanent commitment to the monastic life approached, there was no soul-searching on my part. I was content and had found joy in the life I had chosen.

I was accepted for Solemn Profession. The ceremony took place, as is customary, three years to the day after Simple Profession, on February 10 1967, the eleventh anniversary of my engagement to Richard. It was also the tenth anniversary of my first American recital in the Phillips Gallery in Washington, DC, of which Frank C. Campbell had written the very favourable review, concluding with the words: "I have little doubt that she will soon be heard in many halls throughout the land. I have every confidence that if we are lucky enough to hear her decades from now, she will sound as wonderfully fresh as she did on first hearing."

Again, as with my Simple Profession, the ceremony for Solemn Profession was somewhat shortened. During the ceremony, three things were presented to the candidate: a breviary, a cowl and a gold ring.

The breviary is the official prayer book of the Church, consisting mainly of the psalms and readings from the scriptures, which is used daily by the Solemnly Professed. The giving of the breviary by the celebrant symbolized that from then on the professed nun was delegated by the Church to pray in her name for all mankind. It so happened that the breviary being presented to me belonged to an elderly member of the community, Dame Anselma, who had once taught me Latin. She no longer used it as she had become too infirm to say the Divine

Office, even in private.

The cowl was a full-length, loose black garment worn over the habit for the liturgy.

The ring stemmed from the bridal concept. In scripture, the title given to the Church is 'Bride of Christ'. 'The contemplative nun's role is to *be* the Church,' writes Sister Maria Boulding, (*Contemplative Nuns – Are They Wasting Their Lives?* (CTS, London, 1976)) '. . . faithful to Christ, sharing his passover, led by His Spirit and listening to His Word'. Shortly before, I'd had my engagement and wedding rings melted down and made into one plain ring. This was to be the one I was presented with.

On the morning of my Solemn Profession, as the community processed silently into church, the death knell gently informed them that Dame Anselma had gone to God. The measured tolling of the bell on the cold February air added an element of poignancy and drama to the event. The community was parting with one of its members and receiving another into its ranks. I was filled with gladness for Dame Anselma and, quite frankly, longed to swap places with her. But my pilgrimage had its own course to run.

My Profession ceremony took place during Mass. My father, my twelve-year-old nephew, Sebastian Barry, and my great friend, Scomo, were there in the sanctuary, serving as acolytes. At times during the ceremony my father and Scomo gave the impression of being lost, but Sebastian seemed to have had a better grasp of what was required of him.

The whole ceremony took about two hours. "Dame" is the title given to a Solemnly Professed Benedictine nun, and from then on I was known in the community as Dame Miriam. In the general reorganization that followed Vatican Council II, the term "Dame" came to be used less frequently and "Sister" became more common. For the rest of that day and for the next two days, the newly professed kept total silence. This concluded a week of retreat which she had entered prior to the Profession day itself. There was always great rejoicing and a festive air in the monastery at the time of a Solemn Profession.

My three guests stayed in the village until my period of silence ended and I could talk to them in the parlour. It was good to see them, but especially Scomo, whom I hadn't seen for five years. He was very happy for me, but he spoke yet again of his sincere regret that my singing was silenced. It was still a hope of his that I might some day make another recording. Reminding him that I had no desire ever to sing again, and besides it wasn't possible to make recordings in an enclosed monastery, he laughed and poked an imaginary microphone through the grille that separated us. I was to see this man of God, my most dear friend, only one more time when he came for a brief visit a few years later with his second wife, Eileen, and their three tiny sons: Jash, Alan and Simon. He died of a heart attack two months before I left Stanbrook: he had been running to catch the last bus home.

My father and Sebastian were still visiting the day Dame Anselma was buried. This time they were permitted to enter the enclosure to assist at the funeral and practise their new-found skills as acolytes. It was a hard bright day and the burial took place in the morning. The community, following the coffin, processed from the church to the cemetery, carrying lighted candles in their hands. The singing of psalms was interspersed with the recurring promise of Christ's: 'I am the Resurrection and the Life. He who believes in me, though he die yet shall he live, and whoever lives and believes in me shall never die.' It was as much a celebration of life as a ceremony of burial. The ground was still hard from frost, and here and there small clusters of snowdrops had poked their way through the hostile earth. In a short while they, too, would be returning to their blind roots in the ground, seeming to die, but only to rise again the following spring. Nature conjoined with the Liturgy in a homily of hope: "In the end is my beginning." Dame Anselma's body was lowered into the grave. The final prayer was said. The nuns quenched those candles that the wind had not already blown out, and they filed quietly back indoors to go about their monastic duties.

A death in the monastery gave cause for peaceful rejoicing because through this doorway the nun had reached her final goal – eternal life with God. To be sure there was sadness mixed with the gladness, for she would be missed by all those who had loved her. But in our sorrow are we not merely grieving for ourselves? When a nun was dying the whole community prayed for her. After she had died she was laid out in her cell dressed in her habit and cowl, and people took it in turn to come to the cell and pray in silence. The stillness and feeling of peace which filled the cell pervaded the entire house, and on each occasion it was a deeply moving and truly awesome experience.

The community strove to be as self-supporting as possible. There was a large vegetable garden, chicken houses, orchards, a bakery, a laundry, and various workrooms for making the nuns' clothing. The community derived income from the work of its artists, writers and printers. Each year the Abbess and her council met to reallocate the work for that year. In other words to have what Thomas Merton called 'the annual shake-up.' At the time of my Solemn Profession I was working in the garden, which involved a wide variety of jobs. I might be hoeing in the morning and that afternoon could find me driving a huge tractor, an occupation which I greatly enjoyed. Driving the little tractor was even more enjoyable. It moved very slowly and was largely used for cutting grass around the enclosure and for bringing the heavier supplies of vegetables in from the garden to the kitchen.

Once a year every able-bodied member of the community participated in harvesting the potatoes. A farmer came in with a special potato-digging machine and the nuns lined up along the drills putting the potatoes in sacks. During my early days as a postulant, one of my jobs was to go round with a tin picking slugs off the winter lettuces. I gave myself the title 'Inspector of Slugs.' Another congenial chore was looking after the muscovy ducks that lived on the pond with the moorhens. In the spring and summer it was very pleasurable working out of doors in the morning, sometimes as early as eight o'clock, picking vegetables for the kitchen or feeding the ducks. In summertime individuals often prayed outside between 5.30 and 6.25 a.m. Come spring and I was sent to sow seed. I was reminded of the parable of the sower in the Gospel. I punned in a letter to my father that I was still broadcasting.

With the passage of time my knowledge of gardening improved though I still made blunders. On at least one occasion I picked the wrong greens, which caused the long-suffering Sister Jane to remark resignedly: "Between Sister Miriam and the pigeons we won't have many green vegetables this winter." The same sorely tried Sister Jane put me in charge of the cucumber greenhouse where, in my ignorance, I painstakingly watered them to death. In those early days I liked working in the garden because I had plenty of energy. But during the final few years I found any physical work a strain. I had become perpetually tired.

Some time after I was Solemnly Professed, I was made Second Cook. It was interesting, if very hard work. My appetite was something of a byword and having to taste the food we prepared, far from reducing my appetite, only served to whet it. It was challenging work. One's wits were taxed to devise appetizing and varied dishes on a limited budget. The food was plain, plentiful, nourishing and quite varied. Preparing and cooking for about sixty or seventy people was strenuous. Added to that was the regular cleaning of the huge kitchen with its stoves and equipment. There was an added happiness in working in the kitchen because there the service to the community was obviously more visible and therefore personally satisfying. But the ascetic strand was still strongly present in my make-up, and even when I was exhausted, I kept pushing myself to the limit. It was the only way I could operate at that time of my life. To have done less I felt would have been ungenerous.

But the true Benedictine life is one of balance and equilibrium: *virtus stat in medio*. I piled my own private discipline on to the monastic one and five years later the load was to prove too much. It was during this period in the kitchen that I began to lose my appetite: unheard of for me. A general feeling of malaise became the norm, and the migraines were becoming more frequent. Lady Abbess, always careful to ensure that no one was overburdened with work, discussed my duties in the kitchen with me in case they were too much for me. But I was unwilling to admit to the strain. She advised me to make full use of the periods of rest allowed for in the ordinary monastic timetable and was prepared to give me as much extra rest as I needed as well. But my policy was never to accept extras of any kind, or mitigations of the Rule, and so things continued as before. I was in the kitchen for fifteen months.

After my Solemn Profession I was appointed Second Chantress. If anything went wrong with the singing in choir the First Chantress was responsible for putting matters right, and the First and Second Chantresses alternated every other week in leading the singing in choir. This was a trial from the start. I had been content to be in the ranks and would have preferred not to be Chantress. Among other things it is easier to pray the Liturgy when there are no distracting responsibilities. Being somewhat absent-minded at times, it was not unknown for me to intone Friday's hymn on a Thursday. In fact I became so conscious of the possibility of getting my days confused that at the slightest cough I would freeze in my vocal tracks, wondering what it was I had got wrong this time, or expecting the First Chantress to wade in with the correct lines. My début as Second Chantress for Benediction was a bit of a fiasco. It was during Advent so there was no accompanying music. For a long time, especially at the beginning, I'd found singing in choir uncomfortably low and, having a relatively high register, I had been solemnly warned, as Chantress, to avoid starting things too high for the choir.

I am not one of those people who can pick an isolated required note out of the air. Nervous and tense, I watched the celebrant's movements for the right moment to start the singing. Choosing what I felt was a reasonable note I started: "Praise we our God with joy . . ." Dead silence. Heavens, I thought, I've started it too high. Another go, an interval of a good third down. "Praise we our God with joy . . ." At this point I could feel my neighbour shaking with suppressed laughter. Still no sound from the community. I was in a sweat. In a last desperate bid to get a comfortable range for the choir, I did a Paul Robeson, singing virtually *basso profundo* dragging the notes up from my monastic sandals. "Praise we our God with joy . . ." By now my neighbour, convulsed, had hidden her face in her sleeves. Terror-stricken at the fact that the choir still hadn't responded, I looked at the altar and realized I had taken not the wrong note but the wrong cue. Afterwards I put in a request for pitch-pipes which were duly purchased and from then on, I am glad to say, were in regular use – possibly my only lasting contribution to the choir.

I'd always stoutly maintained that it is raised hearts and not voices that the Lord looks for and that if he is willing to put up with out of tune and dispirited singing, the least we can do is to follow his example. Singing in a monastic choir (which must of

213

necessity include many non-singers) is a vehicle for prayer and cannot, and indeed ought not in any way to be compared with professional singing. It has been, and will ever remain a mystery to me why down the ages the Church has encouraged a sung Liturgy expecting non-singers to sing. More extraordinary still is the fact that so many non-singers love to sing.

While I was an ordinary member of the choir and didn't have the responsibility of Second Chantress, choir practice was bearable, but after I became a Chantress I had, among other things, to become much more involved with the technical and non-prayer side of choir and this increased my general problem with tension. During the latter part of the sixties the Catholic Church was experimenting with new forms of liturgy, necessitated in particular by the change from the use of Latin to the vernacular. Here my difficulties regarding the monastic choir were increased. When I entered Stanbrook the community was wholly absorbed in the Latin liturgy and Gregorian Chant. Although in line with the Church's thinking we moved to the vernacular, no radical change could be made concerning the Chant. (Vespers still continues to be sung in Latin at Stanbrook.) It was a period of readjustment and adaptation. The situation for me became acute when, after I was made Chantress, I was also asked along with others to contribute music for the new English Liturgy. The community, including the other members of the music commission, was part of a long tradition steeped in plainsong, which was generally revered and loved. I myself was totally uninfluenced by it. Each member of the commission was given English words to set to music, and while everyone else, especially at the beginning, produced music unmistakably like the Chant, my contribution was a complete departure from it. I felt that Gregorian Chant was meant for Latin and could not happily be wed to another language.

In singing the Chant in choir, the only time I felt free (or permitted myself any vocal liberty) was when I had solo bits, which I treated as my instincts prompted me they should be treated. Once we had Dom Bernard McElligott, an authority on Gregorian Chant, come to Stanbrook for a few days to help with the singing. I was working in the kitchen at the time and was excused from attending his sessions. As Chantress it happened to be my week for singing the Brief Responsory solo at Vespers. Next morning during his first talk Dom Bernard remarked: "Whoever it was who sang the Brief Responsory solo at Vespers last night did it well. That's the way the Chant should be sung." He did not know me, and when the remark was relayed to me later, I must admit I felt vindicated. He was surprised when Lady Abbess told him afterwards that the one he'd referred to did not actually like Plainchant.

After my time in the kitchen, I was appointed First Portress for two consecutive years. This was a considerably less strenuous job than that of Second Cook. It involved fetching nuns when they were wanted on the phone or in the parlour, and letting such people as had to come inside the enclosure in and out. For those two years my afternoon work period was spent in the orchards. In wintertime it was generally relatively light work involving ladders and secateurs. Scything in the summer months and making compost heaps called for more muscle. We had a few compost heaps located around the enclosure and for easier identification I gave them names like Etna and Vesuvius, after various volcanoes. There were times when I climbed apple trees that were quite tall, and the delight of the operation made me wonder why I'd waited till I was thirty before attempting to climb trees.

Once or twice since I'd entered, Lady Abbess had broached the subject of having copies of my records in the monastery, but since I objected to the idea, she did not press the point further. After I'd been there about eight years, someone from the novitiate approached me for permission to play a record of mine which had been lent to them by a visitor. Eventually I reluctantly agreed, and then forgot about the matter. A few days later while I was on duty as Portress, an unsealed package passed through my hands, being returned to a visitor. I recognized the package to contain a record album and it suddenly struck me that it *might* be one of mine. Looking inside, I saw the cover of 'Songs of Érin', the first long-playing record I had made. It was recorded in the Decca studios in London three weeks after I was married, and Richard had been present during the recording. I felt weak at the knees and had a strong urge to listen to it. I spoke to Lady Abbess and told her that I'd opened a package which I shouldn't have opened and that, with her permission, I'd like to listen to the record before I sent it out. So together the two of us listened to the record in her room and I was totally unprepared for my strong emotional reaction. I was strangely affected by what I heard. I'd never listened to my records without feelings of discomfort, being keenly aware of my flaws and imperfections. But this time it was as though I was listening objectively to someone else. I was struck by the sincerity of the performance. The words of "My Lagan Love" and "Danny Boy", for instance, together with the recollection of the circumstances under which it was recorded, combined to move me to tears. Deeply understanding as she was, Lady Abbess let me have "a good cry" as she put it. We discussed the record, and I told her that this was the first time I had come to recognize that my singing probably did give pleasure to many people. Gently she said: "My dear Sister, I've been trying to tell you that for the past eight years." There and then I told her that yes, she could indeed go ahead and buy my albums for the community. Later on when they arrived and were played, many of my sisters came and affectionately thanked me.

Ever since I entered Stanbrook, Lady Abbess had encouraged me to keep up singing and playing the harp, but my heart was elsewhere and I paid no heed to her advice. Only on two major occasions, and under great duress, did I unpack my harp during my first years in the monastery. One was on Lady Abbess's Feast Day and the other was for an ecumenical Carol Service which was held in the monastery Church. In preparation for this latter event, I squeezed in whatever practice I could get in my free time, but I was still acutely nervous. I was to sing and play the harp beside the grille on a narrow step on the sanctuary. Everything went fine during rehearsals, but all of us forgot that during the actual ceremony the grille was opened, and when I came to reach the top notes of the harp I couldn't, because the opened grille had gobbled up all available elbow room. There was a moment of embarrassment for everyone, and something akin to terror for me, while proceedings were halted and stool, chair, harp and nervous nun were re-positioned. But in spite of that the evening was a success and the singing of various local non-Catholic choirs enjoyable.

As a result of listening to my album with Lady Abbess and our subsequent conversation, my interest in singing with the harp started to revive. Now I felt willing to start again, and I took my harp out of its cover in the attic, where it had safely waited, observing the rule of silence for almost eight years. I started re-stringing it in my free time.

Just about then the French Benedictine monk Dom Jean le Clerc came to visit us to give talks. Here was a singularly joyful man, at times patently drunk with the Spirit of the Lord and radiating godliness. During one of his talks he recited:

I danced in the morning when the world was begun
And I danced in the moon and the stars and the sun
And I came down from Heaven and I danced on the earth
At Bethlehem I had my birth.

Chorus:
Dance, then, wherever you may be
I am the lord of the dance, said he
And I'll lead you all wherever you may be
And I'll lead you all in the dance, said he.

I danced for the scribe and the pharisee
But they would not dance and they would not follow me
I danced for the fishermen, for James and John
They came with me and the dance went on.

Chorus

I danced on the Sabbath and I cured the lame
The holy people said it was a shame
They whipped and they stripped and they hung me high
And they left me there on a cross to die.

Chorus

They cut me down and I leap up high
I am the Life that will never, never die
I'll live in you if you'll live in me
I am the lord of the dance, said he.

Chorus:
Dance, then, wherever you may be
I am the lord of the dance, said he
And I'll lead you all wherever you may be
And I'll lead you all in the dance, said he.

The words bowled me over, for they succinctly articulated the

217

things that mattered most to me. A million bells were set ringing inside me. Those words emphasized so beautifully what I think Christianity is all about: the unavoidable presence of the Cross transformed by the certainty and joy of the Resurrection. When I discovered later on that the words were set to music, I could hardly wait to get at the song and adapt the piano accompaniment for the harp.

Around about 1970 the business of the Mount Street tapes was becoming tiresome and distracting and an unavoidable correspondence was eating into my precious time, so much so that Lady Abbess decided I had better listen to them for myself and find out what the fuss was all about. She also felt that they should be available as records for people to hear and enjoy. I contacted John Nice, a professional friend and music publisher in London, to see if he could help by bringing equipment to Stanbrook so that we could listen to them. He explained that this was not possible as they could only be played on special machines which were available only in recording studios. So Lady Abbess further decided that I had better go to London to hear them. I very much wanted to bring Sister Raphael with me for the sake of getting a second, less subjective opinion on the tapes. I felt strongly that Sister Raphael would be indispensable for several reasons, as indeed she proved to be. She was musical, a singer herself, sympathetic towards my work and had shown from her pertinent observations about my records after she'd listened to them that she also possessed a knowledge and understanding of the technical side of the production of records, something which I lacked. Not only was she one of my closest friends, but she was also a good organizer. When I asked Lady Abbess to allow Sister Raphael to accompany me, she was very reluctant at first, but later agreed and sought the necessary permission for both of us. When the leave came through, I approached Sister Raphael. She was very willing to accompany me but asked, "Why me?"

"Because if needs be, you can be bossy," I said. "And you may be called upon to exercise that trait."

Very early on the morning of November 2 1970, the Feast of All Souls, we duly set out for London, driven by Joan Slade, a close friend of Sister Raphael who happened to be visiting the monastery at the time. Joan decided that on the way we should stop off at St Aloysius Church in Oxford, so that we could attend Mass and say the Morning Office there. She was completely unaware that it was in that very church that Richard and I were married, fourteen years previously.

We reached Oxford at about nine o'clock. As we were ready to leave I walked quietly to the front, where I had stood with Richard for the wedding ceremony. Kneeling there in stillness, a powerful feeling of joy swept through me – "the joy that sits still with its tears on the open red lotus of pain."* Gratitude welled up inside me and my whole being silently cried out its thanksgiving and the certainty that one day, with Richard, I would see God face to face. Sister Raphael came to tap me on the shoulder, but seeing my emotion understood at once, and discreetly withdrew. A few minutes later I joined the others and we continued on our journey. For the rest of the trip, although I had a great feeling of peace within, I felt absolutely drained.

In London we were graciously received at Decca House by John Nice, taken to lunch and then into the studio. The deference with which we were treated was, I suspect, mixed with curiosity. It must be rare to have two nuns in black maxis quietly invading the Decca recording studios. Sister Raphael gathered from the chance remark of one of the technicians that the studio we were assigned was not a very good one. Adopting an authoritative, nay, a bossy tone, Sister Raphael made it known that we wanted the very best facilities and in no time had them book a top quality studio for the following morning.

After hearing all the tapes, Sister Raphael had compiled pages of detailed notes, which were enormously helpful. Her assistance was invaluable, as I had known it would be. Someone in Decca had done a very bad job of reprocessing the original mono tapes for stereo. This had been the root of much of the trouble. Now Philip Wade, another of the Decca engineers, very kindly offered to re-do the job properly. John Nice put me in contact with Mervyn Solomon in Belfast, whose company, Emerald Records, had a tie-up with Decca, and the records were eventually released as 'Mary O'Hara's Ireland' in 1973, 'Mary O'Hara's Scotland' in 1974 and 'Mary O'Hara's Monday, Tuesday – Songs for Children' in 1977.

* Rabindranath Tagore: Gitanjali LVIII, *Collected Poems of R. Tagore* (Macmillan, London)

There was one more piece of business to be attended to before getting back to Stanbrook. Photographs would be needed for the sleeves, and we hoped that the studio in Wigmore Street, where I'd had photographs taken around 1960, would still have the negatives. When we got there we found it had changed hands. It wasn't exactly a warm welcome we got from the new owner, whose first words were: "What have you come to beg for?" The hostility was humiliating.

I remained silent and Sister Raphael, with a cool, business-like air, took over. Ignoring his remark, she explained our reason for coming, finishing with: "These photographs were taken some years ago. Of course, she was not in her present disguise then."

It had been an eventful two days and we'd got a lot done, but we were both very relieved to find ourselves on the train heading back to Stanbrook. We had been out of our element and Stanbrook was where we belonged.

As soon as I was Solemnly Professed, my father went off to work in the US. Every now and then, a particularly lovely autumnal leaf, indigenous to whatever part of North America he was in, would arrive from him in a letter. He would pick them up on his rambles, press them and send them on to me. They were so attractive that I took to sticking them on to cards and using them as markers in my choir books. One day Sister Hildelith, who had seen my leaves, asked me if I'd join forces with her and produce some leaf cards for the annual display of the handmade gifts from members of the community for Lady Abbess on her Feast Day, and I agreed. However, shortly after that, Sister Hildelith had to drop out of the project because of other commitments, so reluctantly I had to continue on my own. Eventually the finished leaf cards went on display among all the other community gifts. It was a lovely surprise to discover that not only did Lady Abbess like them, but so did other people including the Cellarer, who asked if I'd produce more for sale in the monastery shop. So I went on happily making leaf-cards in my free time, little thinking that it was to develop into a fascinating hobby. Until then I was not well acquainted with the flora in our grounds, but gradually, I became more knowledgeable. At first I just culled at random, experimenting with lots of things. Although I never used flowers as such, apart from the heads of conparsley, hogweed or fennel, I sometimes picked a flower after the petals had fallen off and the flower had assumed a different appearance. Clematis, for instance, after the petals have dropped off, becomes 'old man's beard.' Pressed at an early stage it remains silky and a shiny pale green for an indefinite time and looks stunningly lovely. Pressed at a later stage it turns out lavender-coloured, very feathery and fragile-looking. I sometimes called these the Eye of God or Ezechiel wheels. To me each leaf I worked with was a new source of wonder because each was a unique creation and something living. The combinations of leaf and paper were myriad. I was in the enviable position of having access to off-cuts, and sometimes whole sheets of what must have been some of the most beautiful hand-made papers in the world, from Japan to England. My sources of supply were all within the monastery walls, and contributions came from the printing room, where they also did Fine Printing, the scriptorium, the bindary and the artists' studio. Besides hand-made paper in white and in various colours, shades and textures, and Japanese veneer, I was also given good quality machine-made papers, sometimes hand-dyed. Soon it became the most fascinating work I've ever done.

A by-product of this was that I became much more observant of the beauties of nature out of doors around the enclosure. Eventually, as the work expanded, I was given a special cell to work in, which I called my 'Leafy Bower', and was also provided with a table, shelves and a guillotine for cutting paper. It was absorbing and enjoyable work. Sometimes I referred to them as my Zen cards.

On the back of each card I wrote 'Maranatha,' which means 'Come, Lord Jesus'. This was the great eschatological cry of the early Christians who longed for Christ's Coming in Glory. Since this longing for the Parousia informed virtually all my thoughts and deeds and I wanted to give my leaf work a direction, this was appropriate. Next to 'Maranatha' I wrote the number of the particular card and 'MS' for Miriam Selig. 'And the leaves shall be for the healing of the nations,' says the Book of Revelations. There was a healing property in the stillness that working with leaves generated. One prayed that the leaves, through their beauty, would bring moments of inner

221

peace to those who received them. As I worked, I was reminded of the words of the leader of the Elves in Tolkein's *The Lord of the Rings*: '. . . for we put the thought of all that we love into all that we make.'

One day we had as a visitor an American psychiatrist named Kaye with a practice in London. A patron of the arts, he had a standing order for the Fine Printing productions from the Abbey Press. As he was about to leave at the end of his visit, he expressed the wish to buy some Christmas cards. He was directed to the display in the shop and had a look at the various printed cards. Seeing my small box of leaves he seized upon them and said excitedly: "This is what I'm looking for." Then he asked to see the person who made the leaf cards, saying he wanted to buy all that were available. Puzzled by all this, I went to the parlour as instructed and was introduced to a quiet, dignified, middle-aged man with the sort of inscrutable face that gives nothing away. But his words were enthusiastic and he began by asking me why I didn't sign the cards. Mystified, I asked why. He replied: "Because each one is a work of art." I felt flattered and very pleased. It didn't end there.

He ordered 150 cards for Christmas. Eagerly I set to and used all my free time to try and meet the order. By then I was making envelopes to match. He didn't seem to mind when I was short of the 150 by the time Christmas came, and was content to have the remainder later. He ordered more for Easter. He wrote to the printer that he liked his leaves so much that he couldn't part with most of them. He had a special cabinet built by another member of the community to house his beautiful Stanbrook books and also my leaf cards. All the cards I made for him were different, as I made a point of never repeating any one.

I met Mr Kaye only once and very briefly in the parlour. His dealing with the monastery was always through the printer. (He died suddenly two months before I left Stanbrook.) In setting myself the task of never making him two of the same cards, I created a challenge which I enjoyed rising to, and it gave my leaf work a focus that it might otherwise have lacked. I thoroughly enjoyed doing this work and it certainly did something for me. It may have even been a substitute for my singing.

One of my most intimate friends in the monastery, Sister Rosemary, looking back on this period, wrote:

The leaves offered a small outlet for your creative gift. Each was a crystallized song. Some were dark laments, some gay little children's songs, some moving love songs. All had the purity and delicacy of your voice and each had its individual rhythm. You took the detailed beauty of each leaf and enhanced it and showed it forth, just as you take those very simple Irish songs "everyone sings" (e.g. "Kitty of Coleraire") and reveal their true beauty and really surprise people with them. Your leaves were like that . . . you revealed something . . . a further dimension was added. You penetrate reality.

All this time the physical troubles were still present and I seemed unable to pull out of them. My appetite was still on the wane and I was sleeping badly. Duties that before I had taken in my stride were becoming increasingly difficult. During Vespers one evening I had a particularly bad migraine attack and I had to leave church and go to my cell, where I became violently ill. Lady Abbess came to see me and for the first time I told her about the recurring headaches I'd been having. She sent me to a homeopathic doctor, who diagnosed the headaches as migraine and gave me a course of treatment. He also diagnosed fibrositis and sent me to an osteopath by the name of Eric Twinberrow. Eric and his wife, Jacqueline, were to become good friends of mine. It was Jacqueline, a charming and vivacious Frenchwoman, who translated 'Scarlet Ribbons' for me into French, and it's now on the album 'Mary O'Hara Live at the Royal Festival Hall'. During the course of conversation sometime during my first treatment, details of my past emerged and Eric casually asked if any of my husband's poems had been set to music. This resulted eventually in my setting 'Among Silence', a prose poem of Richard's, to music. That, too, is on the Royal Festival Hall album.

But my health did not improve, and in fact deteriorated even further. Very concerned, Lady Abbess arranged for a complete medical examination. The result of this was that I was sent away to another Benedictine monastery for a complete rest. Lady Abbess suggested that it would be a good idea for me to take the harp and get some practice done, since I would have plenty of free time. The community there was loving and welcoming and had already been acquainted with my work prior to my entering Stanbrook. While I was there I gave a few recitals for them, brushed up on some of my repertoire and tried my hand at composing. These were pleasant days, but recovery was slow and it was a good two months before the authorities considered me sufficiently improved to return to Stanbrook. The sea air and the wholesome Jersey milk had partly restored my appetite, but sleeping still remained a problem. I had not yet fully unwound.

Back in Stanbrook I was very gradually eased into the monastic routine again. Lady Abbess, a woman of great compassion, had acquired a good deal of medical knowledge during the time before she was elected Abbess, when she worked in the Stanbrook infirmary. The Benedictine Rule is strict but never harsh, and Lady Abbess made every effort to see to it that the work-load was evenly distributed and that everyone had a reasonably balanced day with enough time for spiritual reading and prayer and sufficient rest for the body. This was essential in a life where each day followed a definite pattern and, except for grave reasons, there were no holiday periods.

Lady Abbess now suggested that it would be a very good thing for me psychologically to start doing a bit of singing each day, and so my afternoon work period was devoted to just that. In the morning I worked at making and mending the monastic habits with Sister Rosemary, whose friendship and keen critical mind were to be of such value to me in coming years. Soon I was back into the mainstream of monastic living. Once or twice on very special occasions I gave a recital to the community, and I continued to build up my repertoire of God-songs, for these were the songs that interested me most.

After about a year I had a sufficient number to constitute half an album, and I started to think about the possibility of recording them some day. I discussed this with Lady Abbess, and she thought it would be a good idea, so I approached John Nice once again. He pondered the matter for a time. We corresponded back and forth, and then he decided that I should go ahead with the recording and that he would make all the necessary arrangements. Lady Abbess obtained permission for me to leave the enclosure for three days, and in August 1974, when I had all the material ready, I travelled up to London. It was very warm weather and midday London was full of noise, swarming crowds and traffic fumes – an uncomfortable contrast with my sequestered life in rural Stanbrook. I was being driven by

24

Solemn Profession Day,
Stanbrook, 1967. Mary in
full battle dress, holding
snowdrops that her father
had sent in that morning.
(One of the rare photos
taken of Mary as a
Benedictine).

(*Left to right*) Dames
Philippa Edwards,
Rosemary Davies, and
Raphael Foster of
Stanbrook Abbey.

25

Lord Moyne, Mary's landlord at Biddesden.

Mary at Biddesden, 1975 – the first summer after leaving Stanbrook, 'getting back into practice'.

Dublin, January, 1976. First publicity photo taken after leaving
Stanbrook in October, 1974.

Left: 'The Dinah Shore Show', California, 1978. Dinah Shore (*seated*) Phyllis Diller (*left*) and Billy Weston on Mary's right.

The Royal Variety Show at The London Palladium, 1978. Mary being congratulated by Her Majesty, Queen Elizabeth the Queen Mother. *Also in the picture* the Nolans, Paul Daniels and Arthur Askey.

Gay Byrne, presenting
'Irish Personality of the
Year' at RTE, 1978.

Below: Mary suffering from
'flu after her Albert Hall
concert.

Mary signing albums in Selfridges, London, 1979. (*On Mary's right*) Sarah Hook 'keeping an eye on things'.

'When I told my neighbour I was writing a book'.

'Who's for tennis?' – in the middle of winter, 1979.

36

Right: Presentation of silver disc for the album 'Mary O'Hara at the Festival Hall'. (*Left to right*) Mary, Louis Benjamin and Richard Afton.

Monday, 2nd June, 1980. Presentation of platinum disc for 'Tranquility'.

37

Mary's appearance on the 'This is Your Life' television programme, December 1978.
Above: Mary with Joyce Grenfell. *Below*: (*left to right*) Dermot, Father, Richard Afton, Joyce Grenfell, Mary, Val Doonican, Mary's mother-in-law, Florence Selig; David Murison, Lily, Lady Mackenzie; Sean Og O Trama, Lesley Findlay, Gay Byrne.

John and Connie McEvoy, and in the midst of London traffic, as we started on our way out to Wimbledon where I was to stay for two nights, I was very sick and vomited almost non-stop for an hour into a plastic bag which Connie had had the foresight to arm herself with. On top of this a monstrous migraine made the journey well-nigh unbearable. I was staying at the Ursaline convent and as soon as I arrived I went to bed, but despite the kind ministrations of Sister Infirmarian, I had a sleepless afternoon and night. I was feeling somewhat better next morning and after breakfast went off to the studio. The recording took two whole days. Despite the debilitating effects of all the sickness on the previous day, my stamina was such that I managed to do the recording successfully without a hitch. Somehow I have always managed to steel myself when necessary and rise to occasions, which I suppose is what Déirdre meant when, years before when we were teenagers, she observed that I had a match temperament.

Side one consisted of secular love songs, a mixture of traditional and art songs ending with Richard's poem 'Eros', and side two had God-songs on it. By the time this goes to press it may be on the market under the title 'Mary O'Hara: Recital'.

After two nights in London I was glad to be back in Stanbrook and in the silence of my own cell. For some time I had again been physically at a very low ebb, and, although I was availing myself of every opportunity for rest, my health did not seem to be improving. I was losing weight and I had little appetite for food. One item of food I was able to get down comfortably was lettuce, of which there was an abundance at the time. I consumed it in vast quantities. This did not go unobserved by an American nun sitting nearby, and one day she commented: "Sister Miriam, I can't make it out. You eat like a longshoreman and look like a wraith."

If my body required extra sleep, it also needed exercise of a more athletic kind than was possible in a monastery. I have always found playing tennis to be not only enjoyable but a great means of unwinding, and for years I missed it at Stanbrook. Also lying flat on the floor, a favourite position of mine for relaxing, was not often possible. These may indeed sound like small things, but in my life I have discovered that they generally work for me. Different people have different ways of

225

relieving tension and strain. Thank God I don't break under stress. I seem to be made of very durable substance, but I can get badly bruised.

It was now almost two years since I'd been away for a rest and my general health, far from getting any better, was worsening. I looked badly, or so I was told. As one elderly nun put it: "Darling Sister Miriam, I look at you across the choir and there you are like a lily among the roses." At times Lady Abbess sent for me or came to my cell saying: "I'm very worried about you, Sister Miriam. How are you feeling?" Answering her questions I was able to tell her that now every day was a constant strain and struggle. Things that went against the grain, but which hitherto I was able to ride, so to speak, were getting – and staying – on top of me. I was exceptionally jumpy, reacting accutely to the slightest sudden sound or movement, and there were nights when I didn't sleep at all.

Deeply concerned, Lady Abbess once again arranged for a thorough medical examination. Two different doctors examined me and gave me various tests. The verdict was that I was suffering from severe physical and nervous exhaustion and once again needed complete rest away from my normal monastic routine. I dreaded the prospect, as my previous two-month break had not really solved anything. Out of the blue one of the doctors said: "How do you feel about continuing with the monastic life?" I was stunned, and for about a minute couldn't say anything. Throughout all the times I had been sick, the idea of leaving the monastery had never for a moment entered my head. When I recovered the power of speech, I replied: "I've always found it difficult, but I've no intention of giving it up."

My first reaction was to go immediately to Lady Abbess to report to her what had happened, but she was away at a monastic conference and would not be back for some time. During the following days I prayed and thought about everything the doctor had said. Very gradually I was beginning to see that the doctor's suggestion about leaving merited serious consideration. I discussed the whole matter separately with two of my closest friends in the community, who knew me better than anyone else there, apart from the Abbess.

When Lady Abbess returned, I went to see her and told her all that had happened and of my realization that I should leave. Lady Abbess, ever solicitous about my well-being, patiently listened to my story. After I'd finished, she gently asked: "Does this mean that you are asking to be dispensed from your vows?" This was probably her way of reminding me of the gravity of what I was contemplating doing.

I answered: "Yes."

She said that if I felt sure I was doing the right thing, might it not be wiser to ask for a year's exclaustration (living outside the monastery, but still a member of the Order) before making the final break? I agreed. She then asked me if there was any particular person I would like to talk to before she finally wrote away for permission for exclaustration. When I mentioned Father Jock Dalrymple, who was known to both of us, she readily agreed.

Jock came to see me. Ironically, it was Scomo's funeral which made it possible for Jock to be in the country and available at that time. I suspect dear Scomo had a hand in this for I felt the loving concern of our mutual friend had not ended with his death. After a lengthy discussion with Jock I felt relieved and happy, for he firmly endorsed my decision to leave. Added to all that, the loving support of Sister Rosemary and Sister Raphael and the fact that they, too, concurred with my conclusion that I should leave, meant much to me and strengthened me. It is no easy matter after twelve years to leave a monastery that one expected to live in for the rest of one's life. I still felt I had no permanent roots anywhere, and in some ways that made leaving easier. Having reached my final decision, all the anguish had melted away and was replaced by an extraordinary sense of peace and, above all, a torrent of inner gratitude which words simply fail to describe.

The arrangement was that I would spend my first week-end with a friend of a member of the community, Vera Keenan, who lived about five miles from the monastery. From there I was to go to Cambridge to stay with Jack and Gwyneth Bennett.

The Cellarer always keeps some secular clothes in the attic and from these, on the day before I left, we got together an acceptable outfit which would do for the time being. Lady Abbess could not do enough for me. With her characteristically maternal foresight she had even made an appointment for me at the hairdresser and arranged for me to be driven to Vera's house. It was not until after Lady Abbess had announced to the community that I was leaving and people came individually to say good-bye, that I realized how strong the bonds of affection were between us.

It was on Saturday afternoon, October 12 1974 that I said good-bye to Stanbrook. I left with Lady Abbess's blessing. I have no regrets. I treasure every hour of those twelve years and would not have exchanged them for anything in the world. Though I emerged from Stanbrook physically depleted, I felt spiritually invigorated and incalculably enriched. I knew that the road back to full vitality and health would not be easy, but with God's help I was prepared for whatever the future might hold.

10   So Far

Close by the hilltop stood a cairn, and each traveller as he passed laid some token by. Some a stone, some a flower and some a song. And the stones fell to dust and the flowers withered, but the songs, the songs laughed and cried and swept into the sky for evermore.

Anon.

I slept very little that first night outside the monastery and rose to a crisp autumnal morning. The local church bells were ringing for Sunday services. Vera, a kind and attentive hostess, took me to nine o'clock Mass in the town. It was a pleasant ten minutes' walk. This was my first experience of Mass sung in English outside the monastery. It seemed to be a family Mass: the atmosphere was more informal than it used to be in parish churches in the late fifties and early sixties, with children moving about at will and parents very relaxed and at ease. Fashions had changed too, and I liked the more casual look.

But it was the liturgy itself that morning that made my heart cry out with joy to the Lord. The theme was thanksgiving and could not have been more apt. The gospel for that Sunday was from St Luke, 17, 11–19 about the cure of the ten lepers, only one of whom came back to give thanks. Every line of the different texts of the proper of the Mass verbalized my own inner experience and spoke to my condition. Spiritually elated, I sat on in church and remained through a second Mass. Once again, of course, thanksgiving was the theme, the only difference being that this other celebrant gave a different sermon. This fresh experience of being permeated with a feeling of gratitude set the seal on my new beginning.

On Monday morning, John Ginger drove me to the hairdresser, and from there on to Cambridge. John, whom I'd known for some while, having met him through a member of the community, is a sensitive person, a writer and a novelist. He had been a contemporary of Richard's at Oxford and had known him slightly. John was the first of a string of kind friends whose generosity and understanding was to help me get back on my secular feet again. He delivered me safely at the Bennetts in Adams Road. Jack Bennett had moved from Magdalen College, Oxford, to Magdalene College, Cambridge, to succeed his friend C.S. Lewis as professor of medieval and renaissance literature.

It wasn't an easy time for Gwyneth to have me. There had been illness in the family and this was the cause of strain and anxiety to her. But she coped nobly and did her best to make me comfortable. I think my inevitable bewilderment and consequent inability to make small decisions were something of a trial to her at times, but she was genuinely concerned that I should be my old self again, as soon as possible. Pragmatist that she is, Gwyneth told me to go shopping and open a bank account the morning after I arrived. My shopping list read: tights, bra, slip, open bank account, cleansing cream, seek out hairdresser, Eden Lilly for skirts (tweed), suede coat, stamps, notepaper and envelopes, tweezers, paper hankies, umbrella. These, I must have deemed, were my immediate needs.

I was accompanied by a French girl, who was staying with the Bennetts at the time. With my friend, John Ginger, I'd felt protected and secure because I knew that he understood what I was going through and the difficulties I was having to face readjusting to the outside world. But it was different with Veronique. There was no communication between myself and this sixteen-year-old schoolgirl, for she had little English and could not be expected to be sensitive to my particular situation. I felt disorientated. To open an account in the bank I had to give my signature. Trying to control the pen was well nigh impossible. Some time ago I had occasion to see that sample signature and I was awed by the great tension evidenced. It was barely legible. From the bank I went to one of the big stores to buy clothes. As soon as we arrived at the skirt department Veronique breezed off downstairs saying she'd meet me there in a little (unspecified) while. After some time I decided on a skirt and moved across to the underwear section. While I was deliberating over some items, I felt a frightening sense of panic take hold of me. I was breaking out in a cold sweat and felt utterly exhausted, longing to sit down. But there were no chairs in sight and I feared that, if I sat on the floor, people might think I was a nutcase. If I went off to look for a chair, Veronique might return, find me gone, and leave. And I didn't know how to make my way back to the Bennetts. Desperately I prayed that Veronique would come back. Just as I'd reached the stage where I thought I couldn't hold out any longer, she turned up. I said nothing to her for neither her English nor her understanding could have coped, and I followed her out of the shop. Walking back through the town and out to Adams Road, I had the uncanny sensation of not being in command of my feet.

In the security and shelter of her house I told Gwyneth of my weird and frightening experience. I voiced the thought that the anti-depressants which had been prescribed for me while I was in Stanbrook might in some way, if not directly, be responsible. Wasting no time, Gwyneth whisked me off to her own GP. Briefly I relayed my case history to her, ending with the words: "If you think these tablets are the cause, I'm ready to stop taking them."

The doctor put out her hand and took the bottle. The doctor who had prescribed these tablets had warned me not to attempt to stop taking three per day for at least six weeks, no matter how well I felt. But I gave them up that very day in Cambridge and have never touched them or their like since. There was no repeat of the stark panic.

My friend, Adrian Hastings, was at that time living at and working from St Edmund's House, a few roads away from me. At a concert together one evening Adrian dropped a veritable bombshell by offering to arrange a recital for me at St Edmund's House. Alarmed at the prospect, I made every sort of excuse. It was too soon; I wasn't well enough yet; I needed more practice; wouldn't it be better to wait and do some work in RTE in Dublin first, perhaps in the spring. But Adrian overrode all these specious arguments and eventually, with much misgiving, I let him go ahead. He arranged the recital for some time in December, before term ended.

About a week after I'd arrived in Cambridge, there was a letter from Father Anselm. Not having been in touch with one another for a long time, he was not aware of my having left Stanbrook. Unsure of his reaction to my leaving, I had delayed writing to him. However, his letter, re-addressed from Stanbrook, dispelled all my unease. He wrote that a friend of his, who had recently seen me in the parlour at Stanbrook, had told him that I looked very frail and ill. He wrote: "If you are as tense as you were two years ago, wouldn't it be a good idea to ask for a year's exclaustration? It can't be God's will for a person to be that strained."

I wrote off at once to say I'd done just what he was counselling and told him how very happy his letter had made me. In his reply Father Anselm said he had only one regret: that he didn't advise me to request exclaustration when I was ill two years previously. But I know I would not have been prepared to come out at that time.

Early in November my father telephoned me to say he was to undergo a serious exploratory operation for suspected cancer. I flew at once to Dublin to be with him. The growth was discovered to be malignant, but the operation was a success. My father recovered quickly in the capable hands of David Lane, the gifted surgeon. He's also an accomplished oboeist, who at one time played with the Radio Éireann Symphony Orchestra. The twin gifts of healing and music go well together. One is reminded of an earlier David, who was sometimes called in with his harp to heal the neurotic King Saul of his black depressions.

Initially I stayed with Joan and Frank in Monkstown. During that visit I moved around a bit, staying a day or two at a time with different people, renewing old friendships. While I was staying with Michael Garvey and his wife, Mercedes Bolger, Gay Byrne, presenter of the "Late Late Show" phoned to ask me if I'd appear on his programme that following Saturday. I'd never seen the show and was very reluctant to take part. Michael – who was controller of programmes at that time – Mercedes and I debated the matter long. Gay said I must let him know my decision by eight o'clock on Saturday morning. The 'Late Late Show' goes out live, and is the most popular programme on Irish Television. Eventually, I agreed to appear.

Michael drove me to the studio. We hardly spoke. His wife Mercedes is a concert harpist, so he understood my need for silence before a performance. Gay did a probing, fairly lengthy interview touching on my life in the monastery; why I went in and why I came out and what my plans were for the future. He had a pleasant surprise for me when he quoted from P.J. Kavanagh's book, *The Perfect Stranger*, where the author describes Richard as 'one of the two best-looking men I've ever known.'

I sang 'The Quiet Land of Erin,' which had become my theme song before I went into the monastery. The viewers' response throughout Ireland was so favourable that I was invited to return the following week, which I did, and sang two more songs. Strangers stopped me in the street to tell me how glad they were that I was back. It was exceedingly encouraging and heartwarming to receive such a welcome.

I had not planned to return to singing so soon. My intention was to rest and get well again over a period of some months before accepting offers of work. That I had to earn my living was obvious; it was only common sense to try to do so by singing, as I had already successfully done before I went into the monastery. As soon as my old producer friend, Ciarán Mac Mathúna, a large, gentle and humble man, heard that I was back in circulation, he offered me radio work. Several times during the next two or three years I recorded songs for inclusion in his tremendously popular Sunday morning programme, 'Mo Cheól Thuú.' There is now a long-playing album of that title on the Gael-linn label. Ciarán's soporific voice introduces the various items of music, poetry and song. "Mo Cheól Thú" is generally confined to Irish and Anglo-Irish material, but I have included English songs and some of my own compositions among my contributions. I also recorded numerous fifteen-minute special programmes for Ciarán and RTE at this period. I am very grateful to him for giving me work and encouragement at that time. *Mo cheól thú a Chiaráin.*

This unplanned return to singing took place amidst daily visits to my father in hospital. I stayed with my sister, whose house was adjacent to the hospital. It was a time of great anxiety and, for a while, the outcome of the operation had by no means been certain.

A couple of days after the 'Late Late Show' I flew to England to visit friends there. The Birmingham bombings had just taken place and people on both sides of the Irish Sea were shocked, and security at the airports in England were particularly stringent. As I was leaving the plane at Heathrow, a middle-aged man in clerical garb asked me if I was Mary O'Hara. He congratulated me warmly on the 'Late Late Show,' admitted to being an admirer of my work for some years and introduced himself as Donal Lamont, Bishop of Salisbury, Rhodesia. At the security check, I discovered that I had no identification, but Bishop Lamont got me through. We travelled together on the bus as far as the city terminal, holding animated conversation about our favourite songs and poets.

First I visited Peter Levi at Oxford. After twelve years Peter had lost his attenuated El Greco look and was heavier in build, but he still had his dark good looks and his fine head of thick black hair. While I was in Stanbrook he'd written verses for me called 'The Clown', which I'd set to music. It eventually went on my Chrysalis album, 'In Harmony.' The clown concept was one which had long fascinated me. In the Edinburgh days Scomo and I had talked about it. When his eldest son, Michael, was a small boy, he told his father wistfully: "I want to be a priest, but if they won't let me be a priest, surely they'll let me be a clown." Richard had written poems about clowns, which I discovered after his death, and he had once done an oil painting of a clown.

Over dinner Peter and I talked about doing some more songs together. We decided that any subject could be considered for a song, when along came the waiter bearing our first course, which was snails. "Snails?" said Peter. And I said: "Yes." Not long afterwards he sent me 'The Snail' which eventually I set to music, and it's now on my Chrysalis album, 'Music Speaks Louder than Words.'

I stayed with Quenna Hunt in Gloucestershire. Quenna, who had recently been widowed, lived in a house of great charm which was part of an old mill, mentioned in the Domesday Book. The couple of days with Quenna in her attractive home were peaceful. She drove me to visit Joyce Grenfell in London. During my time in Stanbrook, Joyce and I had kept in touch, and that summer of 1974 she had written sleeve-notes for the 'Mary O'Hara: Recital' album. She received me warmly and we talked for a long time together. She'd only just retired from the stage and while I was with her she phoned her ex-agent, who had started out on her own, and arranged a meeting between us. Joyce was enthusiastic about my re-starting a career again and predicted that I had another good twenty-five years of song left in me. This was especially enouraging since Sydney MacEwan had advised me against it, saying I should train to be a music teacher because there was no audience for my sort of singing any more. Before I left, Joyce took me to her wardrobe and presented me with two beautiful full-length Thai silk evening dresses, and some beads, which she didn't intend ever to wear again.

Her encouragement and touching concern continued even during the last few months of her life, when unknown to most of us, she was dying of cancer. Without my having referred to them, she had sensed my distress over problems in my professional life and had written to me at great length about them. She was a pillar of strength, a true friend.

While I was in Stanbrook I'd had a brief correspondence with Lord Moyne, who had written to invite me to sing at the Salisbury Arts Festival in 1975. At the time, of course, this was out of the question. Now that I was outside of the monastery, I contacted him and received a very enthusiastic and warm reply, assuring me that the engagement at the Salisbury Festival still stood and inviting me to Knockmaroon, his Irish country estate.

It happened that I had agreed to take part in a concert, which included other musicians, to mark the publication of a harp book by Nancy Calthorpe. (Nancy had taught me the piano when I was about nine years old.) It was a private concert before an invited audience, and I was asked if I wished to invite anyone special. Knowing Lord Moyne liked my work, I gave his name to the organizers and they invited him and his family.

A few days before the concert, my very good friend, Caroline Mahon, brought me along to meet Mary O'Donnell, well-known as a dress designer on both sides of the Atlantic. By the time I'd left her boutique, I was the happy recipient of a blouse of white, hand-made lace and a skirt of peacock blue Thai silk. On the morning of the concert I purchased a pair of silver, sling-back evening sandals with high heels. That evening, as I walked towards the stage, I found to my consternation that the sling-back part kept slipping off my heel. Keeping my shoes on more or less by means of sheer willpower compounded the tension that is normally part of a public appearance, and slowed down my progress. As I settled myself on stage, I caught a glimpse of Cearbhall O'Dálaigh, then president of Ireland, seated directly opposite me in the front row. We were old acquaintances since my pre-Stanbrook days, and his warm smile and welcoming nod encouraged me on this, my first re-appearance in thirteen years on a concert platform.

When I first knew Cearbhall O'Dálaigh, he was a judge, a noted linguist and a Gaelic scholar, deeply interested in all aspects of Irish culture. After the concert we had a pleasant reunion. It was there that I met Lord Moyne for the first time. His beautiful daughter, Tamsy, was with him. Though other members of his family were at the concert, I wasn't to meet them until some time later when I dined with them at Knock-maroon on New Year's Eve. Lord Moyne is the poet, Bryan Guinness, a man of exquisite manners and great gentleness in whom there is not a vestige of guile or arrogance.

On New Year's Eve, Lord Moyne collected me from my sister's house and, as we were driving across the city and through the Phoenix Park, he told me a little about each of his children. To start with I had thought there was only one daugh-ter, Tamsy. By the time he had got to mentioning four, for some reason I concluded that that was the lot and remarked: "What a nice-sized family." But I was still remarking "What a nice-sized family" by the time he had accounted for eleven chil-dren. Of course, none of them are children now.

Lady Moyne had been at the concert, but it was only now at Knockmaroon that I met her for the first time. She is a strik-ingly handsome woman with the loveliest laugh I have ever heard. I think one might hear its like in Lothlorien. She is an ardent lover of children and horses. Tamsy, Kieran, Erskine, Catriona, Fiona and Mirabel were there that night. After dinner I sang in the drawing room and Tamsy drove me back. It was a memorable evening, and I was to meet the rest of the family and to get to know them all better during the next few years at Biddesden on the Wiltshire border in England, where I had the use of one of the worker's cottages on Lord Moyne's estate.

Just after the first appearances on the 'Late Late Show', Déirdre wrote me hoping to see me if I was free. Déirdre had been working in Cork the year before I left for Stanbrook. We had made several attempts to meet, but each time something got in the way, so it wasn't until I was in the monastery that I wrote to tell her what I had done. In the intervening years we had exchanged letters once a year. In 1964 she married Pat Kelleher and that happy marriage had produced four very attractive children: Now Déirdre and I met once again and our friendship has taken on a new lease of life growing in depth all the time. She is an attractive, resolute woman with beautiful hands and an hour-glass figure. Highly intelligent and exceptionally articulate, she has a determination and loyalty to those she loves that few can match.

My father was making very good progress and early in January he was discharged from the private convalescent home. It was time for me to return to England.

I had consulted various people in the music and entertainment worlds and the consensus of opinion was that, if I wanted to re-establish my singing career again, my best bet was to base myself in England. For a year after I left Stanbrook, I was receiving a monthly allowance from the monastery, and there was a small income from my record royalties. Money was slowly starting to come in again from the odd concert and TV and radio work in Ireland and elsewhere. Once it became known that I was available for engagements again, old producer friends in the UK were getting in touch.

The recital at St Edmund's was a success, and gave me the added confidence I needed to go on singing. Lord Moyne wrote inviting me to join the family and their friends for the local hunt ball in Wiltshire and to bring my harp. I travelled with it as far as London, but found it too heavy for me in my weakened condition and had to leave it with my friend, Lyn Marks, who was on the look-out for a suitable flat for me in London.

Dinner at Biddesden was splendid, but the hunt ball was unexciting – though I love dancing. Lord Moyne knew that I was looking for a place to live and generously offered the use of the gardener's cottage on his estate. I considered the matter for a couple of weeks and then decided to accept the kind offer and moved from Cambridge to Biddesden towards the end of January 1975. I stayed with the family for over three months, during which time, I spent a couple of hours each day in the late afternoon in the cottage doing a bit of house painting and decorating. I went up and down to London fairly frequently and stayed with Lyn.

My old friend Fred Macaulay, senior Gaelic producer in the BBC in Scotland, had me do some radio broadcasts from Glasgow. I was also preparing more programmes for RTE radio.

There hadn't been an opportunity to relax thoroughly since leaving Stanbrook, and I felt a great need to get away where there was quiet, sun and sea. Peter Levi suggested the tiny Greek island of Antiparos, so I arranged a three-week holiday there late in March 1975. It would have been preferable to have had a companion, but all my friends were working, so I went ahead and booked a holiday for myself. The sum total of my knowledge of Greek was *"kyrie eleison,"* so travelling in Greece wasn't all that simple.

Armed with a Greek phrase book and, hoping for the best, I flew to Athens where I stayed the night. Next morning I set out for the ferry to the Cyclades. No one spoke a word of English and I couldn't read their language, so I had no way of knowing which island to get off at. My phrase book didn't help. Having a cabin, I slept for a little while because I knew I would be a good twelve hours at sea. When we started calling at the islands I tried to find out which one was mine. Nobody understood what I was trying to ask. My attempts at communication must at times have resembled charades, but I eventually happened upon a lawyer with enough English to understand me. When we reached Paros he called me, and together we made a dash down the crowded pier to catch the small motor-launch, in which he deposited me and my luggage. The boat took off immediately for Antiparos. Within half an hour I was lodged in the only hotel on the island.

For most of the time I was the only visitor on Antiparos. When I wasn't swimming or reading, I walked for hours across the rocky hills which were brightly covered with exquisite tiny spring flowers. The yellow camomile was in flower all over the village. I became friendly with some of the islanders and used to have regular "conversations" with one old lady on the outskirts of the village. Neither of us knew the other's language, but we managed to communicate effectively. She was a widow like myself. Her sons were in America and she was eighty years old.

I became friends with the Athenian wife of the local doctor and we used to go swimming together. Breakfast was in the fishermen's café beside the wharf, and the rest of my meals I took in the kitchen of the hotel owner's family house. My appetite revived and I came back to England in much better shape than when I'd left.

Shortly after I returned from Greece, I moved into the cottage, though I had by no means finished painting it. At first I lived, practised music, entertained, ate and slept in the larger of the rooms upstairs. It didn't matter how loudly I sang or played, or at what hour, for there was nobody to be disturbed, except the horses in the stables around me. In fact I was told that my equine friends enjoyed my music and became biddable while I was singing. I might add that those noble beasts made their own noises, whinnying and kicking their stalls when they felt like it, regardless of the hour. Across the farmyard the dairy herd of about 200 cows sometimes struck up their own chorus when the mood took hold of them. In the end I got used to the farmyard symphonies and slept right through them.

It was at this time that I met Pat O'Toole who, already acquainted with my work, now took a keen interest in helping to get me re-established again. Amazed that I did not have as much as a single brochure about my work, he immediately set about producing the first publicity packet I ever had. Nor did I have a copy of any of my records to show him. He sent me to a music shop to order copies of each of my albums. Together with a friend of his, Seán Trodden, he organized a concert at St Edmund's Art Centre in Salisbury, and another in Bath. Pat's efforts on my behalf made my comeback to singing much easier than it might otherwise have been. A man of many talents, outgoing and adventurous to a fault, he was described to me by his friend, the Irish poet, John Montague, as 'an untetherable bird'. For eight years he had worked in Africa where he was founder and for a time principal of a co-educational Moslem high school and lived in the so-called palace of a Moslem *emir*, who had ten wives. Back in Ireland he had edited a religious magazine for a few years, trained as a radio and TV producer in Dublin, and done some freelance journalism on the side. Later he went on to do his doctorate in education at the University of Toronto in Canada, and while there found time to arrange a number of concerts, radio engagements and TV appearances for me in Canada and the US. He has a staggering capacity for work, and his steady, unstinting support strengthened my resolve to forge ahead in the difficult days during the first few years after Stanbrook. Apart from Lord Moyne, no one has done more to re-establish my career than he. To both of them I owe a debt of gratitude which I can never hope to repay.

Lord Moyne arranged for my appearances at a number of important venues, among which were the Salisbury Arts Festival and the Wexford Music Festival. In Wexford, on the evening of my recital, Lord Moyne had at the last minute persuaded me to join him and his other guests for dinner. Eating and socializing is the last thing I need before I give a concert. The others had already started eating when I arrived, so I missed the introductions. I was very nervous, as is usual with me before a performance and, seeing this, the gentleman on my right asked me what I was doing at the festival. I told him I was giving a recital. After some further small talk I asked him who he was, but amidst the surrounding chatter I didn't quite catch the name, though I thought it had a decidedly Russian ring about it. So I said: "It's interesting that you should have such a definite Irish accent, yet a Russian name." He just smiled. He went on to tell me that he, too, got very nervous before making a speech. I had to rush off and before I departed I asked him to say a special prayer for me that the concert would go well, and he kindly promised he would do so. Afterwards I discovered that my companion's name was no more Russian than my own. In fact what he had said was: "Brendan Corish, An Tánaiste". In other words he was deputy premier of the Republic of Ireland and leader of the Labour Party, and even the youngest Irish high school child would have recognized his face immediately. Déirdre, who was with me, had been eavesdropping on the conversation and risked internal injuries in her efforts to contain her laughter. In any case, Mr Corish came backstage afterwards and reminded me that we had met briefly many years before.

John Paddy Browne, the noted authority on folk music, had been writing favourable reviews about my records from the beginning. Hearing that I was to take part in the Salisbury Festival in summer 1975 (he could hardly believe his ears) he arranged to interview me for the magazine, *Folk Review*. That first meeting was the start of a warm friendship between himself, his attractive red-headed wife, Jacqueline, and myself. John is another person who has strongly supported my return to music, doing everything in his power to get my name circulating again and letting me borrow at will from his prodigious record collection. He took great pains to produce an extremely tasteful, glossy brochure, and presented it to me before one of my visits to the US. He is someone I know I can rely on at any time and be sure of a sympathetic and discerning ear. A cartographer by profession, he is the father of two children, writes widely about music, edits a folk magazine and runs a folk club in Southampton. He is currently involved in writing a biography of the famous collector of Irish folk songs, Herbert Hughes, many of whose excellent piano arrangements I have adapted for the harp and frequently use. It was after the concert John organized for me in Southampton that I had a happy reunion with his friend, Brendan O'Dowda, who was generous in his advice about restarting my singing career. The last time I'd met Brendan was on the set of the 'Ed Sullivan Show' in New York City in 1961.

My first reappearance on BBC Television was from Scotland that summer of 1975 on 'McCalman's Folk.' The following summer I appeared on their programme again. That autumn I sang at the Newcastle-on-Tyne Arts Festival. My friend, Lucy Broughton, drove me there and back – Lucy's introduction to the rigours, the fun and the frustration of touring, for she was subsequently to become my personal assistant during my earlier tours of the UK and Ireland. Lucy, one of the most colourful characters I know, takes delight in flouting convention, and in her company her good humour is infectious. She has raised her family of six, has two grandchildren, does part-time teaching when she feels like it or needs the money. Thoroughly English, she once told me that her father was one of the last British Army sergeant majors in Ireland before that country's independence. Part of her early childhood was spent on Bere Island, off the south coast of Ireland. Lucy adores touring Ireland with me and says that the only drawback is having the concerts get in the way. Seriously, though, she shows exemplary patience during last-minute crises before a concert and is thoroughly unflappable.

At Carnegie Hall early in 1976 I took part in 'The Best of Ireland,' an event organized by Irish-Americans to commemorate the bicentennial of American Independence. The programme was also televised.

At this event I met The Chieftains for the first time. We were all staying together at the Statler Hotel, Madison Square Garden. Peadar Mercier and Derek Bell shared the same room, and one day after rehearsals I went with them to look at Derek's harp box. I left my harp on Peadar's bed and the three of us went out. Next morning when I went to fetch my harp the following lines penned by Peadar were attached:

Mary O'Hara

Upon my made-up bed
I laid your harp, Mary
Upon my word!
I was disturbed, a chroí,
To see it resting there.
For where this coming night
Might I seek sweet repose,
For those as suceptible as I
Even an eiderdown, from *nó éadtrom*,
Can frown at displaced imagery.
As surely as my bed has springs
As surely as your harp has strings
As surely will I sit all night
Voluntarily, Mary
My pillow be your willowy form
I'll be of this sweet madness shorn
By early morn.

Peadar

The "*nó éadtrom*" refers to a bilingual TV programme called 'Trom agus Éadtrom' on Irish television that I had appeared on a few times.

Back in England after 'The Best of Ireland', I found work was piling up. Three more times during the remainder of 1976, I was over to the US and Canada for engagements in places as far-flung as Montreal and California. Of one concert in

Toronto I have a lovely momento: an Inuit soapstone carving, specially commissioned by Russ Kempton and presented to me by himself, on stage, at the end of that concert. He had travelled all the way for the concert from Moose Factory in the frozen north, where he worked as a doctor among the Inuit and Indians.

I found myself going back and forth to Dublin appearing on television programmes, recording radio broadcasts, giving concerts, sometimes in beautiful settings such as Slane Castle, where I shared the programme with Lord Moyne and Richard Murphy reading their poetry. (Richard, looking remarkably youthful, astonished me by quoting verbatim things I'd said at The Bailey restaurant on the evening in 1955 when he and his wife had joined Richard and me for coffee.)

Through the autumn and winter of 1976 and into 1977, I travelled around Ireland, north and south, east and west, giving recitals in schools and public concerts in the evening for the Music Association of Ireland (MAI). This was a valuable experience, children being notoriously critical and unable to 'pretend' to respond favourably to what does not interest or delight them – especially when they are in groups by themselves. For that reason I started out doing these schools' recitals more nervously than usual, but I need not have worried. They were wonderful audiences. They were also thrilled to get off class!

During these protracted visits to Ireland I usually stayed with my friend Eibhlín Ní Chathailriabhaigh. Eibhlin, a retired civil servant, has a zest for living that would wear out many half her age. She is a Gaelic scholar and gives adult classes in the language. She is also secretary of Caírdre na Cruite, the Harp Association of Ireland, and a dominant figure at every Celtic Congress. Aspiring young musicians in the Celtic field find in Eibhlín untiring encouragement.

Driving a battered Renault, Eibhlin accompanied me on the MAI tours round the country. We had a hilarious time and enjoyed every hour of it. We seldom arrived on time anywhere because Eibhlín was not exactly a speed merchant. She would say lovely fairy-tale things such as "Mary, I have a very definite feeling that this road is going somewhere," when in actual fact we were sometimes cruising in the opposite direction to that

243

intended, because some practical joker with a misguided sense of humour had decided to turn the signpost round. At that time I hadn't got my own driving licence, but the first time I had the pleasure of chauffeuring Eibhlín anywhere, a tree fell on my car. Considerable damage was caused to the vehicle, and it was a miracle that we were unhurt, but we managed to get some laughter, even out of this.

Lugging the harp here and there, especially along interminable airport corridors, has always been a physical endurance test. After the first couple of yards the dragging weight tends to play havoc with the shoulder and neck muscles. On one occasion when I was struggling along Kennedy airport, a stranger heading in the same direction thoughtfully offered me her trolley. Suddenly, dashing after us came Aidan and Brid Molloy. Aidan was head of the Irish Mission to the United Nations, and I had dined with Aidan and Bríd and Mollie Rogan a couple of nights before. In fact, they were coming to say a last-minute good-bye to Naomi Kidney, and it was she who had so considerately lent me her trolley. We were introduced, and that was the beginning of a new friendship. Since then I've often stayed and played tennis with Naomi on the brand-new court she has built beside her rambling house in Ballsbridge. This dynamic and adventurous woman of singular good looks, widowed at the age of thirty-nine, is the mother of twelve children.

There was no shortage of work, but it was getting ever more difficult to keep up with correspondence and the organization that the business side of singing unavoidably entails. Concerts and television took me to France, Luxembourg, Germany, and yet again across the Atlantic. The BBC television people came and did a documentary on me, and on Southern Independent Television I had a series of seven late-night programmes with Alec Taylor. Alec's life and work are imbued with his strong Christian beliefs, and it was refreshing to get to know such a competent and personable young man in the media, who is not ashamed to talk about his convictions.

Once when I was singing as soloist with the Radio Éireann Light Orchestra as a teenager I came across Charles Kennedy for the first time. An attractive man with a lovely, lyrical tenor voice, he was a household name in Ireland, and I had admired him from afar. Early in 1976 he contacted me through Lord Moyne, and it was arranged that I would take part in a concert organized by Irish Heritage in London. Charles was on the staff of the Irish embassy and with his wife, Ethna, he organized and produced Irish cultural events in England. Charles, Ethna and myself became good friends, and it was a shock to be told of his sudden and premature death in the summer of 1979. I had grown fond of the gentle, fun-loving Charles. He and Ethna gave me every encouragement and support in my renewed career, and his untimely death has left Irish culture in England bereft of one of its more devoted champions.

In 1977 I took on a manager who arranged a recording contract for me with Chrysalis records, which entailed more frequent visits to London. Living in the country can be idyllic, but for someone whose work necessitates constant travel, rural life has its drawbacks. Having struggled with taxis, trains and buses for a couple of years, I felt compelled to acquire my own transport, but first I had to take a driving test. All my friends predicted that I'd have to do the test at least twice, but, as a result of patient instruction from Ken Simpson, the driving instructor in my local village, I passed my test first time. I was jubilant. To commemorate the success, my instructor presented me with a Jubilee coin, and we celebrated with mugs of coffee in a Salisbury café. Passing that driving test first go did more for my ego than being told that my album 'Tranquility' had gone platinum (sold over a quarter of a million copies).

I christened my new car 'Marco the Red Dragon', but have him well tamed. My newfound mobility enabled me, among other things, to visit Stanbrook occasionally. This is not because of any desire to return to monastic life, but because the friendships I forged at Stanbrook are very precious to me.

The one event that gave the greatest single impetus to my work at this time was my appearance on 'The Russell Harty Show' on London Weekend Television. What took place that night is best described by Russell Harty himself in an *Observer* article, which was subsequently reproduced on the sleeve of my Royal Festival Hall album. The appearance provided invaluable publicity for my forthcoming concert at the Royal Festival Hall in London on November 5 1977. As was the case with the 'Late Late Show' on RTE/Irish Television, so also with 'The Russell Harty Show' – I was invited back the following week and again a third time before the season ended.

I was also filmed and interviewed for the BBC 'Tonight' programme by David Lomax, who came to the cottage with a film crew and a jar of delicious honey from the bees he keeps. To my astonishment the BBC, as already mentioned, had unearthed a snapshot of Richard and me in deckchairs on the *Queen Elizabeth II*, as we sailed to New York in 1956. The picture belonged to Peter Hayworth, a friend of Richard's at Magdalen, who was also on the *QE II*.

Peter had subsequently married Elspeth, whom he'd met on board. They were great friends of David and Judy Lomax in fact, Judy, whom I'd met briefly in the Hayworth's flat in 1961, had written to me after hearing me being interviewed on "Woman's Hour" one day.

The Royal Festival Hall was my first major concert since leaving the monastery, and it was recorded on a Chrysalis album. Within three weeks this album was available in the shops, sold very well and quickly 'went silver.' At the time I didn't know what "going silver" signified – I'm still not all that clear what it means. The concert was sold out two weeks beforehand, and on the night itself the tension was heightened by the possibility of a power cut, which threatened to plunge the whole place into darkness at any moment. For this reason it was announced, before the concert began, that there would not be an interval. This left me with just a few minutes in which to change dresses and proceed with the second half.

On the eve of the concert, a reception was held for me at the Irish embassy, and in the midst of the proceedings I was handed a giant greeting card which Stanbrook had sent to me via the embassy. It contained individual messages of affection and encouragement from virtually every member of the community, and it assured me that they would be praying for me. As I stepped on to that stage the following night, I was surprised by a distinct awareness of being supported by their prayer. I address myself to the Almighty before each of my concerts, but at the same time I also rely on the special efficacy of the loving prayer of others.

The few months after the Royal Festival Hall concert were hectic, what with publicity for the new record, the London

Weekend Television special, and in February a concert tour of the UK, Dublin and Belfast. I lost track of the number of press, TV and radio interviews. During the "Pete Murray Show" on Radio 2, we got into a lively discussion on the subject of silence and its importance. We both agreed that silence can be positive and creative, and just as the interview ended, as if on cue, the station went off the air for a minute or two. How obliging of those responsible to have timed their industrial action to emphasize my point.

Hotels, no matter how many stars they boast, are something I reluctantly tolerate, and if it is at all possible, I prefer to travel home after a performance. One rule I strictly adhere to: never give a concert on the day I travel. Travelling is tiring. I don't feel that I can give my best if I'm tired, and audiences deserve the best that a performer can give. For this reason when I'm on tour I sing only every second night.

On tour, after my usual bout of callisthenics, I have breakfast, followed by a practice of that night's programme. After that, if at all possible I like to play tennis or walk. From lunchtime on, I am incommunicado. I relax, take a nap, wash my hair and get ready to go to the concert hall or theatre for the sound check. Two hours before the concert is due, I eat a light meal. This consists of a lightly boiled egg, a couple of slices of brown bread, toasted, and light tea or lemon and honey. I have been doing this since I first took part in concerts in my teens. Lucy became expert at spiriting away the buttered toast from the dining room after breakfast, and we generally travelled with a supply of fresh farm eggs from my cottage, fresh lemons or a bottle of lemon juice, a jar of honey and tea bags. This meal nourishes and sustains, but doesn't tax the digestive system. I need to have complete control over my diaphragm and abdominal muscles in order to deal with nervousness and control my breathing. All my energies are concentrated on the two-hour performance.

Before a concert I am extremely nervous and walking on to the stage is akin to walking on to a tightrope. It's essential for me to have time to be totally alone just before the concert begins, so that I can get myself inwardly together, concentrated and attentive, my mind focused on what I am about to do. Once the concert is over, I am elated and relieved, and a sociable person again. It's only afterwards that I become aware of how the expenditure of so much nervous energy has left me drained. In a full, two-hour concert (which includes a twenty-minute interval), I usually do twenty-five songs, half of which I sing solo with the harp; whilst for the rest of the songs I am joined by my accompanying musicians.

Catching a cold is an occupational hazard facing every singer and can be particularly disastrous during a tour. The singer's voice is her instrument. Using a damaged instrument, such as the vocal chords when one has a cold not only detracts from the listener's enjoyment, but also risks causing long-term, and perhaps irreparable damage to the singer's voice.

One of my major concerts after my return to singing was given at the Royal Albert Hall in London. Two days before that concert I developed a severe sore throat. I was staying at the Aer Lingus Tara Hotel in London, and Mr Dillon, the manager, sent for a doctor. After examining me, the doctor gave me anti-biotics and next morning put me in touch with Mr Holden, a Harley Street throat specialist. Lucy and I took a taxi to Charing Cross Hospital where Mr Holden diagnosed the "red flu" and prescribed appropriate treatment (there was an epi-demic of the red flu in England at the time). That night I hardly slept. I had difficulty breathing properly, and my throat and sinuses were badly inflamed and very painful. The Albert Hall was sold out, and the next day I had to decide whether to go ahead with the concert or not. It was a difficult and momentous decision. By mid-day I still hadn't improved, I telephoned Lady Abbess at Stanbrook. She was most sympathetic and promised that the community would pray specially for me for the rest of that day. Buoyed up by this and armed with throat sprays (which I loathe using), I decided to go ahead with the concert. Mr Holden was in the audience ready to leap to my as-sistance if need be, and came backstage during the interval to administer more sprays. I had with me on stage a hot lemon and honey drink, and on Mr Holden's advice (as a precautionary measure), I warned the audience.

After a few songs I said: "I bet some of you are wondering what's in the mug." They laughed. "Lemon and honey," I told them. "I'd like to tell you that I've been informed by my doctor that I'm suffering from the red flu." And I continued with the concert. I'll never know how I got through that night: as I started each song I did not know if I would finish it. But the audience was happy and the reviews next day in the London papers were all good. The critic in the *Telegraph* commented: '. . . if she hadn't mentioned the fact that she had the flu, we would never have known;' the *Times* critic wrote in a similar vein: '. . . neither the problems created by a heavy cold nor the acoustic vagaries of the Albert Hall could dim the almost ethereal purity of Mary O'Hara's voice, throughout even the most taxing song of her concert last night'.

There was one other time I had to sing with bad laryngitis. I was a guest on one of James Galway's BBC TV specials, and until the very last moment it was not certain that I could get my voice out. Already on antibiotics for my cold, I was plied all day with various remedies for my throat and, when these had no effect, at the last moment I was given massive injections with a view to reducing the swelling on the vocal chords. As far as I was concerned the drug did not work, but I got through the songs somehow. It's disconcerting to have to perform for an audience which rightly expects the best when you know you can't give it to them. After the James Galway programme it took nine weeks of rest, visits to the Harley Street specialist and a special trip to Dublin to consult with Sister Angela, my old singing teacher, before my voice got back to normal.

Sometimes I have dreams about things going wrong before a concert. In the dream, the audience is waiting for me to come on stage, but I've forgotten the harp accompaniments and I can't even remember what I am supposed to sing. I rush around frantically wringing my hands and pleading with everyone in sight. "What am I going to do?" But nobody does anything about it.

Audiences have been very appreciative everywhere I go. Sometimes they start off rather shy, perhaps not knowing what to expect, but by the time I've reached the second half they have warmed to me. There is something special about the enthusiastic response of a Belfast audience that I can't quite put my finger on. Despite the potentially dangerous situation in that city which the kindness and cheerfulness of the inhabitants makes one forget, I love singing to them. Belfast is always included in my Irish tours, and on one such tour the Belfast concert which was to start at 7.30 pm was inexplicably delayed until 8 pm. It was not until afterwards that I heard that the hall was practically empty at 7.30 because a bomb had exploded two streets away and the army had cordoned off the area, restricting all traffic. The ban was lifted at about 7.40 and the hall was full by 8.00.

People from my distant past keep turning up when I'm on tour. My first evening at the Great Southern Hotel in Galway, the phone rang. I picked it up to hear: "Miss O'Hara, I think you're absolutely marvellous. I'm the mayor of Galway, and I'd like to say what a fantastic privilege it is to welcome you to our city."

Something told me that I'd heard that voice before, and suddenly I knew: "Would that be any chance be a rogue called Pascal Spelman?" Mayor of Galway, my foot. It was a very pleasant reunion with my old pal Pascal, who looked no different (except more prosperous) from the days when he and I used to take part in the same variety concerts in the provinces while I was still in my teens. Pascal is still a very popular comedian in the west of Ireland and a very endearing person.

Soon after the Royal Albert Hall and that spring tour, I flew to the US and Canada to do promotional work for concerts at Carnegie Hall in New York City, and Massey Hall in Toronto. The 'Mike Douglas Show' was my introduction to the American version of the chat show. While in America I was surprised by what I can only describe as the professional autograph hunters, who lie quietly in wait for the celebrities who appear on these shows. After the 'Dinah Shore Show' as I had just finished signing my name for someone, he said: "By the way, who are you, anyway?"

The two concerts were successful, but the publicity surrounding them was pretty heavy going. For instance, in New York I did sixteen press interviews in two days, all in one room.

I arrived in New York a few days before the Carnegie Hall concert with the greater part of my luggage missing. Besides the stage dresses, all the music and spare harp strings were lost. In fact, it was three weeks before my luggage turned up, and by then I had finished my tour and was staying with my friends, Ray and Joyce Byrne, in their charming hideaway cottage outside Toronto. Scouring New York for strings for a Celtic harp was like looking for the proverbial needle in a haystack.

With the dress I was more fortunate. Once again Mary O'Donnell was to come to the rescue. By sheer accident I discovered that she was in New York. She had a multi-coloured dress which, with a few minor adjustments, fitted me, and I bought it there and then. I've got great mileage out of that dress, wearing it for those concerts and also at the Palladium, in London for the 'Royal Variety Show' at which Her Majesty Queen Elizabeth the Queen Mother and Princess Alexandra were present. When, a few months later I gave a private recital for the Queen Mother in someone's home, it was again a Mary O'Donnell that I wore for the occasion.

Lucy Broughton, who had accompanied me on my earlier English tours, was unable to come with me on my most recent ones. She was replaced by Sarah Hook, who unexpectedly walked out of the Wiltshire night into my life about a year ago. Sarah's car had broken down and, seeing the lights, she knocked at the cottage door for assistance. Later she returned and borrowed some books, and thus began a close friendship. Sarah is never moody, and has a well-developed comic streak, an attribute that is highly appreciated at any time, but especially on tour. I can rely on her loyalty. She is also good at handling delicate situations. Sarah has an air of authority, and with her striking Anglo-Saxon good looks, she gets away with most things. With her around, travelling becomes fun, and simple episodes can turn into adventures.

Cities, hotels and crowds are unavoidable in my work, but I am most content when I can get back to the bucolic surroundings of my cottage. There I feel relaxed and free. Normally I get up reasonably early, between eight and nine o'clock, and find my way downstairs where I sit on the mat inside the door and examine what the postman has brought. Then I do some callisthenics, followed by breakfast: fruit juice and a bowl of porridge mixed with pure bran, wheatgerm and honey.

After breakfast I tackle the mail which is interesting and quite varied. There are a certain number of business letters which I get out of the way first, and then I read my fan mail. Although I have the good intention of replying to each individual letter, I find that bundles of them keep accumulating unanswered. Many of those who write simply want information about tours, radio and television broadcasts and records, and all that is now readily available through a club, which Sarah has organized, but I still try to answer as many as possible myself. By and large the letters make heart-warming reading. However, there is the odd disgruntled writer, like the one who heard me playing 'When I'm Sixty-Four' on a BBC radio programme.

Dear Miss O'Hara,

I was half asleep when your programme on Sunday December 10th was ending. But I did hear you play that terrifying record "When I'm SixtyFour."

Nothing annoys me more than to be reminded that I am getting older. Not a day goes by without someone on the radio making some remark to remind us that we are getting older.

Curse you for playing that bloody record! When my birthday comes round I curse the bloody day and if anyone sent me a birthday card I would kick them. That is how much it annoys me.

Yours with contempt.
M.J.P. Aggleton

Many people imagine that a singer's work is only on stage or in the studio, but hours of hard work lie behind every successful performance. Often I practise late into the night. But whatever else I do, I try to make sure of a daily one or two hours' walk across the fields or through the woods, collecting wild flowers and grasses on the way. On these rambles one rarely encounters another human, but there is no shortage of cattle, sheep, horses and sometimes even deer. Each season has its own charm, but summer is especially beautiful and I bring home bunches of wild flowers to decorate the cottage. Now and then friends come to visit and stay a while, but apart from that I prefer to live a very private life. I'm not a party-goer, and the social whirl associated with the entertainment world holds no attraction whatsoever. It never did. In interviews I'm sometimes asked about my ambition in life. I haven't any, really. In a way I would like to have been a ballet dancer, but I am fully content as I am. People often ask if I enjoy singing and remark that I certainly seem to. 'Enjoy' is not the right word, for there is a certain agony involved in performing. But it also has its fulfilment and rewards. It's as though one has been given a talent that must be exercised and accounted for. Laurens Van der Post expresses this admirably: "It is not a gift I chose, or a gift I sought. It is a gift that chose me. A gift inextricable, as Virgil might have said." I will continue to sing as long as there are people who want to hear me.

One September afternoon when I was on Lord Beaulieu's estate in Hampshire filming a scene for television, Éamonn Andrews appeared out of nowhere to announce: "Mary O'Hara, this is your life." I was driven to the Southern Television studios in Southampton to be confronted with some of the key people in my life to date. It proved to be a programme punctuated with laughter and tears. My father was brought from Dublin; Dermot (whom I hadn't seen since Christmas 1961 in Nigeria) from Calgary in Canada; Florence, my mother-in-law, from Washington, DC; Lesley and Gavin Scott-Moncrieff and David Murison from Scotland; Déirdre, Gay Byrne and his wife, Kathleen, Seán Óg O'Tuama, Val Doonican, Joyce Grenfell, Richard Afton and Lady (Lily) Mackenzie, all in their turn greeted me with affection and sometimes emotion. My sister Joan, Joan Baez, Sister Angela and Sister Petra from Sion Hill, unable to be with me in the studio, sent their greetings via television film. There were inevitably some gaps. Lord Moyne and Pat O'Toole, significant people in my life and my return to music, were not present. Nor was there anyone from those Oxford days with Richard. However, it was a moving experience for all present, and at the end of the programme a smiling Éamonn handed me the big red book engraved with the words: 'This is your Life'. And so it was in many ways my life. So far, thank God, so very good.